D0537056

GOLF 365 DAYS

A HISTORY

ROBERT SIDORSKY

GOLF 365 DAYS
A HISTORY

ABRAMS, NEW YORK

Sept. 1894

CONTENTS

INTRODUCTION AND ACKNOWLEDGMENTS

When I started out to write an illustrated history of golf, I was unsure whether 365 entries would be sufficient to recount such a long and glorious story. As it turns out, 365 is just about right for telling the story of this remarkably rich and alluring game—not by any means in encyclopedic detail—but allowing enough space for some interesting digressions and pleasant diversions while catching most of the highlights along the way.

This volume spans the several centuries over which golf has been played, beginning with the origins of the game in the fifteenth century and even earlier, and coming up to the present day. It also seeks to incorporate the various aspects of golf that contribute to its complexity and appeal. These include the social element of the game, the often overlooked area of golf course architecture and the development of great courses around the world, and, of course, the exploits of golf's champions, both men and women, which have defined the history of the sport. The story is truly international in scope. Golf has been spread by its disciples and devotees to the far corners of the globe, and these pages explore the genesis of the game in many different countries as golf continues to expand around the world.

Unique to this volume is the interplay between the text and the illustrations, which were drawn from a variety of mediums, including photographs, paintings, vintage posters, and postcards. These illustrations not only enhance and enliven the text but capture the personalities of golf's most memorable figures and evoke the essence of its most hallowed courses.

TITLE: Padraig Harrington, the eventual winner, and Sergio García on the third playoff hole during the 2007 British Open, held at Carnoustie Golf Club.
CONTENTS: Old Tom Morris surveys the putting contest held on the ladies' putting green at St. Andrews, known as "The Himalayas," in 1894.
OPPOSITE: Advertising poster for Dunlop golf balls.

While theories abound as to how golf began, and several countries lay claim to being its birthplace, golf as we know it was first played on the linksland of tussocky dunes where the sea meets the land along the Scottish coast. There are references to golf on the links of St. Andrews, Leith, and Dornoch dating from the sixteenth and early seventeenth centuries. In 1603, King James VI of Scotland and his courtiers brought the game to England when he became King James I. By the mid-nineteenth century, the game was well established at the golfing meccas of St. Andrews, Musselburgh, North Berwick, and Prestwick, each of which produced its famous golfing dynasties of professionals and clubmakers, with the first Open Championship held at Prestwick in 1860.

Scottish and English army officers, engineers, and civil servants spread the game throughout the British Empire and Europe. The game took hold in the United States in the 1880s, introduced by upper crust Americans who had been exposed to golf on their travels to Scotland and visits to Biarritz and Pau in France.

The 1890s was a boom decade for golf, with the game growing by leaps and bounds in the United States as well as the British Isles. A wave of Scottish professionals emigrated to America to take up positions at the new clubs. Some began laying out courses, most notably Donald Ross, a native son of Dornoch, who designed hundreds of courses from his base in Pinehurst, North Carolina. Great golfers seem to come in threes, and the 1890s also saw the emergence of the Great Triumvirate in Britain of Harry Vardon, J.H. Taylor, and James Braid. Each in his own way contributed significantly to popularizing the game, with Vardon, the winner of a record six British Opens, becoming the first international golfing celebrity.

Golf in the United States came of age in 1913, when Francis Ouimet, an unsung amateur who had grown up across the street from The Country Club in Brookline, Massachusetts, won the U.S. Open there in an epochal play-off over Vardon and Ted Ray, the other leading English professional of the era. By the

time golf resumed after World War I, Walter Hagen had emerged at the top of the professional ranks, and American golfers never again played second fiddle to their British counterparts.

In the Art Deco decade of glamorous sporting stars, there was no more transcendent figure than Bobby Jones. A lifelong amateur who defined golf's beau ideal, Jones dominated golf during the 1920s. He retired from competition in 1930, after winning the Grand Slam by capturing the British Amateur, British Open, U.S. Open, and U.S. Amateur in a single season. Shortly thereafter, working with course architect Alister MacKenzie, he began creating the Augusta National Golf Club, which hosted the inaugural Masters Tournament in 1934. Hagen, the brash showman and bon vivant, was the professional foil to Jones, joined by Gene Sarazen, the other great luminary of the decade, who became the first golfer to win all four of the modern majors when he won the 1935 Masters following his double eagle on the fifteenth hole. The 1920s also saw the flowering of women's golf, with England's Joyce Wethered and America's Glenna Collett becoming the game's stylish trendsetters.

The 1930s witnessed the emergence of the U.S. professional tour and the continuation of the transatlantic competitions established during the 1920s—the Ryder Cup between the pros from the U.S. on the one hand and Great Britain and Ireland on the other; the Walker Cup Match for the men amateurs; and the Curtis Cup for the women. The Dustbowl Era also saw three American originals come to the scene—Byron Nelson, Sam Snead, and Ben Hogan. Nelson retired young, not long after his miracle season of 1945, when he won eleven straight tournaments. Snead, on the contrary, enjoyed unequaled longevity, winning a record eighty-two PGA events. It was Hogan who became the dominant figure of the decade after World War II, forever burnishing his name in 1953 when he won the Masters, the U.S. Open, and—in his only appearance there—the British Open. The

ABOVE: Poster for *Collier's* magazine by Edward Penfield, 1915.

postwar era also saw the formation of the Ladies Professional Golf Association, led by pioneering stars such as Babe Didrikson Zaharias, Patty Berg, and Louise Suggs.

In the late 1950s, it was an open question who would succeed Hogan as the supreme golfer, which Arnold Palmer answered in 1960, charging to victory with a final-round 65 to win the U.S. Open at Denver's Cherry Hills. The telegenic Palmer, with his army of loyal fans, gave golf a mass appeal it had never enjoyed before. Palmer was soon joined by his great rival on the golfing stage, the burly, crewcut, power-hitting Jack Nicklaus. With South Africa's Gary Player, who was driven by a fierce desire to succeed, they formed golf's Big Three in the go-go Sixties. On the Women's Tour, Mickey Wright stood at the apex of the game, winning thirteen majors during her career. In the world of golf course architecture, Robert Trent Jones put an American stamp on the many courses he designed around the world.

During the 1970s and into the 1980s, Nicklaus eclipsed every golfer who had gone before him. The Golden Bear amassed eighteen professional majors, the record that Tiger Woods is currently chasing, with his final PGA victory coming at the 1986 Masters. Nicklaus faced a series of noble and determined challengers during his career, his memorable rivalries with Lee Trevino, Johnny Miller, and Tom Watson defining both his career and theirs. In the women's game, New Mexico's Nancy Lopez lit up the LPGA, winning nine tournaments in her 1978 debut.

The 1980s and early 1990s were marked by golf entering an international era, both on the men's and women's tours, while American golf course architects increasingly began to design visually dramatic marquee courses in the U.S. and around the globe. A new wave of European players, led by Spain's fiery Severiano Ballesteros, reinvigorated the Ryder Cup, with the Europeans winning at The Belfry in 1985 and on U.S. soil at Muirfield Village in 1987.

In the mid-1980s, Australia's Greg Norman became the game's most charismatic superstar even while suffering a series of dramatic setbacks in the majors. At the same time, Nick Faldo carried English golf to new heights, winning six majors and displaying a sangfroid that served him well as he became the Number One player in the world.

The Solheim Cup kicked off in 1990 as a competition among the top women professionals on each side of the Atlantic, while the Presidents Cup was founded in 1994 as an international competition along the lines of the Ryder Cup, pitting the leading U.S. pros against the rest of the world outside of Europe.

New stars such as Phil Mickelson, South Africa's Ernie Els, and Fiji's Vijay Singh established themselves at the top of the game in the mid-1990s in the pre-Tiger Woods era. Then Tiger turned pro in 1996 and forever changed the face of the game—starting with his runaway victory at the 1997 Masters and taking golf to a level of power, skill, and artistry that had been previously inconceivable.

Woods's 2000 season—in which he won the U.S. Open, British Open, and PGA in triumphant fashion—stands as one of the greatest achievements in the history of the game. He followed it up by winning the Masters in 2001 for the so-called "Tiger Slam." Entering the 2008 season with thirteen major victories and in hot pursuit of Jack Nicklaus's record, Woods's command of the game has never been greater. He continues to shatter records with every tournament, tying Ben Hogan's record of sixty-four PGA victories, third on the all-time list, with a come-from-behind win at the Arnold Palmer Invitational in March.

The LPGA Tour is also flourishing, with Sweden's Annika Sörenstam matching—and even surpassing—Woods's dominance in the early years of the new century. Mexico's Lorena Ochoa has recently emerged as a vibrant and charming megastar, seeming destined to set new standards on the Women's Tour.

I am grateful to many individuals at Harry N. Abrams for their enthusiastic support for publishing a history of golf on this scale. In particular, I would like to thank Margaret L. Kaplan, Editor-at-Large, for her overall vision, careful editing, and steadfast determination to make the book a success in every respect. I was also fortunate to have Robert McKee as a designer who devoted enormous attention to the layout and integrated the text and range of illustrations into a strikingly harmonious design.

I would like to thank Janis Lewin for her diligent photo research and unerringly good judgment with the selections. Emily Kronenberg also provided invaluable assistance in this area and Gina Bartlett has been a steady source of support. I would also like to thank Jaime L. Mikle, the USGA's Photo Archive Liaison, for all of her time given to this project, as well as Nancy Stulack and Patty Moran of the USGA Library. I owe a debt of gratitude to each of the photographers who provided images, including Leonard Kamsler, Mike Klemme, Larry Lambrecht, Eric Hepworth, Russell Kirk, Aidan Bradley, David Scaletti, Ken May, Dick Durrance, Martin Miller, and Jim Urbina, as well as to Nancy Grinnell at the Newport Art Museum, Gill Sheldon of the Phil Sheldon Golf Picture Library, and Margaret Hobbs of the Hobbs Golf Collection. Mark Morosse did a consummately professional job in photographing many of the works on paper that appear in the book.

I would also like to thank my wife, Hilary, as well as my children, Alexander, age five, and Julia, age three, whose devotion to hitting balls at the Poxabogue driving range in Wainscott, Long Island, was very inspiring to me during my labors. Finally, I would like to thank my father for his encouragement throughout, and I am glad that I was able to include a reference to the golfing passage in Marcel Proust's *Remembrance of Things Past* that he has been quoting to me for the past twenty-five years.

Robert Sidorsky
New York City, March 2008

THE ORIGINS OF THE SCOTTISH GAME

1 | THE SHEPHERD'S CROOK

Golf, at least in the popular imagination, was born when a Scottish shepherd used his upturned crook to knock a stone through the dunes until he succeeded in getting it into a rabbit hole. How golf actually began will forever remain a mystery. There were several early stick-and-ball games dating back to the Middle Ages, including *chole* in Belgium, *jeu de mall* in France, and *gambuca* in England. Even before that, the Roman game of *paganica* was played with a curved stick and leather ball filled with wool or feathers. One theory is that *paganica* was brought to Scotland by the foot soldiers of the Emperor Severus in around A.D. 140 and then subsequently evolved into golf as we know it. *Chole* or *choule*, which is depicted in illuminated manuscripts, is often cited as a forerunner of golf, but was played by two opposing teams trying to knock the ball into the opponent's net, so the game appears to have been a closer predecessor of hockey than of golf. **OPPOSITE:** Detail showing the game of *choule* from the Book of Hours of Adelaide of Savoy, Duchess of Burgundy, c. 1460. **BELOW:** *Choleurs* at play in the town square.

A game similar to golf known as *colf* or *kolf* was very popular in the Netherlands from the Middle Ages until it disappeared in the beginning of the eighteenth century, transformed into a game played with larger wooden balls and heavier clubs on an indoor court. *Colf* players are conspicuous among the whir of skaters on the frozen canals in numerous Dutch winter landscapes from the sixteenth and seventeenth centuries by artists such as Hendrik Avercamp, Peter Bruegel the Elder, Adriaen Van de Velde, and Lucas van Valckenborch. *Colf* was also played off the ice, with one of the first recorded matches taking place on a course of four "holes" in 1297 in the environs of the Castle of Kronenberg, near Utrecht, in commemoration of the execution of the Lord of Kronenberg, the assassin of the Count of Holland and Zeeland. **OPPOSITE:** *View of Antwerp from the Left Bank During a Snowfall* by Lucas van Valckenborch. **BELOW:** *Portrait of Young Maurice de Hiragières Holding a Kolf Club,* by Adriaen van der Linde, 1598.

3 | BANNED IN SCOTLAND

Golf was already well established as a royal pastime when Charles I received news of the Irish Rebellion in 1641 on the Links of Leith, outside Edinburgh. During the fifteenth century, three Acts of Parliament—under the Scottish Kings James II, III, and IV—had banned the game on the grounds that it interfered with archery practice during the time of the wars with England. The first of these decrees, in March 1457, declared that "the fute ball and golfe be utterly cryed downe and not to be used." In 1491, the Parliament of James IV, who was to perish fighting on foot on the Field of Flodden, renewed the ban imposed by his father and grandfather, declaring that "in na place of the Realme there be used Futeball, Golfe, or uther sik unproffitable sports." In 1567, Mary Queen of Scots, the mother of the future James VI, was charged with unseemly conduct for playing golf and pall-mall on the grounds of Seton House only a few days after the murder of her husband, Lord Darnley. With the end of hostilities, golf was no longer banned, and when James VI of Scotland became James I of England in 1603, he and his court brought golf with them to Blackheath Common outside London. **OPPOSITE:** Charles I receiving the news of the outbreak of the Irish Rebellion while golfing on the Links of Leith in a drawing by Sir John Gilbert, 1875.

Golf had been played on the Bruntsfield Links beneath Edinburgh Castle since before 1450. The links was shared for more than a hundred years by members of the Bruntsfield Links Golfing Society, formed in 1761, and the Edinburgh Golfing Society. The Edinburgh Golfing Society, which became the Royal Burgess Golfing Society of Edinburgh, was founded in 1735, making it the oldest continuously established golfing society or club in the world, predating both the Honourable Company of Edinburgh Golfers and the Royal and Ancient at St. Andrews. The Bruntsfield Society took the initiative in organizing the first interclub tournament, which was held at St. Andrews in July 1857, with the Blackheath golfers defeating the Royal and Ancient in the final. The Bruntsfield Golfing Society moved in 1898 to its present home course at Davidson's Main in Edinburgh, while the Royal Burgess moved to its present home course at Barnton, five miles west of Edinburgh, in 1894. **OPPOSITE:** *Golfers on the Old Bruntsfield Links,* watercolor by Paul Sandby, c. 1746.

The Old Course at St. Andrews, in the Kingdom of Fife, is golf's most sacred site. The course evolved over the centuries on the sickle of linksland between the old gray medieval town and St. Andrews Bay. The first written reference to golf at St. Andrews appears in a license dated January 25, 1552, which granted the right to graze sheep on the links. The course is configured in the shape of a shepherd's crook, running out to the Eden Estuary, with the Swilcan Burn rilling through the fairways. Originally there were twelve holes, played "out" and "home" along the same fairway, for a total of twenty-two. In 1764, the first four holes were reduced to two, for a total of eighteen holes, which over time became the accepted standard. The most distinctive features of the course are the immense, leveed double greens, with only four holes having their own green. The links is pocked with bunkers, most of which have their own name and distinct history, such as the Principal's Nose, the Beardies, Hell, Coffin, Grave, Strath, and Walkinshaw's. The instantly recognizable stone clubhouse, the most famous in golf, was originally designed as a symmetrical neoclassical structure by George Rae, and was completed in 1854. It has been expanded over the years. The Old Course is one of nine courses that currently are part of the rotation or "rota" that hosts the British Open, with St. Andrews holding the tournament every five years. Tom Kidd won the first Open played at St. Andrews, in 1873; Tiger Woods won it in 2005. **OPPOSITE:** Railway poster for St. Andrews by H.G. Gawthorn.

The Honourable Company of Edinburgh Golfers, with its championship course at Muirfield in East Lothian, dates back to 1744, when the provost of the City of Edinburgh presented the Gentlemen Golfers of Edinburgh, as they were originally known, with a silver club for their annual competition. The winner of the competition became "Captain of the Golf" and had to present a gold or silver coin or ball to be attached to the trophy, a tradition that is maintained to this day. The Club established a set of rules for the competition that were also adopted by the Royal and Ancient Golf Club of St. Andrews when it was founded in 1754, and which have served as the basis for the rules of golf ever since. Muirfield is the third home of the Honourable Company of Edinburgh Golfers, who played over five holes at the Links of Leith before moving to Musselburgh in 1836 and then farther down the coast to Muirfield in 1891. **OPPOSITE:** Muirfield Golf Club, eighth hole. **BELOW:** *Prize of the Silver Golf,* pen and watercolor by David Allan, 1787.

Prize of the Silver Golf at Edr 1787.

The Society of St. Andrews Golfers was formed in 1754 by twenty-two gentlemen "being admirers of the ancient and healthful exercise of the Golf." In 1834, the club applied to King William IV for permission to take the name of the Royal and Ancient Golf Club, which was granted, and the king agreed to become the first captain of the newly named club. The battle royal at the R & A's annual meeting in 1841 is depicted in a famous painting by Charles Lees, completed in 1847, showing all the St. Andrews luminaries at the time, from the gentlemen golfers to club and ball makers and caddies. Sir David Baird, in the black top hat leaning forward, was partnered with the red-coated Sir Ralph Anstruther in the central group to the left of the hole. Their opponents were Major Playfair, who has just putted, and John Campbell, coolly smoking a cigarette. The famous St. Andrews caddie Sandy Pirie is in the foreground, while the great professional and ball maker Allan Robertson is standing behind Baird on the left to offer advice. **OPPOSITE:** *The Golfers,* by Charles Lees, 1847.

Royal Blackheath lays claim to being the oldest golf club in the world, tracing its origin to 1603, when King James I moved his court to the south from Scotland. James and his courtiers played golf on a portion of Blackheath near the Royal Palace at Greenwich. While Blackheath's claim is open to dispute, since golf was being played in Scotland in the fifteenth century, it was unquestionably the first golf club in England. In the mid-eighteenth century, when the members were mostly Scots, the course consisted of only five holes, which were later extended to seven. In 1923, Royal Blackheath moved to the existing course of the Eltham Club, which was redesigned at the time by James Braid as a first-rate parkland course. **OPPOSITE:** Woodblock engraving of a match between the Royal Blackheath and London Scottish Clubs at Wimbledon. **BELOW:** *Portrait of George Glennie,* a Scot and the foremost of the nineteenth-century Blackheath golfers.

Musselburgh Links in East Lothian is one of the oldest clubs in Scotland, dating from 1774, when it began with seven holes, and is the oldest course where golf has been played at the same site. The existing, full nine holes came into play in 1870. Besides Royal Musselburgh, Musselburgh was home during the nineteenth century to the Honourable Company of Edinburgh Golfers, the Bruntsfield Links, and the Royal Burgess Club, all of which departed for their own home courses in the 1890s. In 1924, Royal Musselburgh moved to a new parkland course in Prestongrange, near the original Links laid out by James Braid. The nine-hole Links, steeped in history, occupies the same land as the Musselburgh race course, with Mrs. Foreman's Inn adjoining the fourth green beside Lord Shand's bunker. It was the home course of two Scottish golfing dynasties, the Dunns and the Parks. Old Willie Dunn became the greenkeeper at Royal Blackheath in 1851. His son, Young Willie, was a professional who designed the original eighteen-hole course at Shinnecock in 1895 and won the first U.S. Open, an unofficial event held in 1894 at Newport. He went on to design several courses in the United States, including the Ardsley Casino Country Club, the so-called "Millionaires Club," where he served as the professional. Between 1872 and 1892, the British Open rotated among St. Andrews, Prestwick, and Musselburgh Links, and was played as four rounds over the nine-hole course. Musselburgh hosted the championship six times. **OPPOSITE:** Musselburgh Links, first hole. **BELOW:** Willie Dunn, Jr., of Musselburgh, winner of the first, unofficial U.S. Open in 1894

Allan Robertson of St. Andrews was the supreme golfer of his era and the first of the game's great professionals, shooting a remarkable course record of 79 over the Old Course in 1859. Short and compact, he was famed for his deft touch around the greens and his cheerful temperament. Like his father and grandfather before him, he was also a club maker and master of the art of making feathery balls, which were produced by boiling a top-hatful of goose feathers and stuffing them into a leather ball that was then stitched closed. Robertson teamed with Tom Morris, who served as his apprentice, in foursome matches, the most famous of which was a Homeric battle waged in 1849 against the Dunn brothers or "twa Dunns" of Musselburgh over the links of St.

Andrews, Musselburgh, and North Berwick, with thirty-six holes played at each course. In the deciding match at North Berwick, after going four holes down with eight to play, Allan and Tom rallied to win the last two holes and emerge victorious. They continued to join forces even after a falling-out that resulted from Morris's experimentation with the new gutta-percha ball or "gutty," introduced in 1844, which incensed Robertson. Robertson died suddenly in 1859 at age forty-four, the year before the first Open Championship was played. **OPPOSITE:** *The Royal & Ancient's Autumn Meeting of 1862,* painted by Thomas Hodge, who was himself a member of the R & A. **BELOW:** Studio portrait of Allan Robertson, the first of the great St. Andrews golfers.

Willie Park, Sr. of Musselburgh was the winner of the first British Open Championship, played over what was then the twelve-hole links at Prestwick in 1860. There were only eight players in the field, all of them Scottish professionals, with Old Tom Morris of St. Andrews finishing second in the three-round event. Park would go on to win the Open three more times, in 1863, 1866, and 1875. His brother Mungo won the Open on the Musselburgh Links in 1874, having returned to golf after serving twenty years as a seaman. Willie Park, Jr., won the Open twice, in 1887 and in 1889, when he defeated Andrew Kirkaldy in a play-off. Willie Jr.'s success was owed in large part to his wizardry with his putter, known as "Old Pawky," and he wrote an early instructional classic, *The Art of Putting*. Park was also the first professional to focus serious attention on the design of golf courses, in which he proved exceptionally gifted, designing courses of great artistry and strategic interest. He produced the first of the great inland courses in the Heath Belt around London, with his masterpieces at Sunningdale and Huntercombe establishing a new type of course checkered with heather and gorse. These courses in turn inspired leading architects such as Herbert Fowler, Harry Colt, and John Abercromby. **OPPOSITE:** Willie Park, Sr., the first Open champion, painted at Musselburgh by John A. T. Bonnar, c. 1887. **BELOW:** Studio portrait of Park, c. 1863.

Old Tom Morris was the pivotal figure in the history of nineteenth-century golf. His career as a professional at St. Andrews spanned the era from Allan Robertson and the feathery ball to that of the Triumvirate of Harry Vardon, James Braid, and J. H. Taylor, and the advent of the modern rubber-cored Haskell ball. Old Tom, who was born on North Street in St. Andrews, started out as an apprentice club and ball maker to Robertson. He went into business on his own after his dispute with Robertson over the use of the new gutty ball, made from gutta-percha—a Malayan tree gum—and in 1851 he took a position as custodian of the links at the newly formed course at Prestwick, on the Ayrshire Coast. In 1865, Old Tom returned to St. Andrews as greenkeeper, where he remained until his death in 1908 at age eighty-seven. **OPPOSITE:** *Tom Morris Putting,* by N. Arthur Lorraine.

During his brief career, Young Tom Morris surpassed the golfing exploits of his father, completely dominating his contemporaries. In 1868, when he was only seventeen, he won the Open Championship at Prestwick, a year after Old Tom had done so, and he repeated again in 1869 and 1870. Young Tom's three consecutive victories earned him the right to keep the championship belt, made of fine morocco leather, which now resides in the clubhouse of the Royal and Ancient. He won the Open for a fourth time in 1872, the year the silver Claret Jug inscribed with the name of the winner was introduced as the championship trophy. In 1875, while playing with Old Tom in a match against Willie and Mungo Park, Young Tom received a telegram that his wife was dangerously ill in childbirth; she and their newborn baby both died before he could reach them. Three months later, on Christmas Day, Young Tom died at age twenty-four, the cause being attributed to a broken heart. A memorial marks his grave in the St. Andrews Cathedral, the final resting place of many famous St. Andrews golfers. **OPPOSITE:** *Young Tom's Last Match,* watercolor by Francis Powell Hopkins showing Young Tom (left), with his father behind him. He is playing against Arthur Molesworth, backed by his father, on a snow-covered St. Andrews in the winter of 1875. **BELOW:** Studio portrait of Young and Old Tom taken in 1875.

Prestwick, on the Ayrshire Coast of western Scotland, held the first twelve consecutive Open Championships, starting in 1860. It last hosted the Open in 1925, when Long Jim Barnes won the Claret Jug, and while it lacks the length and the facilities to hold a modern tournament, it remains an open-air museum of many of the distinctive and entrancing aspects of early Scottish golf course design. Its notable features include the massive Cardinal Bunker, the Saharas, the Alps, and, most famous, the sleepers or railroad ties that shore up the faces of the greens and bunkers. After the American golf course architect Pete Dye visited Prestwick in the early 1960s as part of a pilgrimage to Scotland, he began incorporating large waste bunkers, deep pot bunkers, and wooden planks and railroad ties into his designs at courses such as Harbour Town and Crooked Stick, creating a revolutionary style of course architecture by reinventing the classic elements of Scottish design.

OPPOSITE: *Prestwick—The Cardinal Bunker,* watercolor by J. Michael Brown.

Old Tom Morris succeeded Allan Robertson as the champion of golfers before himself being overtaken by Young Tom. Old Tom won the Open Championship four times, in 1861, 1862, 1864, and 1867, when it was contested over the twelve-hole links at Prestwick. In his later years, with his flowing white beard and ever-present pipe, he was a revered figure at St. Andrews. His services were also much in demand as a designer of courses, and he had a propensity for pronouncing each of the sites that he was given to work with as specially created by the Almighty for the playing of golf. While they have been much altered over the years, Old Tom was responsible for laying out such famous and far-flung links as Lahinch, Royal County Down, and Rosapenna in Ireland; Machrihanish on the Mull of Kintyre; and Muirfield near Edinburgh. W. W. Tulloch wrote an engaging biography of Old Tom published in 1908, and his portrait by Sir George Reid, painted in 1903, hangs in the clubhouse of the Royal and Ancient. **OPPOSITE:** View of Balcomie Links and the old Coast Guard station, the home course of the Crail Golfing Society, where Old Tom Morris laid out nine holes along the sea in 1895.

Royal North Devon Golf Club, known as Westward Ho! after the novel by Charles Kingsley, was founded in 1864, making it the oldest of English links or seaside courses. The course is protected from the waters of Bideford Bay by the Pebble Ridge; the dominant hazard is the famed Great Sea Rushes—impenetrable beds of spiky assegais. Westward Ho! also claims to have been the home of the first women's golf club, formed in 1868. While the St. Andrews women founded their own club one year earlier, play was limited to a putting green known as "The Himalayas." The ladies at Westward Ho! were also restricted to using only putters, but played over a nine-hole course with holes ranging from 50 to 150 yards. The golfing artist Francis Powell Hopkins (*Major Shortspoon*), a retired navy officer, was an early member of Westward Ho!

OPPOSITE: *The Ladies of Westward Ho!* by Francis Powell Hopkins, 1880.

Jamie Anderson was born into one of the illustrious families of St. Andrews golfers, like the Morrises, Kirkaldys, Auchterlonies, and Herds. His father, David Anderson, known as "Old Daw," was a legendary greenkeeper and caddie at the Old Course. He operated the ginger beer stand near the fourth hole from which the hole takes its name. Jamie, who was known for his accuracy, won the Open Championship three years running, from 1877 to 1879, and was also highly regarded as a club maker. His win in 1878 at Prestwick featured an ace on the seventeenth hole, the first recorded in championship golf. In H. Thomas Peter's *Golfing Reminiscences*, Anderson is described as a "beautiful player" who was "short and burly but drove a long ball, and was deadly with iron and putter. He was calm in temper and of firm nerve." **OPPOSITE:** The Swilcan Bridge on the Old Course, St. Andrews. **BELOW:** "Old Daw" Anderson serving a refreshment to Old Tom Morris from his ginger beer stand near the fourth hole of the Old Course.

Bob Ferguson of Musselburgh picked up where Jamie Anderson left off, winning the Open Championship three times running, from 1880 to 1882, a record only equaled by Young Tom Morris, Anderson, and, in modern times, by Peter Thomson. His first victory came at his home links of Musselburgh, followed by wins at Prestwick and St. Andrews. A powerful man who was known as a bad-weather player, he defeated Anderson at Prestwick in a torrential downpour. Ferguson almost won the Claret Jug a fourth straight time in 1883 at Musselburgh, finishing with three straight 3s to tie Willie Fernie, only to lose in the thirty-six-hole play-off by one shot when Fernie made an incredible eagle on the final hole. Fernie was the pro at Felixstowe and later, starting in 1887, Troon, where he redesigned the course, and was a great favorite and boyhood hero of golf writer Bernard Darwin. As for Ferguson, after recovering from typhoid, he finished his career as custodian of the Musselburgh Links and golf teacher to the boys of the Loretto School. **OPPOSITE:** Royal Troon, fourteenth hole.

Ben Sayers will forever be associated with the famed links of North Berwick. He was born in Leith in 1856 and at age twelve moved to Haddington, in East Lothian, where his father was a basket maker. One of Scottish golf's most engaging and colorful personalities, Sayers was a professional acrobat before turning to golf full-time, and would perform cartwheels on the green after winning a big match. Sayers made his mark as the professional at North Berwick, giving lessons to members of the royal family and the upper crust of English society, who came to play Scotland's most socially fashionable links each summer. His pupils included the amateur champion Dorothy Iona Campbell and the Frenchman Arnaud Massey, who won the Open Championship in 1907. The bow-tied Sayers never won the Open Championship himself, but was a regular competitor for more than forty years, entering the field for the first time in 1876. Sayers's forte was match play, and he frequently teamed up with his friend and fellow professional Andrew Kirkaldy. At five feet three inches, "Wee Ben" was accompanied into battle by his caddie and aide-de-camp, the massive Harry "Big" Crawford, who also ran the ginger beer stand at North Berwick. **OPPOSITE:** Ben Sayers playing at the 1915 U.S. Open at Baltusrol Golf Club in New Jersey.

The small town of Carnoustie, on the northern shores of the Firth of Tay, boasts the most fearsome course in the British Open rota. While golf has been played over Carnoustie's linksland since the sixteenth century, the course dates from 1850, when it was laid out by Allan Robertson of St. Andrews. It was extended to eighteen holes by Old Tom Morris twenty years later. Carnoustie was substantially revised by James Braid in 1926, but the fiendish three finishing holes, where the Barry Burn insidiously snakes its way into play, were the satanic creation of James Wright, a local man, in 1937. In the 1999 Open, the fairways were engulfed by a Sargasso Sea of rough that overwhelmed the field. Jean Van de Velde unforgettably came to the eighteenth hole needing only a double bogey six for victory, but a series of blunders and bad luck left the Frenchman barefoot in the Burn, lying three. He was forced to take a drop as the waters rose, and only a courageous up and down from the bunker in front of the green left him even with Justin Leonard and Paul Lawrie, the play-off winner. Van de Velde bore his crushing disappointment with Gallic good humor. Eight years later, Padraig Harrington came to the final hole and provided a Gaelic reprise of the woes of Van de Velde, finding the Burn not once, but twice, escaping with a double bogey only after a skillful up and down of his own. Harrington, however, righted the ship in the play-off, sailing to victory over Sergio García. **OPPOSITE:** Carnoustie Golf Club, seventeenth hole. **BELOW:** Jean Van de Velde ponders his fate while standing in the Barry Burn on the eighteenth hole of Carnoustie in the 1999 British Open, which he lost in a play-off to Paul Lawrie.

Ben Sayers started in business as a ball maker in 1876, turning out gutties made from Malayan tree gum that he sold in his small shop on the West Links at North Berwick overlooking Point Garry. Later, he began inventing and making clubs. Sayers also designed a number of courses, including Rothesay with James Braid on the Scottish island of Bute, the Craigielaw Links for Kilspindie Golf Club, and the picturesque links of Castlerock in Northern Ireland, not far from Londonderry. Sayers's two sons, Ben Jr. and George, expanded the club-making business, turning Ben Sayers & Son into a world famous manufacturer of golf clubs. Young Ben developed the "Dreadnought" driver in 1906, which had an extra-large head, and the company manufactured the "Benny" putter, which was used by Henry Cotton. In 2003, the Ben Sayers factory in North Berwick closed after 124 years, with production transferred to China. **OPPOSITE** and **BELOW:** Railway posters for golf at North Berwick by Andrew Johnson.

NORTH BERWICK

ILLUSTRATED BOOKLET FROM TOWN CLERK NORTH BERWICK
OR ANY L·N·E·R ENQUIRY OFFICE

LNER

Royal Dornoch is the regal and remote golfing oupost of the Scottish high-lands, overlooking Embo Bay on the east coast of Sutherland. The club was founded in 1877 as successor to the Sutherland Golfing Society, with Old Tom Morris laying out the original nine, and an added nine three years later. In 1901, Andrew Carnegie presented the Carnegie Shield for the club's annual competition, and in 1906, through the good graces of Duchess Millicent of Sutherland, the club was granted the royal charter by King Edward VII. A favorite of connoisseurs of links golf, it was introduced to American golfers by Herbert Warren Wind in his 1964 *New Yorker* article "North to the Links of Dornoch." In 1981, Tom Watson, who is now an honorary member, came to play one round and enjoyed the course so much that he stayed for three. Golf was played over Dornoch's linksland for centuries before the golf club was founded, with the first written reference dating from 1616. This makes Dornoch the third of the Scottish links to be documented, after St. Andrews in 1552 and Leith in 1593. Sir Robert Gordon, in his *History of Sutherland*, published in 1630, pointed out: "About this toun there are the fairest and largest links of any pairt of Scotland, fit for archery, Golfing, Ryding, and all other exercise; they do surpass the fields of Montrose or St. Andrews."

OPPOSITE: Royal Dornoch Golf Club, third hole.

THE SPREAD OF THE GAME

23 | GOLF SPREADS TO THE EMPIRE

It comes as no surprise that the history of golf in India is closely intertwined with the history of the British Raj. The Royal Calcutta Golf Club dates from 1829, making it the oldest golf club in the world outside Great Britain. The original course was located in the suburb of Dum Dum and was known as the Dum Dum Golfing Club; a second course was built at Tollygunge in 1895. Royal Calcutta was followed by Royal Bombay, which is no longer in existence, and then Bangalore in 1876. Shillong Golf Club, a relative newcomer founded in 1878, is set in Upper Assam in northeast India. The course is nestled in the Khasi and Jaintia Hills, near the Himalayas, at an altitude of five thousand feet, with fairways wreathed in pine and rhododendron. Popular with the local Scottish tea planters and visitors looking to escape the heat of Calcutta, the course billed itself in the 1920s as the "Gleneagles of India." **OPPOSITE:** Program cover for the 1964 Open Golf Championship of India, played at the Delhi Golf Club. **BELOW:** Railway poster for Shillong Golf Club.

THE OPEN GOLF CHAMPIONSHIP OF INDIA
1964

OFFICIAL SOUVENIR PROGRAMME

Pau Golf Club was founded in 1856, making it the oldest course in Continental Europe by a considerable margin. The club owes its beginnings to a group of Scottish army officers who had fought in the Peninsular Campaign against Napoleon and eventually retired to the spa town of Pau on the plain of Billère, beneath the Pyrénées. The club remained a British bastion for many years, the original founders including the Duke of Hamilton and Colonel Hutchinson, father of amateur champion Horace Hutchinson. Pau and the other early French courses at fashionable resorts, such as Biarritz and Etretat, played an important part in the origin of golf in the United States. It was there that well-heeled Americans touring the Continent first learned of the game and became determined to take it up when they returned home. The Scottish golf writer and watercolorist Garden G. Smith painted the course in the 1890s, showing the crossing over the River Gave, which runs through the course, and the characteristic poplar and horse chestnut trees. **OPPOSITE:** *Crossing Jordan,* watercolor of golf at Pau by Garden G. Smith, 1892. **BELOW:** Englishman Joe Lloyd, winner of the 1897 U.S. Open, and the professional at Pau.

"Crossing Jordan."   Garden G. Smith. R.S.W.

PAU. 1895.

Royal Montreal Golf Club, founded in November 1873, is the oldest golf club in North America, Queen Victoria granting it royal status in 1884. For the first twenty-three years of its life, the club was located at Fletcher's Field on the eastern slopes of Mount Royal. In 1881, Willie Davis came over from Hoylake in England to become the club's first pro. Davis laid out early courses at Newport and Shinnecock Hills, two of the original five founding clubs of the USGA. In 1896, the club moved to Dorval on Lake St. Louis, ten miles from downtown Montreal. In 1953, the club hosted the inaugural Canada Cup, an event founded by Canadian industrialist John Jay Hopkins to promote goodwill among nations, in which two-man teams compete every year representing countries around the world. In 1967, the name of the event was changed to the World Cup. Since 1958, Royal Montreal has had its home at Île Bizard, with two championship courses, the Blue and the Red, designed by the American golf architect Dick Wilson. The Blue Course was recently substantially remodeled by Rees Jones in preparation for the 2007 President's Cup competition. **OPPOSITE:** Royal Montreal Golf Club, seventeenth hole.

Golf in Sri Lanka (formerly Ceylon) had its birth on March 13, 1879, when the Colombo Golf Club was founded by British golfers at Galle Face Green; it became Royal Colombo in 1928. The fourth-oldest club outside Great Britain, its current Ridgeway Links was named for Governor Sir Joseph West Ridgeway and opened in 1896, with the colonial style clubhouse completed in 1905. The fairways run through tall pines and around ponds blooming with water lilies, with the landmark Kelani Valley Railway Line traversing the course. Nuwara Eliya Golf Club followed in 1888, laid out at an altitude of 6,200 feet amid the tea plantations surrounding the hill station of Nuwara Eliya (City of Light), with fairways clustered with rhododendron, cypress,

golden wattle, and kina trees. It was here that the first Amateur Championship of Ceylon was held in 1891, two years before the U.S. Amateur began. Several other courses flourished in the early years, including ones around the fort at Jaffna and in the ruins of Anuradhapura, but those have disappeared. In 1997, the Victoria Golf Club opened near the ancient capital of Kandy, Sri Lanka's second-largest city, designed by noted English architect Donald Steel. The course tumbles through mara trees, jack forests, and coconut palms overlooking the Victoria Reservoir, with views of the mist-laden mountains of Kandy.

OPPOSITE: Cover of the program for the 1962 Open Amateur Golf Championship of Ceylon, held at Nuwara Eliya Golf Club.

OPEN AMATEUR GOLF CHAMPIONSHIP OF CEYLON

CEYLON

Golf

UNION

1962

NUWARA ELIYA GOLF CLUB COURSE, 27th OCTOBER

Golf in Ireland officially began in 1881 with the founding of Royal Belfast by George Baillie, a Scot, and since 1926 the course has been terraced along the tranquil shores of Lough Belfast in Craigavad. The two towering championship courses of Northern Ireland, with their two distinct personalities, are Royal County Down and Royal Portrush. County Down was founded in 1889 in Newcastle, with Old Tom Morris brought over from St. Andrews to lay out the links "at a cost not to exceed £4." The course as it evolved is one of staggering beauty and constant challenge, its fairways bobbing with flotillas of flowering gorse along the curve of Dundrum Bay, beneath the mottled greens and purples of the Mountains of Mourne. The club has hosted many important competitions, from the British Ladies' Championship of 1899 through the 2007 Walker Cup. Royal Portrush lies farther north, along the majestic Antrim Coast, not far from the thousands of trunks of stone that form the Giant's Causeway. Founded in 1898 at the Victorian seaside resort, the modern course was largely the work of Harry Colt in the early 1930s. The championship, or Dunluce, course, is named for the ruined sixteenth-century castle that teeters on the nearby cliffs. The fairways swirl through dunes wrapped in a thick coat of sea grasses embroidered with wild roses, running out to the limestone formations high above the Atlantic. Portrush hosted the 1951 British Open, the only time the championship has been played outside Great Britain. **OPPOSITE:** Royal County Down in Northern Ireland, looking back from the third green at Newcastle and the Mountains of Mourne.

Royal Dublin, located at Dollymount, is the second-oldest golf club in Ireland after Royal Belfast, having been founded in 1885 by John Lumsden, a Scot, and his friends. Golf was forbidden on Sundays at Royal Dublin, which led to the formation of the Island Golf Club in 1887, when four of the Dollymount members took a rowboat from Malahide across the Broadmeadow Estuary in order to play on the Sabbath. Portmarnock Golf Club followed a few years later, becoming the championship course of the east of Ireland. The course was laid out on a spit of land across the estuary from Dublin that was also reached by the club's founders by rowboat, in this case on Christmas Eve 1893. Overlooking Dublin Bay, Portmarnock has hosted numerous noteworthy events over the years, including the 1991 Walker Cup. Lahinch, in County Clare, dates from 1891. Founded by army officers who first played at Limerick racecourse, the course was laid out by Tom Morris in 1893 with the original links overlooking Liscannor Bay. The course was substantially revised by Alister MacKenzie in the 1920s, but two of the original holes, the fifth—known as "Klondyke"—and the sixth—named "The Dell"—survive as outdoor museum pieces. Ballybunion, the supreme test of the southwest, in County Kerry, facing the Atlantic on the southern shore of the Shannon Estuary, goes back to 1893. Originally only twelve holes, it was not extended to eighteen until 1927. **OPPOSITE:** Royal Dublin Golf Club, eighteenth hole.

After Pau became the first bastion of golf on the Continent in 1856, it was another thirty-two years before Old Willie Dunn laid out the famous course at Biarritz under the gaze of the lighthouse on a promontory of the Côte Basque. Golf got its start on the Riviera at Cannes Mandelieu in 1891, founded by the exiled Grand Duke Michael of Russia—brother to Czar Alexander III—who had been smitten by the game after spying golfers on the Old Course at St. Andrews while on a partridge shoot in Scotland. The club was laid out through corridors of parasol pines and across the River Siagne, and the early members wore a distinctive golfing costume of black-and-white stripes. Golf courses sprang up along the Côte d'Azure, starting with the Palmiers or Palms course at Hyères in 1894, followed in short succession by Cagnes-sur-Mer, Sospel, Costebelle, and the Monte Carlo Golf Club. Of these, the lone survivor is Monte Carlo, with its magnificent views of the Mediterranean out to Corsica from its fairways tucked along Mont Agel in La Turbie, France. In 1895, Lord Ashcomb founded Valescure Golf Course, a parkland course in the English style laid out amid the pine forest of Saint-Raphäel, not far from the Roman ruins at Frejus, which continues to thrive. **OPPOSITE:** Travel poster for Monte Carlo Golf Club by Elio Ximenes. **BELOW:** Travel poster for Hyères (a course no longer in existence) by Roger Broders.

Golf in Belgium has been very much a royal pursuit, beginning with King Leopold II in the early 1900s, followed by Leopold III and his son, King Baudouin. Royal Antwerp, founded in 1888, has the distinction of being Belgium's first club, set in the pine and heath of Kapellenbos. Leopold II made land available for Royal Golf Club de Belgique, founded in 1906, and donated the château of the manor farm at Ravenstein for the clubhouse. He also made land available for Royal Ostend Golf Club, established in 1903, a links course nestled in the dunes at Coq sur Mer. Golf also took root in the dunes of Knokke, where the first players were a band of retired Englishmen; the first course at Royal Zoute opened in 1908. By 1930, Royal Zoute had

three courses, all destroyed by the Germans during World War II and later restored. The English influence on golf in Belgium remained strong in the years between the two world wars, with Tom Simpson designing the revised Royal Antwerp and Royal Golf de Belgique, as well as the Royal Golf Club des Fagnes at Spa, with the front nine laid out over the old Sart racecourse. Henry Cotton and Aubrey Boomer, two of the leading lights of British golf, were the successive pros at Royal Waterloo during the late 1920s and 1930s. **OPPOSITE:** Travel poster by Henri Cassiers showing golfers in 1898 at the Belgian seaside resort of Coq sur Mer, near Ostend. **BELOW:** Postcard showing golfers at Royal Zoute in Knokke.

LE ZOUTE. KNOCKE s/Mer. BELGIQUE. Plage. Dunes. Golf.

CHEMINS DE FER DE L'ETAT BELGE · BELGISCHE STAATSPOORWEGEN · BELGIAN STATE RAILWAYS

LA PLAGE BOISÉE ET FLEURIE

GOLF, TENNIS, COURSES, etc.

Pour tous renseignements :
s'adresser au " SYNDICAT D'INITIATIVE "
1° à BRUXELLES, 58, rue Bosquet - Téléphone 154.56
2° au COQ-SUR-MER, Villa *Les Géraniums Rouges*,
avenue Léopold - Téléphone 28 ▪▪▪

LE COQ-SUR-MER EN 1898

 COQ SUR MER

PRÉS D'OSTENDE

AFF. D'ART. O. DE RYCKER & MENDEL. BRUXELLES.

Golf in Denmark had its official beginning with the founding of the Copenhagen Golf Club in 1898, although even before then the game was played on the private estates of a few members of the aristocracy, and at the Fælled, or commons, on the island of Amager near Copenhagen by a Danish family that had brought clubs and balls back with them from a visit to England. Fanø Golf Links was established in 1901 on the small North Sea island of Fanø off Denmark's southwest coast, near the country's oldest *krø*, or inn, at Søderho, which dates from 1722. Set in dunes swathed in heather and lyme grass, the course was designed by a Scot named Dunlop; it was expanded to eighteen holes in 1930. Denmark has produced one of Europe's top pros in Thomas Bjørn, who looked as if he was about to win the British Open at Royal St. George's in 2003, when his lapse on the greenside bunker at the sixteenth hole cost him the Claret Jug. Bjørn also finished tied for second at the 2005 PGA Championship, behind Phil Mickelson. **OPPOSITE:** Travel poster for golf at Fanøe. **BELOW:** A dejected Thomas Bjørn after failing to get out of the bunker at the sixteenth hole in the 2003 British Open at Royal St. George's.

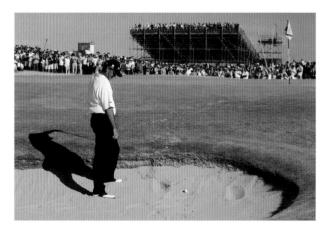

Horatio Gordon "Horace" Hutchinson, born in 1859, was the renaissance man of golf at the turn of the nineteenth century. He was a champion golfer, a prolific and accomplished author, and an all-round authority on the game. Hutchinson, whose name will forever be linked with his beloved home course of Westward Ho!, won the British Amateur Championship in 1886 at St. Andrews and the next year at Royal Liverpool (Hoylake), where he defeated John Ball on his home turf. His fourteen books include *Golf* for the Badminton Library sporting series, which did much to popularize the game, and *British Golf Links*, which he edited, a cornucopia of information and photographs of the leading courses of the 1890s. In 1908, he was elected the first English captain of the Royal and Ancient. **OPPOSITE:** Westward Ho! (Royal North Devon Golf Club), fifth hole. **BELOW:** Sketch of Horace Hutchinson by John Singer Sargent.

Royal St. George's Golf Club, founded in 1887 at Sandwich in Kent, rollicks through the rough-and-tumble sand dunes overlooking Pegwell Bay. The club owes its start to Dr. Laidlaw Purves, a Scottish eye specialist and die-hard golfer. Purves first gazed upon the spine of sand hills when he climbed to the top of St. Clement's Church in Sandwich with a group of friends, and recognized that they would make an ideal golfing ground. The course was greeted with acclaim, and in 1894 Sandwich, as it was popularly known, hosted the first Open Championship to be held outside Scotland, with J. H. Taylor the winner. In 1930, the club was the site of the first Walker Cup Match to be held in England. Most recently, St. George's hosted the 2003 Open, at which Ben Curtis of Ohio, playing in his first major championship, drained a clutch putt on the seventy-second hole to become one of the most improbable winners in the history of the event. Not long after St. George's opened, it was joined by its two illustrious neighboring courses, Prince's and Royal Cinque Ports. **OPPOSITE:** *Members of Royal St. George's, 1892,* by Allen C. Sealy and Charles Spencelayh, depicts many of the early members, and two of their wives, with W. Laidlaw Purves, the founder of the club, shown standing directly behind the kneeling caddie.

John Reid is credited with having introduced golf in the United States, earning him the title "Father of American Golf." Reid was born in Scotland in 1840, but only took up the game in 1888, when he was given a set of clubs and two dozen gutta-percha golf balls that his friend and fellow Dumferline native Robert Lockhart had ordered at the golf shop of Old Tom Morris on a visit to St. Andrews in the late summer of 1887. Reid and his friends started playing the game on a three-hole course laid out on a pasture across the street from Reid's home in Yonkers. The Saint Andrew's Golf Club was established at a dinner at Reid's home in November 1888, with Reid elected president. A large apple tree circled by a bench served as the first "clubhouse," and the small band of America's first golfers has been known ever since as the "Apple Tree Gang." **OPPOSITE:** The earliest photograph of golf in America, taken at Saint Andrew's Golf Club in Yonkers in 1888, with John Reid at the far right **BELOW:** A portrait of John Reid by Frank Fowler, c. 1900.

Saint Andrew's Golf Club expanded from its original three holes to six in a larger pasture owned by Henry Tallmadge, who became the first secretary of the USGA. By 1892, the club had moved to an apple orchard on Palisades Avenue, and in 1897, an eighteen-hole course was established in Hastings-on-Hudson. The club's current course, designed by Jack Nicklaus, opened in 1985. The Stanford White–designed clubhouse is home to some of the clubs and balls used by the original members, John Reid's red coat, and a branch from the fabled apple tree. Saint Andrew's is not alone in its claims to be the oldest golf club in America in continual operation. The Dorset Field Club had its genesis when a dozen men from Troy, New York, began playing golf on summer visits to Dorset, Vermont. On September 12, 1886, a 1,892-yard, nine-hole course was laid out across a series of pastures. The current eighteen-hole course was designed by Steve Durkee in 2000. Foxburg Country Club, overlooking the Allegheny River in western Pennsylvania, owes its origin to a trip by Joseph Mickle Fox to Scotland in 1884 while representing Merion Cricket Club in a series of matches between the visiting Americans and English teams. Fox was introduced to golf by Old Tom Morris at St. Andrews and brought back clubs and balls. Fox initially laid out a three-hole course on the lawn of his western Pennsylvania estate in 1885. In 1887, five holes were constructed on the club's current site, with sand greens and tomato cans for holes, which were expanded to nine holes a year later. Foxburg's clubhouse also houses a museum of golf history. **OPPOSITE:** *The Old Apple Tree Gang,* by Leland R. Gustavson. **BELOW:** A portrait of Henry O. Talmadge, c. 1900.

While Saint Andrew's and other clubs can lay claim to being the oldest golf club in continuous operation in the United States, the honor of the oldest golf course in the United States belongs to Oakhurst Links, a nine-hole course laid out in 1884 in White Sulphur Springs, West Virginia, on the Oakhurst estate of Russell Montague. After graduating from Harvard in 1872, Montague became a member of the Massachusetts bar and was introduced to golf on a visit to St. Andrews and other Scottish courses while studying law in London during 1874 and 1875. He only practiced law in Boston for a year before his failing health led him to move to West Virginia, where he became a farmer and raised sheep. The Oakhurst golfers were Montague and his Scottish neighbors, who were instrumental in laying out the course. The original course was abandoned around 1909, and thereafter Montague and his friends played at the Old White Course at the Greenbrier Resort, designed by C. B. Macdonald and Seth Raynor in 1913. In 1994, the original Oakhurst Links was restored for play by owner Lewis Keller and golf course architect Bob Cupp, with visitors using replicas of hickory-shafted nineteenth-century clubs and gutty balls.
OPPOSITE: Keeping the fairways trimmed at the restored Oakhurst Links in West Virginia.

Shinnecock Hills Golf Club had its genesis in a chance encounter during the winter of 1890–91, when William K. Vanderbilt and his friends from the Southampton summer colony, Duncan Cryder and Edward Mead, witnessed the Scottish pro Young Willie Dunn hitting shots to the green of the famous Chasm hole at the Biarritz course on the Côte Basque. Vanderbilt remarked: "Gentlemen, this beats rifle shooting for distance and accuracy. It is a game I think would go in our country." Cryder then wrote to another friend from Southampton, Samuel Parrish, about starting the new game in Shinnecock Hills. Parrish was traveling in Italy at the time, collecting the Renaissance art that would form the basis of the museum he founded in Southampton in 1897. When he returned to Southampton, he arranged for Willie Davis, the pro at Royal Montreal, to come to Southampton in 1891 and lay out what would be a twelve-hole course. In 1895, Willie Dunn, who had arrived from France, laid out an eighteen-hole course built by 150 of the local Shinnecock Indians, who cleared the thick scrub oak and blueberry bushes. Parrish also enlisted another Southampton summer resident, Stanford White, the preeminent architect of the Beaux Arts era, to design the clubhouse. Shinnecock's symmetrical, shingled clubhouse, with its wraparound porch framed by Doric columns, became the first golf clubhouse in America when it opened in June 1892. It remains the archetype of the American clubhouse. **OPPOSITE:** *The First Clubhouse in America, Shinnecock Hills,* by Leland R. Gustavson. **BELOW:** Some scenes of old Southampton on Long Island's South Fork.

For many years, the introduction of golf in Boston was attributed to a "young lady from Pau." The anonymous young lady was actually Florence Dumaresq Boit, who brought her golf clubs with her when she returned to Boston from France in 1891. Florence's parents, Edward and Mary Louisa Boit, were at the pinnacle of Boston society, but after graduating from Harvard Law School, Ned Boit decided to become a painter, inspired by an exhibition of Corot's work at a Boston gallery. The family moved to Paris, where the Boits were friends with John Singer Sargent and Henry James, and lived in the expatriate world chronicled by James. Florence and her three sisters are the subject of Sargent's great masterpiece *The Daughters of Edward Darley Boit*, painted in the family's Paris apartment in 1882. Florence, the oldest of the girls, leans against a huge Ming vase in the shadowy background. Julia, the youngest of the four, nicknamed "Ya Ya," sits in the foreground holding her doll "Popau," named for the French politician and duelist Paul de Cassagnac. Julia Boit became an accomplished landscape painter like her father, painting in her childhood sketchbook a watercolor of girls playing golf. **OPPOSITE:** *Girls Playing Golf,* watercolor from Julia Overing Boit's sketch book, c. 1898. **BELOW:** *The Daughters of Edward Darley Boit,* by John Singer Sargent, 1882, which is now in The Museum of Fine Arts, Boston.

When Florence Boit brought her clubs with her from France and discovered that no one else in Boston played golf, a makeshift course was set up on the grounds of the Wellesley estate of her maternal uncle, Arthur Hunnewell, using flowerpots as cups. Hunnewell and Lawrence Curtis, who had played golf on the Hunnewell lawn, then gave an exhibition of the new game at The Country Club in Brookline in 1893. The members were impressed, and six holes were laid out that year. The following year, the Scottish pro Willie Campbell was brought over and expanded the course to nine holes; by 1899, there was an eighteen-hole course. The Country Club, the first such institution of its kind, had originally been established by Malcolm Forbes in 1882 as a club for horse racing and for shooting. It was modeled after the country club on Bubbling Well Road in Shanghai, where Forbes had lived while overseeing his family's lucrative shipping trade with China. Lawrence Curtis became the second president of the USGA in 1897 and encouraged his cousins, Margaret and Harriot Curtis, to take up the game. Both became amateur champions and founded the Curtis Cup competition. In 1913, The Country Club was the site of Francis Ouimet's historic upset victory in the U.S. Open over Harry Vardon and Ted Ray. **OPPOSITE:** Francis Ouimet lines up the final putt in his play-off victory over Harry Vardon and Ted Ray at the 1913 U.S. Open, held at The Country Club.

Charles Blair Macdonald was a central and strong-willed figure in the birth of golf in the United States. Macdonald was reared in Chicago but attended St. Andrews University in the 1870s, where he was introduced to golf by none other than Old Tom Morris. He returned home severely smitten with the game. In 1895, Macdonald won the first official U.S. Amateur Championship, at Newport Golf Club. He had been upset in the finals of unofficial events played the year before at Newport and Saint Andrew's in Westchester and challenged the outcomes, calling for the formation of an official governing body, which led to the creation of the United States Golf Association. An organizational meeting was held on December 22, 1894, at the Calumet Club in New York City, attended by representatives of Saint Andrew's, The Country Club, Shinnecock, Newport, and Chicago Golf Club, with Newport's Theodore Havemeyer elected the USGA's first president. In 1896 and 1897, the winner of the Amateur Championship was Henry J. Whigham, who subsequently married Macdonald's daughter and consulted with Macdonald on his design of the National Golf Links of America in Southampton. Whigham, who was descended from one of Prestwick's oldest golfing families, had come to the United States in 1895 and was employed as the drama critic of the *Chicago Tribune* when he won his amateur titles. He later worked as a foreign correspondent covering the Spanish American War and the Boxer Rebellion, before becoming the first editor of *Town & Country* magazine. **OPPOSITE:** *The First Amateur Golf Championship Held in America, 1894,* lithograph after a 1931 painting by Everett Henry, showing Charles Blair Macdonald teeing off at Saint Andrews. The spectators included John Reid, on the far left, smoking a pipe. **BELOW:** Henry J. Whigham, U.S. Amateur champion in 1896 and 1897.

The Newport Golf Club opened on July 4, 1893, and by 1894 consisted of a nine-hole course at Rocky Hill Farm laid out by Willie Davis, the pro at Royal Montreal, and a short six-hole course for beginners, women, and children. The driving force behind the club was Theodore Havemeyer, who became enraptured with the game at the Pau Golf Club in France and was elected the first president of the newly formed USGA in December 1894. Havemeyer formed a syndicate to purchase 140 acres for the course, whose members were the social elite "400" that included Cornelius Vanderbilt, Oliver H. P. Belmont, and John Jacob Astor. The magnificent Y-shaped Beaux Arts club-house was one of the first commissions of the young architect Whitney

Warren, who won a competition for the design. He went on to found the renowned firm of Warren & Wetmore, whose buildings include New York City's Grand Central Station, the New York Yacht Club, and the Westchester Biltmore Hotel—which serves as the clubhouse for the Westchester Country Club. After hosting the inaugural U.S. Amateur in 1895, Newport Country Club held the centennial U.S. Amateur in 1995, with Tiger Woods taking home the Havemeyer Trophy that is presented each year to the amateur champion. **OPPOSITE:** Newport Country Club before hosting the U.S. Women's Open in 2006. **BELOW:** A portrait of Theodore Havemeyer by George Holston.

THE AGE OF THE GREAT TRIUMVIRATE

42 | THE GREAT TRIUMVIRATE

Harry Vardon, James Braid, and J. H. Taylor, known as "the Great Triumvirate," were the three golfing superstars of the early twentieth century. Born within a year of one another, all three came from humble, working class backgrounds. Vardon was born in 1871 in Grouville, on Jersey in the Channel Islands, and started out as a caddie at Royal Jersey. He won a record six Open Championships, beginning in 1896 at Muirfield, the same year he became the professional at Ganton. Braid was a lanky Scot with a dry sense of humor from the village of Earlsferry, who learned the game at the nearby course in Elie. Between 1901 and 1910, he won the Open Championship five times. John Henry Taylor was born in Northam in Devon, and started out as a caddie on the links of Westward Ho! J. H. won five Opens, beginning in 1894 at Sandwich, the first time the championship was held in England. **OPPOSITE:** Left to right, Harry Vardon, Ted Ray, James Braid, and J. H. Taylor in June 1922 at Gleneagles in Scotland.

The first ladies' golf clubs had been founded in Britain in the 1860s. The St. Andrews Ladies' Putting Club held its opening meeting on September 5, 1867, and the following November played for a challenge trophy consisting of a St. Andrew's cross made from pebbles. The earliest women's competition on record was a match during the eighteenth century held annually on New Year's Day among the fishwives of Musselburgh and Fisherrow. The open women's golf competition at Musselburgh dates from 1811, played on a putting course, with the winner receiving a prize of a creel and a skull (a small fishing basket) and consolation prizes of "two fine silk handkerchiefs from Barcelona." The August 25, 1894 issue of the *The Illustrated American* featured a design by Aubrey Beardsley for an invitation to the opening of the Prince's Ladies Golf Club on Mitcham Common in Surrey on July 16, 1894. Beardsley's art nouveau design displays a highly stylized interpretation of the female golfing costume of the era, with Pierrot serving as the caddie. **OPPOSITE:** Cover of the *The Illustrated American*, August 25, 1894.

THE ILLUSTRATED AMERICAN

Vol. XVI. No. 8

Whole Number 236

A Weekly News-Magazine

For the Week Ending August 25, 1894

CONTENTS

Copyright, 1894
BY LORILLARD SPENCER
5 and 7 East 16th St., New York
ENTERED AT POST OFFICE AS SECOND-CLASS MATTER

Price 10 Cents

AVBREY
BEARDSLEY

Charles Blair Macdonald, the imperious patriarch of golf in the United States and a native Chicagoan, organized the Chicago Golf Club in 1892, after local interest in the game was raised by the English delegation to the Chicago World's Fair held that year. The initial course consisted of seven short holes, but a year later Macdonald created an eighteen-hole course in the suburb of Wheaton, making it the first eighteen-hole course in the United States. Macdonald's layout, which is essentially unchanged, remains a masterpiece of strategic design. The Chicago Golf Club hosted three early U.S. Opens—in 1897, 1900, and 1911—as well as the 1928 and 2005 Walker Cup Matches. The winner in 1897 was Englishman Joe Lloyd, the pro at Essex Country Club in Massachusetts, who spent his winters at Pau Golf Club in France. In 1900, the great English player Harry Vardon took the title while on his first exhibition tour of the United States. In the 1911 Open, Johnny McDermott won in a three-way play-off, becoming the first American-born player to win the national championship; he successfully defended his title the following year. McDermott, who played out of the Atlantic City Country Club, had learned the game in the hardscrabble caddie yards of Philadelphia, and his victories foreshadowed the new era in American golf ushered in the following year when Francis Ouimet defeated Harry Vardon and Ted Ray to win the U.S. Open at The Country Club. **OPPOSITE:** Chicago Golf Club. **BELOW:** John J. McDermott, winner of the U.S. Open in 1911 and 1912.

The beautiful Lady Margaret Scott, in her signature tam-o'-shanter and long, flowing skirts anchored by lead weights and webbing to prevent any petticoats from showing, was the first star of women's golf. Her style of play was described as dashing, fearless, fascinating. She won the first three British Ladies' Championships, beginning with her victory at the nine-hole ladies' course at Royal Lytham and St. Annes in 1893. Her next two championships were at Littlestone, overlooking the Channel Coast at the edge of Romney Marsh, and Portrush, on the Antrim Coast in what is now Northern Ireland.

Following her victory in 1895, Lady Margaret, who was the great-granddaughter of the first Earl of Eldon, the influential Lord Chancellor during the reign of George IV, retired from competitive golf. Portrush produced a bevy of leading women golfers in the 1890s. It was the home course of the Hezlet sisters—May, Florence, and Violet—and of Rhona Adair. May Hezlet won the British Ladies' Championship in 1899, 1902, and 1907, while Adair was the victor in 1900 and 1903. **OPPOSITE:** Lady Margaret Scott, winner of the British Ladies' Championship from 1893 to 1895.

Golf in France has a long and rich history, with the early clubs serving as enclaves for English and Scottish golfers. Several of the fin de siècle courses were established at the fashionable resort towns of the Normandy Coast and Pas de Calais, where the English influence was the strongest. In Normandy, there were early clubs at Dinard, founded by retired British army officers returning from India and Egypt, with the course designed by Tom Dunn in 1887, followed by Dieppe, Deauville, Cabourg, and Etretat. The Dieppe course at Pourville dates from 1897 and is the handiwork of Willie Park, Jr. The Old Course at Deauville, laid out in 1899, is no more, but the New Course, designed by Tom Simpson in the 1920s, is alive and well, with views of the Seine estuary and a timber-framed clubhouse that was an eighteenth-century cider brewery. Golf de Cabourg, founded in 1907, is a links-style course running through marshland near the resort that became the fictionalized Balbec in Proust's *Remembrance of Things Past*. Proust depicts a band of golfers leaving the course, with one of the male players announcing that Andrée shot a 77, "a course record." Golf d'Etretat, begun in 1908, spreads across the top of the soaring chalk cliffs of the Alabaster Coast, high above the sea. **OPPOSITE:** Travel poster for Golf de Sarlabot (a course in Cabourg, no longer in existence), by René Vincent. **BELOW:** Travel poster for Dieppe.

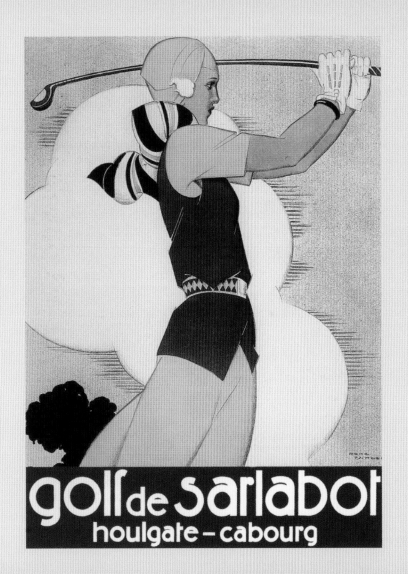

There is a ring of wonderfully remote links in Donegal, a mix of the new and antiquarian, surrounded by the stark, stony grandeur of Ireland's windswept northwest. Ballyliffin Golf Club on the Inishowen Peninsula boasts two courses. The Old Links was designed by Eddie Hackett in the early 1970s, while the Glashedy Links, named after Glashedy Rock bubbling out of the Atlantic, was completed in 1995, created by Pat Ruddy and Tom Craddock. Portsalon Golf Club, which hugs the sandy shore of Lough Swilly beneath the Knockalla Mountains on the Fanad Peninsula, dates from 1891, but was revamped in the 1990s by Ruddy, Ireland's leading contemporary course architect. Old Tom Morris laid out the rumpled links at Rosapenna in 1891, sandwiched between the scenic splendor of Sheephaven and Mulroy Bays facing Muckish Mountain. Over a century later, Ruddy fashioned the new Sandy Hills Course at Rosapenna, sculpted from the vast chain of sand dunes that runs above the old course. **OPPOSITE:** The Sandy Hills Course at Rosapenna, third hole, overlooking Sheephaven Bay.

The English brought golf to the coast of Calais, on the French side of the Channel, in the early 1900s, where the game continues to flourish at the seaside resorts of Wimereux, Le Touquet, and Hardelot. Wimereux, established in 1901 near Boulogne sur Mer, is a true links that straddles the dunes, with views across the Channel to the white cliffs of Dover. The course was rebuilt after World War I by the English architect and golf historian Sir Guy Campbell with Cecil Hutchinson. Le Touquet Paris-Plage is a seaside resort that dates from 1876, when it was created by the owner of *Le Figaro* newspaper, but it became a golfing destination par excellence after it was acquired and developed in 1903 by the English linoleum magnate Sir John Whitley. In 1904, the British prime minister Lord Balfour, an ardent golfer, inaugurated the La Forêt Course designed by Horace Hutchinson. The seaside La Mer Course, designed by the august Harry Colt, made its debut in 1930. In the 1920s and 1930s, Le Touquet became a fashionable getaway for the English literati and smart set, including Noël Coward and P. G. Wodehouse—who built his villa "Low Wood" in 1934 and was living there during World War II when he was interned by the German army. The original Hardelot course was founded in 1906 by Whitley, who walked the entire length of the Côte d'Opale in search of an ideal site. The present-day course carved through the pines was designed in 1931 by Tom Simpson and restored after the war.

OPPOSITE: Railway poster for Wimereux, by Leon Dupin. **BELOW:** Railway poster for golf at Le Touquet Paris-Plage, by Edouard Courchinoux.

County Sligo Golf Club, known as Rosses Point, was founded in 1894 and is the championship course of Ireland's northwest, set in the landscape of Irish myth that inspired the poetry of William Butler Yeats. Located four miles north of the harbor town of Sligo on the promontory of Rosses Point, the course plunges down to the Atlantic beneath the somber tabletop mountain of Ben Bulben to the north and Knocknarea to the south. The site of the course, originally leased from Yeats's maternal uncle Henry Middleton, found its way into one of Yeats's verses: *"My name is Henry Middleton, I have a small demesne, A small forgotten house that's set, On a storm bitten green."* The original nine was laid out by George Combe, the first honorary secretary of the Irish Golfing Union, who was responsible for much of the design of Royal County Down, with the present course the work of Harry Colt during the 1920s. The Tudor pavilion of a clubhouse, designed by the Dublin architect George O'Connor, dates from 1912. After turning from the sea, the course runs along the estuary across from gray-walled Lissadell House, the childhood home of Yeats's friends the poet and suffragist Eva Gore-Booth and her sister Constance, one of the leaders of the 1916 Revolution, who are the subjects of one of Yeats's greatest poems. The finishing holes look across the estuary to the steeple of the old Drumcliffe church, where Yeats is buried. **OPPOSITE:** County Sligo Golf Club (Rosses Point), eleventh hole, facing Ben Bulben and Drumcliffe Estuary.

Golf has a long tradition in Switzerland, with sporty alpine courses featuring spectacular vistas. Engadine Golf Club, founded in 1898 at Samaden, not far from St. Moritz, was the first of the Swiss courses. Laid out high above the Engadine Valley, at an elevation of 5,700 feet, the course is flat but laced by a stream and raked by the winds that blow through the Maloja Pass. In Lucerne, the Dietschiberg Golf Club, popular with British visitors, was founded in 1903, overlooking the Lake of the Four Cantons. Golf came to Crans-sur-Sierre in 1905, courtesy of Sir Arnold Lunn, one of the pioneers of alpine skiing, who built the Palace Hotel at nearby Montana. The new course at Crans was built in 1923 above the Rhône Valley, with breathtaking views of the Matterhorn and Monte Rosa. It has hosted the Swiss Open, now known as the Omega European Masters, since 1971, and is a favorite stop on the European Tour. **OPPOSITE:** Travel poster for Engadine Golf Club at Samaden, the first course in Switzerland. **BELOW:** Travel poster by Emil Cardinaux for golf at Crans-Montana, the site of the Palace Hotel.

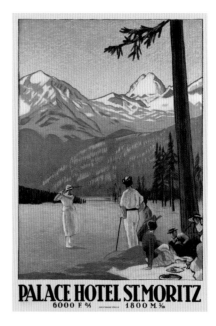

SAMADEN
18 HOLE GOLF LINKS
ENGADINE · 5670 ft. · SWITZERLAND

Golf in Italy began in 1903 at Acquasanta Golf Club, laid out among the filigreed evergreens of the Roman countryside near the Appian Way and in plain view of the towering arches of the ancient Claudine Aqueduct. Most of the leading courses are clustered in the Lake District of the north, along the shores of Como, Menaggio, and Garda. Menaggio e Cadenabbia, the second-oldest course, was founded in 1907 by four Englishmen in the hills high above Menaggio on the western shore of Lake Como, with views over the rooftops of Croso out to the mountains. The quaint Victorian clubhouse is the unlikely home of one of the world's great golf libraries, its twelve hundred volumes including many books on early British golf. Next oldest is Carezza al Lago, created in 1914 above the iridescent green waters of Carezza in the Dolomites. The Villa d'Este course, near the famous hotel with its palazzo on Lake Como, dates from 1926, running along the shore of the small Lago di Montofano. Then there is Varese, established in 1934, another of the splendid courses of the Lake District, where Peter Alliss won the Italian Open in 1958. Its fairways are lined with firs and chestnuts, overlooking Lake Varese and beneath the Monte Campo dei Fiori, with a frescoed clubhouse that was a twelfth-century Benedictine convent. Continuing to the west, Biella, popularly known as Le Betulle, or The Birch, is one of Italy's top-ranked courses, cascading through thousands of white birches above the village of Magnano. It was designed by the English architect John Morrison. **OPPOSITE:** Travel poster for Cadenabbia on Lake Como, the site of the Menaggio e Cadenabbia Golf Club. **BELOW:** Travel poster for the course at Carezza al Lago.

In 1896, Shinnecock Hills Golf Club in Southampton, New York, hosted the second official U.S. Amateur and U.S. Open Championships, the inaugural events having been played at Newport. The Amateur, which was considered the main event at the time, was won by H. J. Whigham. Controversy broke out before the Open began when some of the Scottish professionals threatened to boycott because of the entries in the tournament of John Shippen, an African-American whose father was a minister and schoolteacher at the Shinnecock Reservation, and Oscar Bunn, a Shinnecock Indian who had caddied at the course. Theodore Havemeyer, the president of the nascent USGA, settled the dispute by declaring that Shippen and Bunn would be allowed to compete even if they were the only two players in the field. The Open was won by

James Foulis, the son of the foreman of Tom Morris's golf shop at St. Andrews, who had emigrated earlier that year to serve as the first professional at the Chicago Golf Club. Foulis was the winner by three shots over the defending champion, Horace Rawlins. Shippen, who had been taught the game by Willie Dunn, was in contention, ending up tied for fifth. He went on to serve as the pro at Aronomink in Philadelphia and nearby Maidstone in East Hampton, and eventually at Shady Rest in New Jersey, a club with a largely black membership, where he was the pro for thirty-six years. **OPPOSITE:** Shinnecock Hills Golf Club, twelfth hole, on the existing course designed by William Flynn in 1930. **BELOW:** James Foulis, the winner of the 1896 U.S. Open at Shinnecock.

The members of Shinnecock Hills encouraged women to play golf, and Beatrix Hoyt of Shinnecock became the leading American woman golfer at the turn of the century. In 1896, sixteen-year-old Beatrix won the U.S. Women's Amateur at Morris County in New Jersey, the second year the event was held, earning her the ornate winner's trophy based on an Etruscan design donated by Robert Cox of Edinburgh. She went on to win the championship again in 1897 and 1898, and was the medalist in the tournament's qualifying round for five straight years. She retired from competitive golf in 1900, at age twenty, after losing to Margaret Curtis in the semifinal round. Beatrix was the granddaughter of Salmon P. Chase, Secretary of the Treasury under President Lincoln and then Chief Justice of the Supreme Court beginning in 1864. In 1890, her mother, Janet (Nettie) Ralston Chase Hoyt, invited William Merritt Chase to establish a summer art school at Shinnecock Hills for plein air painting, modeled after the art colonies she had seen in France. Other Southampton residents, including Samuel Parrish, provided land for the Art Village, with a large studio designed by Stanford White surrounded by residential cottages. Chase's school opened in 1891 as the "American Barbizon," the same year that the Shinnecock Hills Golf Club was founded. **OPPOSITE:** Lady golfers in front of the Shinnecock clubhouse in 1901. **BELOW:** Beatrix Hoyt, c. 1895.

Golf in Mexico began in 1897 with a nine-hole course, christened San Pedro Golf Club, that was founded by American William Townsend on a barren strip of land in Puebla, forty-five minutes southwest of Mexico City by mule-drawn streetcar. In 1907, construction began on Mexico City Country Club, with 1899 U.S. Open champion Willie Smith, one of the famed trio of Scottish-born golfing brothers, serving as the first pro. Smith met a sad and untimely end when the club was shelled and ransacked in 1915 during the Mexican Revolution and he was critically injured. When the political climate improved, the Chapultepec Golf Club was organized in 1923, designed by Willie's brother Alex. John Bredemus, the architect of Colonial Country Club, came down from Texas to lay out a number of nine-hole courses in the 1920s, including Guadalajara Country Club and Monterey Golf Club. The godfather of Mexican golf was Percy Clifford, whose English parents had settled in Mexico City. A six-time Mexican Amateur champion between 1928 and 1938, Clifford designed the thirty-six-hole Club de Golf Mexico in 1947, Mexico City's premier course and the site of the 1966 World Cup. He went on to design more than forty courses in Mexico, including such well-known layouts as Vallescondido in Mexico City and the Fairmont Pierre Marques course in Acapulco. **OPPOSITE:** The cover of the program for the 1937 Mexico Amateur Golf Championship, held at the Mexico City Country Club and the Chapultepec Golf Club.

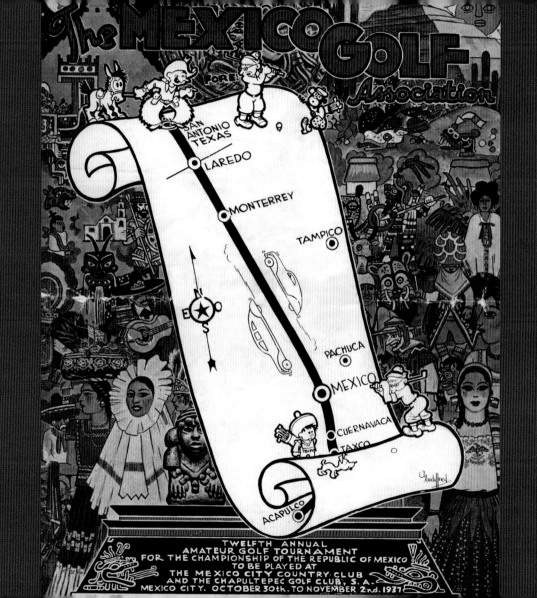

The MEXICO GOLF Association

SAN ANTONIO TEXAS
LAREDO
MONTERREY
TAMPICO
PACHUCA
MEXICO
CUERNAVACA
TAXCO
ACAPULCO

TWELFTH ANNUAL
AMATEUR GOLF TOURNAMENT
FOR THE CHAMPIONSHIP OF THE REPUBLIC OF MEXICO
TO BE PLAYED AT
THE MEXICO CITY COUNTRY CLUB
AND THE CHAPULTEPEC GOLF CLUB, S.A.
MEXICO CITY, OCTOBER 30th. TO NOVEMBER 2nd. 1937

As the game caught on, the number of golf courses in the United States during the 1890s spread like wildfire. In 1894, the first American golf magazine, *The Golfer*, began publication in New York. During that decade, literary magazines such as *Harper's*, *Ainslee's*, *Leslie's*, and *Collier's Weekly*, which catered to a growing middle class, also featured articles about golf and covers depicting golfers, further popularizing the game. Edward Penfield, who made his mark as the master of the American art poster by designing advertising posters for *Harper's* magazine, created popular golf calendars for 1899 and 1900. The 1899 calendar featured a cover and nine golf holes, displaying the fashionably dressed and serious couples on the course that are the hallmark of Penfield's style. **OPPOSITE** and **BELOW:** Two pages and the cover from the *Golf Calendar* for 1899, by Edward Penfield.

Argentina has an illustrious golfing tradition. As in most locales around the globe, the British were in the forefront in introducing the game, with English and Scottish executives from the Argentine Southern Railways first playing in the dunes of Playa Grande on the Atlantic coast, leading to the founding of the fine links at Mar del Plata in 1900, where the sea is visible from every hole. The course was designed by Juan Dentone, the first Argentine professional, with camels used for much of the construction. The Lomas Athletic Club in Buenos Aires laid out its course in 1896, making it the earliest golf club. Córdoba Golf Club in Villa Allende, the home of 2007 U.S. Open winner Angel Cabrera, is a rolling, oak-lined course at the foot of the Sierras Chicas, laid out in the late 1920s by amateur Hector Bozzachi. In 1935, the Jockey Club in Buenos Aires opened its Red and Blue courses designed by the renowned Alister MacKenzie. Other leading courses around the capital include Olivos, famous for its fast and rolling greens, Hindu, Martindale, and, more recently, the Buenos Aires Golf Club, which hosted the 2000 World Cup. There is also a vintage nine-hole layout on the grounds of the landmark hotel in Rosario de la Frontera (Rosary of the Frontier). The area is famed for its hot spring baths, drawn from the thermal springs that were called *Inti Tacu* or "Waters from the Sun" by the Incas. In 1905, the first Argentine Open, originally known as the Open Championship of the River Plate, was held in Buenos Aires, with Scotland's Mungo Park the winner. **OPPOSITE:** Travel poster for Córdoba, Argentina. **BELOW:** Travel poster for the Rosario de la Frontera resort.

John Ball, Jr., of the Royal Liverpool Golf Club, or Hoylake, was the first great British amateur golfer, winning the British Amateur Championship a record eight times between 1888 and 1912. Shy and unassuming, his great rivals were Harold Hilton, also of Hoylake, and Freddie Tait of St. Andrews. Ball's father was the proprietor of the Royal Hotel at Hoylake, which served as the club's original clubhouse. In 1890, Ball pulled off a legendary double, winning both the Amateur Championship at Hoylake and the British Open at Prestwick—making him the first amateur and the first Englishman to win the Open. In 1899, Ball defeated Tait in their historic battle at the Amateur Championship at Prestwick, with Ball prevailing on the first hole of sudden death in the thirty-six-hole final match. Many years later Bernard Darwin wrote in *Green Memories* that "the more matches I watch the more I think that this was the greatest, the most prostratingly exciting of them all." **OPPOSITE:** A portrait of John Ball, Jr. by R. E. Morrison from 1899, which hangs in the Hoylake clubhouse. **BELOW:** An early photograph of Ball.

Frederick Guthrie Tait, the son of a professor at Edinburgh University, was killed leading his regiment of the Black Watch into battle at Koodoosberg Drift in 1900, during the Boer War. He learned the game over the Old Course at St. Andrews, where he was a popular figure. Tait was a leading amateur of the 1890s, and while he never achieved victory in the Open, he won the British Amateur crowns at Sandwich in 1896 and Hoylake in 1898. In 1899, he lost to John Ball on the thirty-seventh hole of the final of the British Amateur at Prestwick after playing a remarkable recovery shot to the green from the flooded bunker on the famous seventeenth or Alps hole while his ball was literally floating. At the presentation ceremony, Tait declared: "I would rather be beaten by Johnny Ball than by any other man in the world."

OPPOSITE: Freddie Tait prepares to play out of the flooded bunker while John Ball looks on in their match in the final of the 1899 Amateur Championship at Prestwick.

The Auchterlonies were one of the great clans of St. Andrews golfers and also renowned for their skill as club makers. Laurence, or Laurie, Auchterlonie, one of the six golfing brothers, came to America in 1899, where he was the professional at Saint Andrew's Golf Club in Hastings-on-Hudson. He won the U.S. Open in 1902 at Garden City, breaking 80 in all four rounds using the new rubber-cored ball invented by Coburn Haskell. His younger brother Willie won the British Open in 1893 at Prestwick, when he was only twenty-one, and remains the youngest winner in the history of the championship after Young Tom Morris. Willie became the honorary professional to the Royal and Ancient for many years, and was succeeded in the post by his son, also named Laurie. It was Willie who founded the family club-making business around 1894 with his brother David, after they had both served apprenticeships with the famous St. Andrews club maker Robert Forgan. Forgan, who pioneered the use of hickory shafts, was the nephew of Hugh Philp, the Stradivarius of St. Andrews club makers. David and Willie Auchterlonie were subsequently joined in the business by their brothers Laurie and Tom, with David eventually departing in 1912 to become the pro at the Czech resort of Carlsbad (Karlovy Vary) and then Potchefstroom in South Africa. Auchterlonies Golf Shop, featuring handcrafted antique wooden putters, remains a bustling enterprise located at Golf Place in St. Andrews to this day. **OPPOSITE:** A bearded Robert Forgan seated in the finishing shop of the Forgan Golf Club Works in St. Andrews, c. 1880, while his son Thomas stands behind the workbench.

Ganton is steeped in history, having been laid out in 1891 by Tom Chisholm of St. Andrews on Sir Charles Legard's Ganton Estate, ten miles inland from Scarborough, in the Yorkshire Wolds. Harry Vardon put Ganton on the map when he became the professional from 1896 to 1903, followed by Ted Ray. Vardon's famous seventy-two-hole home-and-away clash with Willie Park, Jr., in 1899 finished with Vardon closing out Park by 11 and 10 over the final thirty-six holes at Ganton. Vardon, Ray, J. H. Taylor, and James Braid all contributed to a major redesign of the course in 1905, and it seems that every British architect of note had a hand in making modifications over the years. The course is characterized by exceptionally deep and profuse bunkers lined with native sand, wild flowering grasses, and cascades of golden gorse, much of which was planted in the late 1930s. Ganton hosted the 1949 Ryder Cup, the 2000 Curtis Cup won by the United States in a tight 10–8 match, and the 2003 Walker Cup won by the Great Britain and Ireland side. **OPPOSITE:** Ganton Golf Club in Yorkshire, fifth hole.

Harold Horsfall Hilton and his phlegmatic counterpart, John Ball, were the two unrivaled British amateurs of the turn of the nineteenth century. Like Ball, Hilton's home course was Royal Liverpool at Hoylake. Hilton, a chain-smoking bantamweight, had a fast swing, a sharp mind, and a well-deserved reputation as a cool competitor. He won two British Open championships, in 1892 and in 1897—when he nipped James Braid—before going on to win the British Amateur in 1900, 1901, 1911, and 1913. In 1911, he also captured the U.S. Amateur Championship, beating Fred Herreshoff in the final at Apawamis Golf Club in Rye, New York. Hilton and Herreshoff finished the thirty-six-hole match all square. On the first hole of the sudden death play-off, Hilton was the beneficiary of one of golfing history's all-time lucky breaks when his second shot to the first hole bounced off a rock and onto the green instead of going over, enabling him to win the match. He also served as editor of the English golf magazine *Golf Monthly*.

OPPOSITE: A painting of Harold Hilton **BELOW:** Hilton (left) with Robert Harris before the final of the 1913 British Amateur at St. Andrews, which Hilton won. Harris was captain of the British Walker Cup team in the inaugural 1922 match and also served as captain in 1923 and 1926.

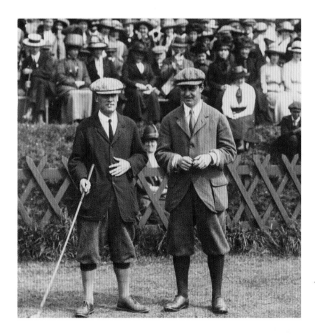

The Machrie Golf Links was laid out in 1891 on the island of Islay in the Hebrides, framed by the sands of Laggan Bay and the peat bogs brimming with wildflowers that give Islay's single malts their distinctively peaty flavor. The course was laid out by Willie Campbell of Musselburgh (who later became the first professional at The Country Club in Brookline, Massachusetts), with revisions by the English architect and golfing authority Donald Steel in the 1980s. Willie Campbell's wife, Georgina, also born in Musselburgh, played and taught golf as well, making her the first woman professional in the United States. Machrie is one of those rare museum pieces of early Scottish golf, sauntering through the dunes while serving up a multitude of blind shots. In 1901, the Triumvirate of Braid, Taylor, and Vardon made the sea voyage to Islay to compete in a tournament for a first-place prize of £100, a princely sum at the time. Nowadays, an old whitewashed farmhouse serves as the hotel and clubhouse; nearby is the village of Bowmore, with its brightly painted houses and the old church built in the round so that the devil would have no place to hide. **OPPOSITE:** The Machrie Links, ninth hole, running along Laggan Bay.

Harry Vardon was the supreme golfer of his generation. His powerful, fluid swing and the Vardon grip remain the basis of the modern fundamentals of golf. Vardon did much to spread the popularity of golf in the United States by playing exhibition matches around the country. On his year-long tour beginning in January 1900, he won the U.S. Open at the Chicago Golf Club, with his rival J. H. Taylor finishing second. In 1913, he returned to the United States, losing to Francis Ouimet in a play-off at The Country Club in the most historic upset in the annals of American golf. In 1920, when he was fifty, Vardon was on the verge of winning the U.S. Open at Inverness, holding a six-shot lead with seven holes to play, when a freak gale swept over the course and caused him to lose the championship by a stroke to Ted Ray. **OPPOSITE:** Harry Vardon tees off on the opening hole at St. Andrews in the 1890s, while a caped Old Tom Morris looks on.

J. H. Taylor was the first great English professional golfer. With a distinctive flat-footed swing, he was runner-up to Vardon in 1900 at the U.S. Open at Chicago, but beat Vardon that same year at St. Andrews to win his second British Open. He won his fifth Open title in 1913 at Hoylake. Taylor was a tireless proponent of golf and played a major role in the formation of the British PGA. He captained the victorious British Ryder Cup team at Southport and Ainsdale in 1933. Although self-educated, he was well read and wrote a highly entertaining and literate autobiography. Taylor was the pro at Royal Mid-Surrey for more than forty years before retiring to a cottage on a hill overlooking the links of Westward Ho!, near where he was born, which he described as having "the finest view in Christendom." **OPPOSITE:** J. H. Taylor putting in 1908. **BELOW:** A caricature of J. H. by Sir Leslie Ward, known as "Spy."

James Braid played golf with what Horace Hutchinson described as "a divine fury." Taylor and Vardon had already won the Open Championship three times before the late-blooming Braid burst on the scene, winning five Opens between 1901 and 1910. Braid was known for understated wisdom and was great friends with Bernard Darwin, who wrote his biography. In 1904, the English course architect Herbert Fowler completed the design of his heathland masterpiece at Walton Heath, and Braid became the Club's first professional, a position he held until his death in 1950. The "Sage of Walton Heath" also made his mark as a gifted designer of golf courses, although he disliked traveling and frequently worked off topographical maps. Two of Braid's most memorable and enduring creations are the King's and Queen's courses at Gleneagles in Scotland, completed in 1919 at the famous golf resort surrounded by the panorama of the Ochil and Grampian ranges. **OPPOSITE:** James Braid blasts out of the rough at Walton Heath in 1922. **BELOW:** Travel poster for Elie and Earlsferry, the village where Braid was born.

Bernard Darwin, born in 1876, is universally regarded as the greatest of golf writers. Darwin, the grandson of Charles Darwin, learned the game on family holidays at the Aberdovey Golf Club, the oldest course in Wales, which had been founded in 1886 by his maternal uncle Colonel Richard Ruck. Darwin called it "the course that my soul loves best of all the courses in the world." He captained the Cambridge golf team, and after a brief and unfulfilling career in the law, decided to pursue his real passion and became the golf correspondent for *The Times* (London) in 1907, a position he held until 1953 while also writing for *Country Life* and *The American Golfer*. Darwin's books include *Green Memories* and *Golf Between Two Wars*, as well as the autobiographical *The World That Fred Made*. He also wrote scores of introductions and club histories, as well as delightful children's books illustrated by his wife, Elinor. **OPPOSITE:** Aberdovey Golf Club in Wales, twelfth hole, the course that Bernard Darwin loved most of all.

GOLF TAKES HOLD IN THE UNITED STATES

67 | A RECORD NEVER BROKEN

Willie Anderson, who won the U.S. Open four times in its early years, was born in 1879 in a house opposite the Abbey Church in the old golfing town of North Berwick, where his father was the head greenkeeper and starter at the West Links. In 1896, Willie immigrated to the United States with his father and his brother, Tom Jr., who became the pro at the Misquamicut Golf Club in Rhode Island. The following year, when he was seventeen, Willie entered the first of the thirteen Opens in which he competed, held at the Chicago Golf Club, and finished second, one shot behind Joe Lloyd. Anderson's first U.S. Open win came at Myopia Hunt Club in 1901, defeating Alex and Willie Smith in the first eighteen-hole play-off in the history of the event. He then strung together three straight wins from 1903 to 1905—the only man ever to win the U.S. Open three times in a row—prevailing in another play-off at Baltusrol in 1903, then winning at Chicago's Glen View in 1904 and again at Myopia in 1905. A slight man who dressed in an oversize tartan wool cap, baggy plaid trousers, and an old tweed jacket, he also won the prestigious Western Open four times. His record of four U.S. Open victories has been equaled by Bobby Jones, Ben Hogan, and Jack Nicklaus, but has yet to be surpassed. Anderson died in 1910 at age thirty-one, at which time he was the pro at the Philadelphia Cricket Club, one of the ten clubs at which he served as the professional during a fourteen-year period; the others included Apawamis, Owentsia, St. Louis, and Baltusrol. **OPPOSITE:** Three early U.S. Open champions: four-time winner Willie Anderson, wearing a bow tie, is seated with his arm around Alex Smith, the U.S. Open winner in 1906 and 1910. Horace Rawlins, winner of the first U.S. Open in 1895, sits on the ground in front of them.

Walter Travis, who emigrated to the United States from Australia, took up the game late in life, and through steely and steadfast determination became the best amateur golfer in the country. In the early 1900s Travis, known as "the Old Man," and Foxhall Keene of Rockaway Hunt Club, the top polo player in the country and an all-around athlete, were the only two scratch golfers in the United States. Travis was a short hitter but uncannily accurate and a deadeye putter. In 1900, 1901, and 1903 he won the U.S. Amateur. In 1904, when he was already forty-two, he became the first American to win the British Amateur, triumphing at Sandwich using a center-shafted Schenectady putter that was subsequently banned in Britain. Travis was a major force in the golf world off the course as well. He founded and edited *The American Golfer* and was an accomplished course architect, his layouts including Ekwanok in Vermont, Westchester Country Club, and the remodeling of the Garden City Golf Club on Long Island originally designed by Devereux Emmett. **OPPOSITE:** Walter Travis in action.

The honor of the oldest golf club in South Africa goes to Royal Durban, laid out within the confines of a horse-racing track in the heart of the city in 1902, and rebuilt in 1932. Durban Country Club, in contrast, is a hummocky links course set beside the Indian Ocean and overlooking the Blue Lagoon estuary. South Africa's top-ranked course, it was designed in 1920 by George Waterman and Laurie Waters, a Scottish pro from St. Andrews, who had served as an assistant to Old Tom Morris before emigrating to South Africa for his health. Waters won the inaugural South Africa Open in 1903, while serving as the pro at Royal Johannesburg and Rhodesia's Royal Salisbury—which

he did for much of his career. Durban has staged sixteen Opens, more than any other club. Humewood Golf Club in Port Elizabeth, fanned by the winds of Algoa Bay, is another outstanding links course. It was created by the British architect Major S. V. Hotchkin in 1931. The South African Golf Union was founded in 1909, when the South African Championship was contested at Potchefstroom in the Northwest province, the first course with grass greens in the South African interior. **OPPOSITE:** Durban Country Club, fourth hole. **BELOW:** Travel poster for golf at Potchefstroom in South Africa.

H. Chandler Egan won the U.S. Amateur Championship in 1904 at Baltusrol when he was still an undergraduate at Harvard, having captured the collegiate championship in 1902. He successfully defended his Amateur title the next year at the Chicago Golf Club. Egan moved to Oregon in 1911 to become an apple grower before settling in California in the 1920s. He also took up golf course architecture, designing several courses in the Pacific Northwest, including the top-notch Eugene Country Club in 1925. (Robert Trent Jones revised it in 1967, reversing the tees and greens.) Egan also worked with Robert Hunter on remodeling Pebble Beach during the 1920s. After a twenty-year hiatus, Egan competed in the 1929 Amateur Championship held at Pebble Beach, making it all the way to the semifinals. **OPPOSITE:** H. Chandler Egan (left) with Bobby Jones.

Oakmont Golf Club is the paradigm of penal golf courses. It was completed in 1904 by Henry Clay Fownes, the golf-obsessed Pittsburgh industrialist, as an austere Scottish-style links on an open plain a dozen miles north of Pittsburgh. In the years following World War II, thousands of trees were planted and the fairways became enclosed corridors, but in the decade leading up to the 2007 U.S. Open the trees were largely removed, returning the course to its Fownesian vision of an open, treeless links. Fownes's son, William Fownes, Jr. (named after his uncle), who won the U.S. Amateur in 1910 and captained the first U.S. Walker Cup team in 1922, continued his father's legacy at Oakmont. Of the many bunkers, which in the old days were lined with furrowed river sand, the ones synonymous with Oakmont's perils are the "Church Pews," the immense blankets of sand between the third and fourth holes that are striped with grassy aisles. But the most nefarious aspects of the course are the multi-tiered greens, hard as marble, that are universally regarded as the most treacherous and terrifying in golf. Oakmont has hosted eight U.S. Opens, with the roll call of winners consisting of Tommy Armour in 1927; Sam Parks, Jr., in 1935, a long shot with local knowledge of the course; Ben Hogan in 1953; Jack Nicklaus in 1962; Johnny Miller in 1973; Larry Nelson in 1983; Ernie Els in 1994; and Angel Cabrera in 2007. **OPPOSITE:** Oakmont Golf Club, seventeenth hole.

Jerome Dunstan "Jerry" Travers, together with his older rival Walter Travis, was one of the two leading American amateurs in the decade prior to World War I. Travers, who came from a well-to-do New York family, started playing golf on the front lawn of his family's estate in Oyster Bay on Long Island in 1896, when he was nine years old. By 1902, he had been taken under the wing of Alex Smith, the pro at the Nassau Country Club in Glen Cove. Alex Smith would himself win the U.S. Open twice, in 1906 at Owentsia and 1910 at the Philadelphia Cricket Club, when he defeated his brother Macdonald and Johnny McDermott in a three-way play-off. Travers, who was known for his ability to scramble and his unruffled temperament, won the U.S. Amateur Championship four times—in 1907, 1908, 1912, and 1913. His 1908 victory included a win in the semifinal match over his great rival, the flinty Travis, at Travis's Garden City home club. **OPPOSITE:** Jerry Travers at the British Amateur Championship.

Arnaud Massy, born in 1877, became the first foreigner and only French golfer to win the British Open when he triumphed at Hoylake in 1907, overcoming heavy winds and torrential rain. (In recent years, Frenchman Jean Van de Velde came agonizingly close to winning the Open at Carnoustie in 1999 before his infamous seven on the seventy-second hole, and Thomas Levet lost in a four-way play-off to Ernie Els in 2002.) Massy, who was of Basque descent, was born in Biarritz and started caddying at the Biarritz course when he was fourteen; he also worked as a sardine fisherman. When he was twenty-one, he began spending summers at North Berwick developing his game under the supervision of Ben Sayers, and married a local woman named Janet Henderson. Their daughter was born during the 1907 Open and they fittingly named her Hoylake. Massey also won the French Open four times, including the inaugural event in 1905 at La Boulie, outside Paris. Later in his career, he was the professional at La Boulie, the first professional at Golf de Chantaco near Biarritz, opened on November 1, 1928, and the private professional to the pasha of Marrakesh in Morocco. **OPPOSITE:** Arnaud Massy playing in the Open Championship at Royal St. George's in 1922.

Golf came to Kenya, which was British East Africa at the time, in 1906, when the Nairobi Golf Club was started with a nine-hole course near the King's African Rifle lines; it became Royal Nairobi in 1935. The course was extended to eighteen holes in 1911, when the new clubhouse was built. Located three miles from the center of the city, the jacaranda trees along the fairways bloom in September and October, and on a very clear day the clubhouse offers a view of Mount Kilimanjaro's outline across the Athi Plains. There are many fine courses in Kenya—two of the best are Karen Country Club and Muthaiga Golf Club. Muthaiga, located in the Nairobi suburb that was a favorite haunt of British society, dates from 1913, becoming eighteen holes in 1926, when the clubhouse was built. The site of the first Kenya Open Championship in 1967, which it continues to host, it is a scenic course renowned for its fine greens. Karen is located in the Nairobi suburb that was once the coffee plantation of Baroness Karen von Blixen, who wrote *Out of Africa* under the pseudonym Isak Dinesen. Founded in 1933, the course is sprinkled with exotic flowering trees and has views of the Ngong Hills. On leaving her farm for good to return to Denmark, von Blixen wrote in *Out of Africa:* "Will the air over the plain quiver with a color that I have on, or the children invent a game in which my name is, or the full moon throw a shadow over the gravel of the drive that was like me, or will the eagles of the Ngong Hills look out for me?" **OPPOSITE:** Muthaiga Golf Club in Kenya.

The Curtis sisters, Harriot and Margaret, were both outstanding amateur golfers from an old-line Boston family, and played out of the Essex County Club in Manchester-by-the-Sea, Massachusetts, where the family had its summer home. Harriot, who was two years older, won the Amateur Championship in 1906 at Brae Burn near Boston, while Margaret was the winner in 1907, defeating her sister in the final at Midlothian outside Chicago. Margaret was victorious again in 1911 and 1912, and continued to compete in the Amateur until she was sixty-five. In 1932, the sisters, who had been introduced to international competition when they competed in the British Ladies' Championship in 1905 at Royal Cromer, donated the

Curtis Cup for a biennial competition between the top women amateurs from the United States and Great Britain, with the inaugural match held that year at Wentworth in England. Harriot was also a leader in the civil rights movement, serving as dean of women at the Hampton Institute in Virginia and secretary of the NAACP. Their portraits were painted by their brother-in-law, the noted portrait artist Charles Hopkinson. **OPPOSITE:** American woman golfers at the 1905 British Ladies' Championship at Cromer, with Harriot Curtis standing in rear center and Margaret Curtis seated far right. **BELOW:** *The Claude Lorraine Glass,* portrait of Harriot Curtis by Charles Hopkinson.

Harry Shapland Colt, born in 1869, established golf course architecture as a recognized profession and art form, weaving natural broadlooms of heather and broom in the Heath Belt around London and creating courses throughout Continental Europe. After graduating from Cambridge, where he captained the golf team, he practiced as a solicitor before becoming the first secretary of Sunningdale in 1900 and setting his sights on design. Colt's masterpieces include Swinley Forest, Wentworth, St. George's Hill, Sunningdale (New Course), and Moor Park around London; Royal Portrush in Northern Ireland, which he redesigned in the early 1930s; and Kennemer and Royal Haagsche in the Netherlands. Colt's design partners for many years were C. H. Alison, who designed courses in Japan and the United States, and J. S. F. Morrison, who worked with Colt on numerous courses in Europe. In the summer of 1913, Colt came to America to consult with George Crump on the design of Pine Valley, the golfing Valhalla in the pine barrens of southern New Jersey. Colt was a strategic designer who worked with the natural contours of the land to frame his holes. He avoided blind shots and had an aversion to straight lines.

OPPOSITE: Sunningdale Golf Club, New Course, designed by Harry Colt.

Dorothy Campbell Hurd was the leading woman golfer of the early 1900s, before the emergence of England's Cecil Leitch. Born in Edinburgh in 1883, the daughter of a metal merchant, she joined the North Berwick Ladies Club when she was thirteen years old and learned the game from the famous professional Ben Sayers over North Berwick's West Links. In 1905, she played in the British Ladies' Championship at Cromer, and was part of the British team that beat a U.S. squad that included the Curtis sisters, planting the seeds for what would become the Curtis Cup competition. In 1908, she lost in the final of the British Ladies', held for the first time at St. Andrews, before a huge gallery, estimated at nine thousand. Old Tom Morris, who was present, died two days later. The following year she won the British Championship at Royal Birkdale and the U.S. Amateur Championship at Merion, becoming the first British-born player to win the U.S. Amateur and the first woman to hold both the British and U.S. Amateur titles. **OPPOSITE:** Dorothy Campbell Hurd (second from right), winner of the 1910 U.S. Women's Amateur at Homewood Country Club in Illinois, poses with the other semifinalists.

W. Herbert Fowler was one of the pioneering English architects of the classic age of design. After distinguishing himself in cricket, hunting, and billiards, he took up golf and quickly became a scratch player. He was given a golden opportunity to prove himself as a designer in 1902, when his brother-in-law, Henry Cosmo Bonsor, director of the Bank of England, obtained the rights to build a course on the six hundred acres of Walton Heath adjacent to his home. Fowler surveyed the site on horseback for several months before creating the heathland masterpiece that opened in 1904, draped with thick swags of purple heather and yellow whins, with the remains of a Roman villa left untouched. Described by Bernard Darwin as "perhaps the most daring and original of all golfing architects," Fowler also worked with other illustrious architects of the era, forming a partnership with Tom Simpson before World War I. They were subsequently joined by John Abercromby and Arthur Croome. Fowler completely redesigned Westward Ho! in 1908. In addition to a second course at Walton Heath, he created another pair of Heath Belt standouts in the Red and Blue courses at the Berkshire in 1928. During and following World War I, he also worked in the United States, creating Eastward Ho! on Cape Cod, and in California designing the Los Angeles Country Club's South and North courses. During the 1920s, he also revised Sacramento's Del Paso and Sequoyah Golf Club in Oakland, another hidden jewel. **OPPOSITE:** Walton Heath, Old Course, designed by Herbert Fowler, fourth hole.

Donald Ross, a native of Dornoch in Scotland, apprenticed under Old Tom Morris at St. Andrews before becoming the professional and greenkeeper at Royal Dornoch. He emigrated to Boston in 1898 at the urging of Robert Wilson, an astronomy professor at Harvard who spent his summers in Dornoch and arranged for Ross to become the professional at Oakley Golf Club in Watertown. While in Boston, Ross met James Tufts, the soda fountain magnate and founder of Tufts University, who hired him in 1900 as the professional at the resort Tufts had recently built at Pinehurst in North Carolina. The sandy pine barrens were an ideal site for shaping inland links-style courses, and in 1907 Ross created Pinehurst No. 2, which he continued to revise the rest of his life. Ross adopted some of Dornoch's design features, such as the crowned greens, angled fairways, and boldly contoured chipping areas. He remained based at Pinehurst and closely associated with the Tufts family for the rest of his career, until his death in 1948. **OPPOSITE:** Donald Ross poses with his Packard automobile in front of the Pinehurst clubhouse.

Golf course architect Tom Simpson was a patrician figure who favored a beret and cloak and arrived at sites in his chauffeur-driven silver Rolls-Royce. A scratch golfer, he studied law at Cambridge and was called to the bar in 1905, but practiced only briefly. After observing the remodeling of Woking Golf Club outside London, a course he frequently played, Simpson turned to golf course design and became partners with Herbert Fowler in 1910. Simpson's courses in Great Britain and Ireland include Cruden Bay in Scotland, County Louth (Baltray) in Ireland, and the revision of Ballybunion. He did much of his most artistic work on the Continent, including Morfontaine and Chiberta in France and Royal Antwerp and Spa in Belgium. Simpson also wrote about golf course architecture with great flair, and insisted that all good design was based on the design principles of the Old Course at St. Andrews. He wrote *The Architectural Side of Golf* with A. N. Wethered, which is illustrated with his own lovely ink and color wash drawings. **OPPOSITE:** County Louth Golf Club (Baltray), designed by Tom Simpson, fourteenth hole.

In 1901, inspired by a series in the British magazine *Golf Illustrated* on the best golf holes, Charles Blair Macdonald became determined to build an ideal course modeled after the great holes of the British Isles. Macdonald, a pioneer of golf in the United States, obtained surveyor's maps of famous holes in Scotland and searched the Eastern Seaboard for just the right terrain on which to build his links. He ultimately acquired 205 acres choked with bayberry bushes on Sebonac Neck in eastern Long Island, just to the north of Shinnecock Hills Golf Club, overlooking Peconic Bay. When the National Golf Links of America opened in 1911, with an exhibition match by the recently crowned U.S. Amateur champion Harold Hilton, it featured Macdonald's interpretation of several legendary golf holes in Scotland, including the Redan and Perfection at North Berwick and the Eden and Road Hole at St. Andrews. Some of the most memorable holes were Macdonald's original creations, such as the Cape Hole and Punchbowl. The course received immediate acclaim and Macdonald continued to reign over the club until his death in 1939. The National has always shunned the limelight, except for hosting the inaugural Walker Cup match in 1922. **OPPOSITE:** The National Golf Links of America, sixteenth hole. **BELOW:** A young Charles Blair Macdonald.

The British railways played an instrumental role in the growth of golf in Great Britain, building and promoting opulent Victorian resort hotels to lure golfers to the courses of the north. The Great North of Scotland Railway commissioned Old Tom Morris to lay out the original course at Cruden Bay, on the east coast of Scotland, in 1899, and built the Cruden Bay Hotel at the same time, a rococo palace of pink Peterhead granite. The course, redesigned by Tom Simpson and Herbert Fowler in 1926, remains resplendent, but the hotel, lauded as "The Brighton of the North," closed in 1932 and was demolished after World War II. The sumptuous Turnberry Hotel, with its distinctive steeply pitched red-tiled roof, was built by the Glasgow and South Western Railway in 1906 on the plateau looking down on the lawn bowling courts and over the sweep of the resort's Ailsa and Arran courses, magnificently restored by Philip MacKenzie Ross after World War II. Gleaneagles, the pleasure palace in the sylvan bower of the Highlands, was the vision of Donald Matheson, general manager of the Caledonian Railway Company. The hotel opened on June 7, 1924, overlooking the intoxicatingly beautiful King's and Queen's courses designed by James Braid, and was joined in the 1990s by Jack Nicklaus's PGA Centenary Course, the site of the 2014 Ryder Cup. **OPPOSITE:** Railway poster for golf at Cruden Bay by Tom Purvis, with the magnificent hotel, since demolished, in the background. **BELOW:** Travel poster for Peterhead Golf Club in Scotland, founded in 1841, where the Craigewan Links dates from 1892. The "New Course," laid out in 1923 as eighteen holes, is now nine.

In 1910, Dorothy Campbell Hurd successfully defended her U.S. Amateur title at Homewood Country Club in Flossmoor, Illinois. The following year, she won her second British Ladies' Championship at Royal Portrush, defeating local favorite Violet Hezlet, the youngest of the three famous golfing Hezlet sisters from Portrush (Campbell had defeated Florence Hezlet to take the trophy in 1909). After marrying an American, Jack Hurd, she moved to the United States in 1913 and largely withdrew from competitive golf. In 1924, after revamping her swing to reflect a more modern technique, she entered the U.S. Women's Amateur held at Rhode Island Golf Club, meeting the former American tennis champion Mary K. Browne in the final. At age forty-one, fifteen years after her first victory, at Merion, Campbell won the match in convincing fashion for her third U.S. Women's Amateur. She was killed in 1945 when she was struck by a passing train while changing lines at Yemassee, South Carolina. **OPPOSITE:** Royal Portrush Golf Club in Northern Ireland, fifth hole. **BELOW:** Dorothy Campbell Hurd, winner of the 1911 Ladies' Championship at Portrush.

Ted Ray was an important and distinctive figure in the major golfing events just before and after World War I, despite being overshadowed by the legendary Triumvirate. Like the great Harry Vardon, he was born on the Channel Island of Jersey, and he succeeded Vardon as the pro at Ganton. Like Vardon, he made the passage in 1913 to barnstorm in America and play in the U.S. Open, in which they were both vanquished by the young Francis Ouimet in the play-off that put American golf on the map. A burly man who held nothing back when he swung, Ray's trademark was a pipe clenched tightly in his teeth. He won the 1912 British Open at Muirfield and the 1920 U.S. Open at Inverness, overtaking the aging Vardon, who fell victim to a freak storm that blew through the course. Since then, Ray and Tony Jacklin in 1970 remain the only English players to win the U.S. Open. The popular Ray was also the captain of the British team in the inaugural Ryder Cup Match played at Worcester in 1927, with Walter Hagen leading the American side.

OPPOSITE: Ted Ray (left) with Harry Vardon at Sunningdale Golf Club outside London in October of 1912.

Charlotte Cecilia Pitcairn "Cecil" Leitch and her four golfing sisters learned the game from their father, a Fife physician, at the remote and romantic links of Silloth-on-the-Solway in Cumberland, near Carlisle. Leitch, together with her great rival, Joyce Wethered, was one of the twin pillars of women's golf in Great Britain in the 1920s, and their contests were closely followed by the British public. A powerful ball striker, she won her first British Ladies' Championship in 1914 at Hunstanton, a charming links near Norfolk in East Anglia that is straddled by the coastal dunes and the River Hun. When competition resumed after World War I, Leitch picked up where she had left off, winning the British Ladies' in 1920, 1921, and 1926, as well as the French Ladies' Open five times between 1912 and 1924. In 1921, Leitch defeated Wethered in the final of the British Ladies' at Turnberry, as well as the French Open at Fontainebleau. She was dethroned by Wethered in the final of the British Ladies' Championship held at Prince's in 1922 and suffered a bitter loss on the thirty-seventh hole of their final-round clash at Troon in 1925. **OPPOSITE:** A young Cecil Leitch driving in the 1913 British Ladies' Championship. **BELOW:** Travel poster for Hunstanton, where Leitch won the championship in 1914.

Baltusrol Golf Club first hosted the U.S. Open in 1903, when Willlie Anderson was the winner. In 1915, Jerry Travers was the upset victor in the U.S. Open at Baltusrol, playing the last six holes in one under par. He declined to defend his title the following year and his golfing career came to a sudden end. The club was founded in 1895 by Louis Keller, the reclusive publisher of the *Social Register*. Set on five hundred acres in Springfield, New Jersey, close to the Watchung Mountains, Baltusrol was named after Baltus Roll, a local farmer who had been the victim of a grisly murder during a robbery at his farmhouse in 1831. The original clubhouse burned down in 1909 and was replaced with the baronial Tudor manse, complete with fluted redbrick chimneys and leaded windows, that is a landmark of American golf. The club has hosted numerous important events, including the 1936 U.S. Open won by Tony Manero on the Upper Course and the 1954, 1967, 1980, and 1993 U.S. Opens, all played over the Lower Course. Ed Furgol was the winner in 1954, while Jack Nicklaus triumphed in 1967 and 1980. Lee Janzen took the prize in 1993.

OPPOSITE: Aerial view of Baltusrol Golf Club.

In golf's enduring version of David and Goliath, Francis Ouimet, a twenty-year-old amateur with a milquetoast mien, beat the two professional titans of British golf, Harry Vardon and Ted Ray, to win the 1913 U.S. Open at The Country Club in Brookline, Massachusetts. Ouimet's victory was not only a fairy tale come true, it was an epochal event in the story of American golf, for it came at a time when the game was still in its formative stage in the United States and proved that homegrown American players could compete successfully with the game's recognized stars from the British Isles. Ouimet, who came into the championship as the unknown holder of the Massachusetts State Amateur title, was from a working class family that lived in a house across from The Country Club on Clyde Street. He had followed in the footsteps of his older brother Wilfred to caddie at the course when he was eleven, becoming enamored of golf. Vardon and Ray entered the tournament as part of a tour of the United States sponsored by Lord Northcliffe, owner of *The Times* of London. After fifty-four holes, Vardon, Ray, and Ouimet were all even, and in the waterlogged final round Vardon and Ray struggled home with 79s. Ouimet then played the final six holes in two under par to tie them. In the eighteen-hole play-off the next day, the phlegmatic and poised Francis, with his irrepressible ten-year-old caddie, Eddie Lowery, serving as his sidekick, pulled away from Vardon and Ray at the end and won convincingly, with a round of 72 to Vardon's 77 and Ray's 78, forever changing the face of American golf. **OPPOSITE:** Francis Ouimet displays his lucky horseshoe as he is held aloft following his historic upset win in the 1913 U.S. Open at The Country Club. **BELOW:** Marching to victory with ten-year old caddie Eddie Lowery.

Francis Ouimet remained a lifelong amateur and a model for those who followed after him. The great English golf writer Bernard Darwin, who served as Ouimet's scorer in the play-off with Harry Vardon and Ted Ray, reported on the action for *The Times* in London as if he were the correspondent on a foreign battlefield, but in the end was completely won over by Ouimet's brave play and rooted him on to victory. The following year, Ouimet traveled to play in Great Britain, where he was the center of attention but struggled at the *Golf Illustrated* Gold Vase tournament at Sunningdale and the British Amateur. Returning to the United States, he beat "The Old Man," Walter Travis, to win the U.S. Amateur at Ekwanok in Vermont, becoming, like Bobby Jones and Johnny Goodman, one of the few players to win the U.S. Open before the U.S. Amateur. With Bobby Jones in his prime during the 1920s, Ouimet was unable to win the Amateur title again until 1931, when at age thirty-nine he triumphed at Chicago's Beverly Country Club. Ouimet was also a mainstay of the American side in the Walker Cup, playing in the first eight matches, twice as playing captain and then as nonplaying captain four times up through 1949. A gracious and humble man, Ouimet in 1951 received the honor of becoming the first American and first non-British captain of the Royal and Ancient Golf Club of St. Andrews. **OPPOSITE:** Francis Ouimet warms up for the 1926 Walker Cup, which the American team won at St. Andrews, on the roof of the Savoy Hotel in London. **BELOW:** An early shot of Ouimet in action.

Walter Hagen was a golfing Houdini, famed for hitting really wild shots and then displaying remarkable powers of recovery from bramble, bush, and bunker. Percy Alliss, the English pro, said of Hagen: "He never hits two bad shots in a row." He made his debut on the national scene as a twenty-year-old at the 1913 U.S. Open, finishing an overlooked fourth in the tournament won by Francis Ouimet in his legendary upset. Hagen was much impressed at Brookline by the wardrobe of Tom Anderson, the lesser-known but much better-dressed older brother of four-time U.S. Open champion Willie Anderson. He began to model his attire after Tom, who sported a white silk shirt with red, blue, yellow, and black stripes, pleated white flannel trousers, a red bandanna, and white buckskin shoes with thick red-rubber soles. In 1914, the U.S. Open was held at Midlothian near Chicago. Hagen opened with a 69, followed by a 68, equaling the Open record despite a bout of food poisoning, and ended up winning his first major. In 1919, he won the first postwar Open at Brae Burn in Massachusetts, taking the eighteen-hole play-off over Mike Brady by one shot after arranging for Brady to be summoned from the clubhouse so that he could witness Hagen hole his eight-foot putt on the eighteenth hole to tie in regulation. **OPPOSITE:** Walter Hagen in 1920 at a golf match between England and America.

Merion Golf Club, in Ardmore, Pennsylvania, on Philadelphia's Main Line, has hosted more USGA championships than any other course. The Merion Cricket Club, from which the golf club split in 1941, had been founded in 1865. In 1911, the club selected Hugh Wilson, a thirty-two-year-old member who had been born in Scotland and educated at Princeton, to design its new course. Wilson prepared himself by traveling to Scotland and England to study the famed links courses, and upon his return he shoehorned his East Course into 126 acres, creating the yawning bunkers that Chick Evans dubbed "the white faces of Merion." Wilson came up with the idea of using red wicker baskets for hole locations instead of flagsticks, based on some of the old courses in the British Isles, and they remain a Merion tradition. Wilson also completed the four holes at Pine Valley that remained unfinished at the time of George Crump's death in 1918, but Wilson himself died young, at age forty-six. Merion remains the only course that testifies to his genius. In 1916, only four years after the East Course was completed, it hosted the U.S. Amateur, won by Evans with fourteen-year-old Bobby Jones in the field. In 1930, Jones achieved the final leg of the Grand Slam at the U.S. Amateur at Merion. In the 1950 U.S. Open, the course was the site of Ben Hogan's comeback from his near-fatal car crash. Merion has hosted five U.S. Opens and six U.S. Amateurs, the most recent in 2005, when Italy's Eduardo Molinari was the winner. The course will welcome the U.S. Open again in 2013. **OPPOSITE:** Merion Golf Club, thirteenth hole, outside Philadelphia.

Charles "Chick" Evans was a gifted amateur from Chicago, who, when he was only twenty, beat a field of professionals in the 1910 Western Open, the oldest and most important tournament at the time next to the U.S. Open. Evans's breakout season came in 1916, when he won both the U.S. Open played at Minikahda in Minneapolis and the Amateur Championship held at Merion, a feat equaled only by Bobby Jones. The 1916 Amateur marked the first major event to be held at Merion, the field including fourteen-year-old Bobby Jones making his Amateur debut. In 1922, Evans lost in the final of the Amateur Championship to Jess Sweetser, who was still an undergraduate at Yale, and who would go on become the first native-born American to win the British Amateur, in 1926 at Muirfield. Evans, who started out as a caddie, established a caddie scholarship fund at Northwestern University that has paid for the education of hundreds of caddies over the years. **OPPOSITE:** Chick Evans putting in the 1916 U.S. Amateur, which he won at Merion. **BELOW:** Evans in 1915 at the U.S. Open at Baltusrol.

Since its completion in 1918, Pine Valley has been perennially rated the greatest golf course in the United States, and possibly on earth. It is an understated oasis for the world's most serious and privileged golfers in the pine barrens in Clementon, New Jersey, thirty miles southeast of Philadelphia. The course owes its creation to the all-consuming passion of George Crump, a Philadelphia hotelier who discovered the property in 1912 while traveling on the Reading Railroad to the Atlantic City Golf Club, where he was a member. Crump moved to the site, living in a tent and then a bungalow as he labored for six years to create a course of sandy washes and eddies stitched with Scotch broom, huckleberry, bluestem, and lyme grass that spill over the rolling fairways. He consulted many experts, including the illustrious English architect Harry Colt, but the course remains his edenically beautiful and demonically punishing vision, with each hole encased in the forest of pine, oak, larch, and hemlock. Crump died suddenly in January 1918, leaving holes twelve through fifteen to be completed by Hugh Wilson, the architect of Merion. As Ben Crenshaw aptly put it, Pine Valley "is eminently fair—and among the two or three golf courses in the country that can be experienced as an expression of art." Legends of Pine Valley's extraordinarily exacting demands are legion, with the standing bet being that no one can break 80 the first time he or she plays the course. It is a very private club, and the course is unable to accommodate large galleries. As a result, the only significant tournaments the club has hosted have been the 1936 and 1985 Walker Cup Matches. **OPPOSITE:** Pine Valley Golf Club, tenth hole, Clementon, New Jersey. **BELOW:** The halfway house.

Long Jim Barnes, who earned his nickname because he stood six feet four inches tall and was, as Herbert Warren Wind described him, "as lean as Chile," was also known for his big drives. A quiet Cornishman who came to the United States in 1905, Barnes was one of the game's early stars, forming the "Big Three" with Walter Hagen and Jock Hutchinson in the years right after World War I. He won the first PGA Championship in 1916, defeating Hutchinson in the final at Siwanoy in Westchester, and he repeated when play resumed in 1919, this time beating Fred McLeod at the Engineers Club on Long Island. More than forty years later, Hutchinson and McLeod teamed up to serve as the honorary starters at the Masters for several years.

In 1921 and 1924, Barnes lost in the finals to the streaking Walter Hagen. He trounced both Hagen and McLeod by nine shots to win the 1921 U.S. Open at Maryland's Columbia Country Club, where McLeod was the club pro. He added to his roster of major wins in 1925, when he won the British Open the last time it was held at Prestwick. Barnes quietly posted a 74 in the final round, while the crowd favorite and native son Macdonald Smith collapsed with an 82, distracted by a huge and unruly gallery that had come out to see him win the championship. **OPPOSITE:** Long Jim Barnes (left) with rival Walter Hagen, c. 1920.

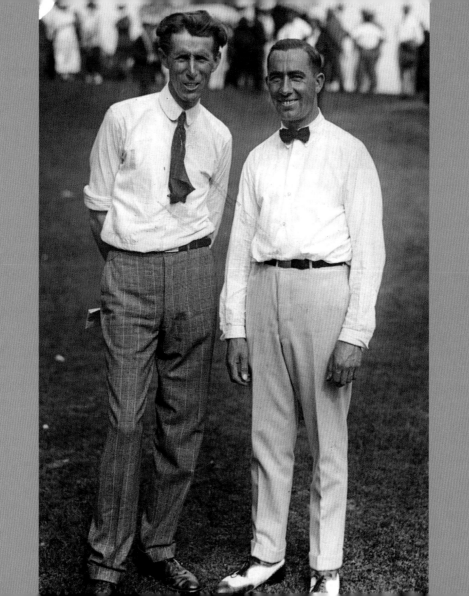

Del Paso Country Club, located ten miles northeast of downtown Sacramento, was founded in 1916 on land that was once part of the 44,000-acre Rancho Del Paso. The original course was designed by a Scot, John Black, and revised by Herbert Fowler in the 1920s. It was recently redesigned and lengthened by Sacramento-based course architect Kyle Phillips, whose creations include the Kingsbarns course in Scotland and The Grove outside London. Del Paso, which is home to many magpies, wanders through valley oaks with a creek cutting through the line of play on several holes. It has a close association with the history of women's golf, hosting the 1982 U.S. Women's Open, won by Janet Anderson for her only LPGA victory, and the 1957 and 1976 U.S. Women's Amateur Championships, won by JoAnne Gunderson Carner and Donna Horton, respectively. **OPPOSITE:** The recently restored Del Paso Country Club in Sacramento, California.

Jock Hutchinson was one of many native sons of St. Andrews who sought greener golfing pastures in the United States. After losing by one hole to Long Jim Barnes in the final of the first PGA Championship in 1916, he was victorious in 1920 at Flossmoor in Illinois, after failing to qualify and getting into the field as an alternate. That same year, he lost out in the U.S. Open by one stroke to Ted Ray, finishing in a four-way tie for second. Hutchinson's crowning glory came in the 1921 British Open at St. Andrews, after he returned to his birthplace in time to play dozens of practice rounds in preparation for his assault on the Old Course. He finished tied in regulation with the British Amateur champion Roger Wethered, and then won the thirty-six-hole playoff by a resounding nine strokes to make him, at least technically, the first American to win the British Open. A nervous and high-strung player who talked to himself on the course, Hutchinson continued to play superbly well into his eighties. He was well known to American golfing audiences for his role from 1963 to 1976 as the honorary starter at the Masters, playing nine holes with fellow Scottish emigré Freddie McLeod, the winner of the 1908 U.S. Open at Myopia Hunt Club and the professional at Maryland's Columbia Country Club from 1912 until 1967. **OPPOSITE:** President Warren Harding presents the Claret Jug to Jock Hutchinson for winning the 1921 British Open in a ceremony at the 1921 U.S. Open at Columbia Country Club in Chevy Chase, Maryland. Long Jim Barnes holds the trophy for winning the U.S. Open. **BELOW:** Fred McLeod (left) and Jock Hutchinson at the Masters in 1971.

Dr. Alister MacKenzie, a Scottish-born physician, became the leading international course architect of the 1920s, with designs ranging from Cypress Point in California, which has been described as the Sistine Chapel of golf, to Crystal Downs in Michigan, the Jockey Club in Buenos Aires, and Royal Melbourne in Australia. MacKenzie's design at Cypress Point greatly impressed Bobby Jones, who selected MacKenzie to collaborate with him on the design of Augusta National. MacKenzie served as a surgeon during the Boer War, and later applied to the design of golf courses camouflage techniques practiced by the Boer soldiers on the treeless veldts. His first foray into course architecture came in 1907 when he met H. S. Colt, who was designing Alwoodley Golf Club in Leeds, where MacKenzie was then living and practicing medicine. Colt was impressed with MacKenzie's suggestions and invited him to work on the design of the course. In 1914, MacKenzie won first prize in the famous competition held by *Country Life* magazine to design a two-shot finishing hole for C. B. Macdonald's Lido Links on Long Island, with Bernard Darwin, Horace Hutchinson, and Herbert Fowler serving as the judges. By the end of World War I, MacKenzie was fully engaged in golf course architecture. **OPPOSITE:** Alwoodley Golf Club in Leeds, eighth hole. **BELOW:** Dr. Alister MacKenzie.

Golf began in Morocco at Tangier, where the first course was laid out in 1917 on land presented in 1903 by Sultan Moulay Abd-el-Aziz to the British diplomatic community to establish the Diplomatic Country Club. The present-day Royal Tangier, with its view from the fifth hole across the Bay of Tangier to the Strait of Gibraltar, was built by the English architect and amateur champion Frank Pennink in the early 1950s. Next came the Royal Golf Club of Marrakesh, framed by the snowcapped Atlas Mountains, which was founded in 1923 by the pasha of Marrakesh, a passionate golfer whose instructor was the British Open champion Arnaud Massy. The third pillar of early Moroccan golf was Fedhala, a links-style course nestled in the dunes of a town near Casablanca; it was renamed Mohammedia in 1959 in honor of King Muhammed V. Originally laid out as a nine-holer by M. Hirigoyen of Biarritz, the course was expanded to eighteen in 1947 with the help of American troops stationed at the nearby military base who enjoyed playing the course.

OPPOSITE: Travel poster for Fedhala Golf Club (now Royal Mohammedia) by Jacques Majorelle.

After moving to Pinehurst in 1900 and designing his uniquely challenging and beguiling Pinehurst No. 2, Donald Ross's reputation as a golf course architect spread far and wide. Ross designed more than five hundred courses throughout the United States as golf boomed in the period between the two World Wars. He employed a team of skilled construction supervisors, most notably Frank Maples, to carry out his designs. Ross's style was to make the most of natural features while creating the complex and challenging greens that are most evident at Pinehurst No. 2. His gems range from Pine Needles, a neighbor of Pinehurst No. 2, to Seminole in North Palm Beach, Oakland Hills in Detroit, Inverness in Toledo, and Holston Hills in Knoxville, Tennessee. Ross is responsible for a horn of plenty in New England, where he made his summer home at Little Compton in Rhode Island. His courses in the area include Brae Burn, Essex, Fall River, Salem, and Winchester in Massachusetts; Wampanoag and Shennecossett in Connecticut; and Wannamoisett, Metacomet, and Sakonnet in Rhode Island. **OPPOSITE:** Misquamicut Golf Club in Rhode Island, designed by Donald Ross, tenth hole. **BELOW:** Program cover for the 1931 PGA Championship held at Wannamoisett Country Club in Rhode Island.

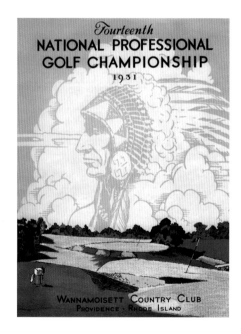

Albert Warren Tillinghast was the sultan of golf course architects during the 1920s. Born into a well-to-do family in Philadelphia in 1874, he was by all accounts an aimless youth until he visited St. Andrews, where he was befriended by and took lessons from Old Tom Morris and became captivated by the game. Tillinghast competed in the U.S. Amateur several times between 1905 and 1915, and in 1909 designed his first course, at Pennsylvania's Shawnee-on-Delaware, for Charles Worthington of the Worthington pump fortune. "Tillie the Terrible," as he became known, enjoyed an extravagant lifestyle collecting art and antiques, drinking heavily, and displaying a genius for golf course architecture, preferring to design his courses in the field dressed in a three-piece suit. By 1918, he had established a reputation as an architect and was hired to design a second course at Baltusrol, which had already hosted two U.S. Opens. With typical bravado, he recommended plowing under the original course, and then designed two new and resplen-dent layouts—the Upper and Lower courses. Tillinghast's creations are the *Mona Lisa*s of championship courses in America, including, in addition to Baltusrol, Winged Foot's West Course and Quaker Ridge in Westchester; Ridgewood in New Jersey; Baltimore's Five Farms; Newport; and Bethpage Black on Long Island. His business collapsed in the Depression and he fell on hard times, working for a time as a course consultant to the PGA before moving to Beverly Hills, where he and his wife ran an antiques store.

OPPOSITE: Image from the cover of the program for the 1929 U.S. Open at Winged Foot, which was won by Bobby Jones. **BELOW:** (left to right) Alex Findlay, Harry Vardon, A.W. Tillinghast, and Ted Ray at Shawnee Country Club in Pennsylvania, the first course designed by Tillinghast. Findlay, who had emigrated from Scotland, played exhibitions throughout the United States with Vardon and Ray and also designed many early courses.

BOBBY JONES AND THE ROARING TWENTIES

100 | THE IMMORTAL BOBBY

Robert Tyre Jones was the golfing immortal in an era of sporting deities, with Babe Ruth on the diamond, Red Grange on the gridiron, Jack Dempsey in the ring, and Big Bill Tilden on the court. Bobby Jones not only dominated golf in the Roaring Twenties while playing as an amateur, but came to personify the ideals and values of the sport. Born in Atlanta in 1902, Jones was introduced to golf in 1907 when his father, Robert Purmedus Jones, known as "The Colonel," rented a house for the summer close to the Atlanta Athletic Club's East Lake Course and his parents began to play. It was at East Lake that Jones learned the game under the eye of club pro Stewart Maiden, recently arrived from Carnoustie in Scotland. Jones was a child prodigy and a national sensation, advancing against well-known players as a fourteen-year-old in the U.S. Amateur at Merion. Between 1923 and 1930, when he retired from competitive golf, Jones won the four majors of his era—the U.S. Open, U.S. Amateur, British Open, and British Amateur—thirteen times, capping his career by winning the "Grand Slam" in 1930 and making him the only golfer ever to capture all four major tournaments in a single season. **OPPOSITE:** Bobby Jones in 1928.

The 1920s was a golden age not only of American sports but of sports-writing as well, and nowhere was this more evident than in the pages of *The American Golfer*. The magazine was founded in 1908 by Walter Travis, who turned over the helm in 1920 to Grantland Rice—the most mythical sportswriter of them all. Regular contributors included Rice's good friend the satirist Ring Lardner; O. B. Keeler, who became known as Bobby Jones's Boswell; Jones himself; and Bernard Darwin. The magazine was beautifully illustrated, with many covers by Montgomery Flagg. Rice, an avid and scratch golfer, also played a big part in popularizing the game through his newspaper columns. He wrote *The Winning Shot* with Jerry Travers and *The Duffer's Handbook of Golf*, with comical illustrations by the cartoonist Clare Briggs—a longtime member of Westchester's Siwanoy. Rice's columns about the teenage Bobby Jones made Jones a national celebrity. They became close friends and Rice played an important role in the development of Augusta National, of which he was a member. It was Rice who wrote: "For when the one Great Scorer comes to write against your name, He marks—not that you won or lost—but how you played the game." **OPPOSITE:** The cover of *The American Golfer* for January of 1928. **BELOW:** Grantland Rice (right) with Bobby Jones on the deck of the SS *Europa* in New York City in 1936.

January 1928   25 Cents

The American Golfer

Edited by ··· GRANTLAND RICE

Alexa Stirling, born in 1897, was a childhood friend and neighbor of Bobby Jones at the summer golf colony of East Lake in Atlanta, where her family lived in a cottage across from the tenth tee. The course had been established by the Atlanta Athletic Club, with the opening ceremony held on July 4, 1908. Her father, a Scot, was a physician and the acting British consul in Atlanta. Like Jones, she learned the game from Stewart Maiden, the taciturn Carnoustie-born professional at East Lake. She would go on to win three consecutive U.S. Amateur Championships, in 1916, 1919, and 1920 (play having been suspended for two years during World War I). As a teenager, she also played in exhibition matches across the country with Jones, fellow Atlantan Perry Adair, and Elaine Rosenthal of Chicago, the four golfing "Dixie Whiz Kids," to raise funds for the Red Cross. **OPPOSITE:** The Dixie Whiz Kids at an exhibition match at Montclair, New Jersey, in 1917. From left to right: Perry Adair, Elaine Rosenthal, Bobby Jones, and Alexa Stirling. **BELOW:** Alexa Stirling.

Walter Hagen was golf's greatest bon vivant, showman, and master of match play; his eleven professional major championships rank him only behind Jack Nicklaus and Tiger Woods in the annals of the game. He was born in 1892 in Rochester, New York, the son of a blacksmith in automobile body shops, and began caddying at Rochester Country Club when he was eight. He left school for good at fourteen by climbing out a window and heading for the golf course, serving as assistant pro and then becoming the club pro when he was nineteen. With his self-confident insouciance, competitive flair, brilliantined hair, and two-tone golf shoes, Sir Walter would forever transform the perception of the professional golfer from the tweed jacket days of Vardon, Braid, and Taylor. Hagen made golf a glamorous sport in the Roaring Twenties. During his career, he won the U.S. Open twice, the British Open four times, and the PGA Championship five times during the 1920s, as well as winning the Western Open three times. During the 1930s, he traveled the world giving exhibitions with the trick shot artist Joe Kirkwood, visiting Australia and New Zealand before heading to India, Aden, and France, followed by exhibitions in Europe, big game hunting in Africa, and then onward to Malaysia, Java, and Japan. **OPPOSITE:** Walter Hagen practicing on the deck of the SS *Mauretania* while traveling to the 1924 British Open at Hoylake, which he would win.

The Olympic Club is the oldest athletic club in the United States, having been established on May 6, 1860, in downtown San Francisco. Golf was introduced in 1918, when the club took over the Lakeside Country Club, which was in financial distress. The Olympic members replaced the existing course in 1924 with the Lake and Ocean courses designed by a Scot, Willie Watson. Construction was overseen by Sam Whiting, who had been an English professor at Berkeley before becoming the pro at Lakeside. Whiting became course superintendent at Olympic, remodeling both courses in 1927. Through his tree planting, he created the canopy of cypress and eucalyptus that overhangs the fairways of the Lake Course as it slopes down to Lake Merced. Olympic has hosted four U.S. Opens, earning a reputation as a course that favors the underdog: Jack Fleck was the ultimate upset winner over Ben Hogan in the 1955 U.S. Open; Billy Casper knocked off Arnold Palmer in 1966; Scott Simpson dashed Tom Watson's hopes in 1987; and Lee Janzen overtook Payne Stewart in 1988. Olympic's Lake Course hosted the 2007 U.S. Amateur won by Colt Knost and will hold the U.S. Open again in 2012. The Ocean Course, redesigned by Tom Weiskopf, reopened in 2000. **OPPOSITE:** The Lake Course at San Francisco's Olympic Club, eighteenth hole.

Gene Sarazen was born Eugene Saraceni in 1902 in Harrison, New York, the son of Italian immigrants, just as Westchester was starting to swell with golf courses. He started out as a caddy when he was eight, but also sold newspapers, scavenged for scrap metal and coal, and worked lighting gas streetlamps. In 1919, while playing golf in Florida, he was offered the job of assistant pro at the Fort Wayne Country Club in Indiana; in 1921, he became the pro at the course in the small town of Titusville, Ohio. Thus, when he arrived for the 1922 U.S. Open at Skokie, outside Chicago, as an unknown twenty-year-old,

he was dubbed "The Man from Titusville" by Bernard Darwin, who was much taken by his direct, energetic personality and Cheshire Cat grin. In the great early burst of his career, Sarazen won the Open at Skokie with a phenomenal final-round 68 to finish one ahead of Bobby Jones. Later that same year, he won the PGA at Oakmont. The following year, he successfully defended his PGA title, defeating the all-time maestro of match play, Walter Hagen, in the thirty-eight-hole final at Westchester's Pelham Country Club. **OPPOSITE:** Gene Sarazen teeing off in 1924.

When Bobby Jones won the 1923 U.S. Open at Inwood Country Club on Long Island he was only twenty-one years old, but it marked the end of a period of frustration in the major events for Jones, who had been expected to win earlier but had struggled to control outbursts of temper and club tossing. Jones needed a play-off to defeat the Scottish-born Bobby Cruickshank, taking a double bogey on the final hole in regulation to finish, as Jones put it, "like a yellow dog." All even coming to the eighteenth hole of the play-off, Jones played a one-iron from a sandy lie over the water hazard in front of the green seven feet from the pin, and his lean years were over. Jones won the first of U.S. Amateurs the following year at Merion. He successfully defended eating his friend from East Lake, Watts Gunn, in the final, but lost en at Worcester Country Club by one stroke in a thirty-six-hole h Willie MacFarlane, a Scottish-born club pro. In an act that he took for granted, Jones had cost himself the tournament by calling a penalty stroke on himself after his ball moved at address. Jones was an exceptionally well-rounded, thoughtful, and intelligent man. He graduated from Georgia Tech in 1922, and then took a degree in English literature at Harvard in 1924 before attending Emory Law School. Jones practiced law while winning his major championships, founding the firm that would become Alston & Bird. In 1927, when he was twenty-five, he wrote his autobiography, *Down the Fairway*, together with *Atlanta Journal* sportswriter O. B. Keeler, who chronicled his exploits. It remains an evergreen classic of golf literature. **OPPOSITE:** Bobby Jones is greeted by jubilant well-wishers upon his return to his native Atlanta after winning the 1923 U.S. Open. **BELOW:** The program cover for the 1923 U.S. Open at Inwood Country Club, the site of Jones's first U.S. Open victory.

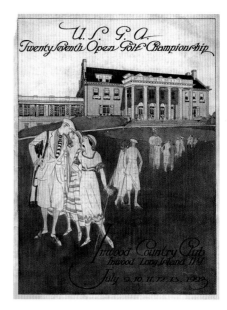

When Walter Hagen, who loved the grand gesture, competed in his first British Open in 1919 at Royal Cinque Ports in Deal, he arrived at the clubhouse in an Austro-Daimler limousine with his footman. After being refused entry to the clubhouse to change, in the days when professionals were still regarded as second-class citizens, he proceeded to park in front of the clubhouse while his footman served him lunch each day. Hagen popularized the style of American golfers making the ocean voyage to play in the Open during the 1920s, and it became his favorite tournament. In 1922, he won at Royal St. George's, becoming the first American-born player to have his name inscribed on the Claret Jug.

Unimpressed by the amount on the winner's check, he handed it to his caddy at the presentation ceremony. In 1924, he holed a seven-foot putt on the final hole for victory at Hoylake, with his wife embracing him on the green. Four years later, Hagen was the winner again at St. George's, by three over the British hero Archie Compston, who only the week before had annihilated Hagen by a score of 18 and 17 over their seventy-two-hole exhibition match at Moor Park. In 1929, he won his fourth and final Open, this time at Muirfield, by a convincing six-shot margin. **OPPOSITE:** Walter Hagen receives a congratulatory kiss from his wife after winning the 1924 Open at Hoylake.

Charles Blair Macdonald, who is credited with coining the term "golf course architect," had strong views on design that were based on the strategic principles of Scottish links golf and the ethical underpinning that a bad shot deserves to be punished. Macdonald hired Seth Raynor, a local Southampton surveyor and Princeton graduate, to work with him on the design of the National Golf Links, Macdonald's testament to Scottish golf. Raynor's father had been the surveyor on the original Shinnecock Hills course in the 1890s, with seventeen-year-old Seth serving as his assistant. Macdonald and Raynor collaborated on several outstanding high society courses of the 1920s, such as Mid Ocean in Bermuda and Piping Rock, the Creek Club, and the famous lost Lido course, all on Long Island. Raynor became a leading golf course architect in his own right and employed the principles of strategic design he learned from his mentor, incorporating variations on classic holes from Scottish courses in his own work. His sublime creations include the Fishers Island Golf Club off the coast of Connecticut, Shoreacres outside Chicago, the Camargo Club in Cincinnati, Yeamans Hall in Charleston, as well as the nine-hole Quogue Field Club on Long Island's South Fork and the Hotchkiss School course in Lakeville, Connecticut. Raynor was engaged to design Cypress Point when he died of pneumonia in 1926 at age fifty-one. **OPPOSITE:** Shoreacres Golf Club in Lake Bluff, Illinois, designed by Seth Raynor, fourth hole.

The International Match for the Walker Cup began in 1922 as a competition between the leading amateur golfers of the United States and Great Britain and Ireland; it has been played in odd-numbered years since 1947. The match, which is cosponsored by the USGA and the Royal and Ancient, is named in honor of George Herbert Walker, President George Herbert Walker Bush's namesake and grandfather, and President George W. Bush's great-grandfather. Walker, who served as president of the USGA in 1920, was an enthusiastic proponent of creating the match as a means to promote international goodwill and fellowship, and offered to donate the trophy. The newspapers, to Walker's embarrassment, began referring to the match as the Walker Cup. An unofficial match was held in 1921, but the first official Walker Cup took place the next year at the National Golf Links in Southampton, where Walker was a member, with the U.S. winning 8 to 4. Every member of the U.S. team, which included Bobby Jones, Francis Ouimet, and Jess Sweetser, would at some point win the U.S. Amateur. Through 1987, the United States dominated the matches, with Great Britain and Ireland's only victories coming at St. Andrews in 1938 and 1971, with a tie in 1965 at Baltimore Country Club. The balance of power has been much more even in recent years, with Great Britain and Ireland winning the Cup in 1999 at Nairn, 2001 at Ocean Forest, and 2003 at Ganton, and the United States prevailing in 2005 at Chicago and by one point in 2007 at Royal County Down, when Jonathan Moore's eagle on the eighteenth hole of the final match was the margin of victory. **OPPOSITE:** The members of the 1959 U.S. Walker Cup team at Muirfield (left to right) Jack Nicklaus, Billy Joe Patton, Deane Beman, Tommy Aaron, Ward Wettlaufer, Frank Taylor, and E. Harvie Ward, the winner of the 1952 British Amateur and 1955 and 1956 U.S. Amateur.

George Thomas, born in 1873, was one of the giants of the golden era of golf course architecture, leaving an indelible mark on the game in Southern California. The scion of a wealthy Philadelphia family, Thomas witnessed the work in progress of his friend Hugh Wilson at Merion and of George Crump at Pine Valley. In 1908, he designed his first course, the Whitemarsh Valley Golf Club, on his family's estate in Chestnut Hill. Known as "The Captain," Thomas served as a pilot during World War I, miraculously surviving three plane crashes. A man of many avocations, he was a leading authority on the cultivation of roses, developing at least forty new species, and moved to Beverly Hills after the war primarily to pursue his horticultural interests.

Thomas created the three crown jewels of Southern California golf, designing Bel-Air, Los Angeles Country Club's North Course, and his masterpiece, Riviera Country Club, during the 1920s. He also designed Ojai Valley and La Cumbre, which have been greatly altered over the years. Thomas worked closely with his construction foreman, William "Billy" Bell, who went on to have a notable career as a golf course architect in his own right. In his later years, Thomas's dedication to course design waned as he pursued interests in Pacific game fishing and yachting. **OPPOSITE:** Program for the 1930 U.S. Women's Amateur Championship held at Los Angeles Country Club, designed by George Thomas.

Bernard Darwin wrote about golf in columns for *The Times* (London) that combine the highest literary standards—including a liberal sprinkling of quotations from Dickens, on whom Darwin was an authority—with a deep understanding of the game and a dash of self-deprecating humor. He was also a very fine, although highly self-critical, amateur golfer. While covering the first Walker Cup Match in 1922 at the National Golf Links in Southampton, he filled in for a member of the British team who had become ill and won his singles match against William Fownes of Oakmont, the captain of the American side. Darwin's classic *Golf Courses of the British Isles* was published in 1910, with striking watercolor illustrations by Harry Rountree. **OPPOSITE:** Bernard Darwin (center) playing in the 1913 British Amateur Championship at Royal St. George's against John Ball, Jr. (right).

William Flynn was at the vanguard of the so-called "Philadelphia School" of golf course design that produced many of the classic courses of the 1920s, and whose members included George Crump, Hugh Wilson, George Thomas, and A. W. Tillinghast. Flynn, who at one time owned part of the Philadelphia Eagles, assisted Wilson with the completion of the East Course at Merion and served initially as its greenkeeper. After World War I, he formed a design firm with engineer Howard Toomey; their courses include Denver's Cherry Hills and the Cascades Course at the Homestead from 1923, the completely redesigned Shinnecock Hills in 1930, and Huntingdon Valley, Manufacturers, and Rolling Green, all in Pennsylvania. Flynn's construction supervisors included Dick Wilson and Robert "Red" Lawrence. Wilson would become a major architect of the 1950s and early 1960s, whose courses include Deepdale and Meadowbrook on Long Island, the Blue Monster at Miami's Doral, and Pine Tree in Delray Beach. Lawrence worked with Flynn from 1921 to 1932 and then became the course superintendent at the Boca Raton Hotel's two courses, designed by Toomey & Flynn. In 1958, Lawrence moved to Arizona and returned to golf course architecture, designing Desert Forest Golf Club in Carefree, the archetype of the desert courses of the American Southwest, with their islands of fairway engulfed by the cactus and sagebrush of the desert floor. **OPPOSITE:** Cherry Hills Golf Club, first hole, designed by William Flynn.

Pebble Beach Golf Links, the most famous and photogenic of American golf courses, hopscotches across the craggy headlands of Carmel Bay on the Monterey Peninsula. Begun in 1918, the course was the brainchild of Samuel F. B. Morse (grandnephew of the inventor of the telegraph), who had taken over Del Monte Properties, operator of the Del Monte Hotel and the original Del Monte Golf Club. Morse, who acquired the land for the course from Chinese fishermen, hired two relative novices to lay out the links, Jack Neville and Douglas Grant, both former California Amateur champions. The course they created was showcased at the U.S. Amateur Championship in 1929, when Bobby Jones, the great favorite, was defeated by unknown Nebraskan Johnny Goodman in the first round. Goodman, who had arrived for the event by cattle car, went on to win the U.S. Open in 1933, making him the last amateur to win the Open. Pebble Beach hosted the U.S. Open in 1972, 1980, 1995, and 2000, with the winners' roll consisting of Jack Nicklaus, Tom Watson, Tom Kite, and Tiger Woods. **OPPOSITE:** Program for the 1929 U.S. Amateur Championship held at Pebble Beach, after a painting by Maurice Logan. **BELOW:** Johnny Goodman (left) is congratulated by Bobby Jones after his victory in their match in the first round of the 1929 U.S. Amateur.

THIRTY THIRD

National Amateur
Golf Championship

PEBBLE BEACH
CALIFORNIA
1929

Walter Hagen, a genius at gamesmanship, was known to nonplus opponents by arriving at the first tee in white tie and tails after having reputedly stayed up all night drinking champagne. The Haig won five PGA Championships contested as match play, including four in a row from 1924 to 1927, making him the only golfer to win a major championship four years running. He won his first PGA in 1921 at Inwood over Long Jim Barnes, who had won the inaugural event in 1916. After losing in extra holes to Gene Sarazen in 1923, he began his streak in 1924, defeating Barnes in the final at the French Lick Springs Resort in southern Indiana—famed at the time for "Pluto Water," a natural laxative. In 1925, he won marathon matches against Al Watrous and Leo Diegel before finishing off "Wild Bill" Melhorn in the final at Olympia Fields. In 1926, at Salisbury Golf Club's Red Course, which is now part of Eisenhower Park on Long Island, Diegel was his victim in the final. Hagen's fifth and final PGA Championship was one of the most spectacular—he battled back against Joe Turnesa in the final at Cedar Crest in Dallas to end up all square going to the final hole. Hagen then drove astray but punched his second shot through the trees and onto the green, while Turnesa bogeyed from the fairway. His winning streak finally came to an end in 1928 at the hands of Diegel, the winner in both 1928 and 1929. In 1937, Hagen captained the U.S. Ryder Cup team at Southport & Ainsdale that was the first to win the match on British soil. **OPPOSITE:** Golfing postcard for the French Lick Springs Resort in French Lick, Indiana, c. 1925, where Walter Hagen won the PGA in 1924.

Tommy Armour, known as "The Silver Scot," was born in Edinburgh and fought with the Black Watch in World War I, during which he was wounded and lost an eye. After accompanying the British team to Southampton on Long Island for the inaugural Walker Cup Match in 1922, he stayed in the United States and turned professional in 1924. Armour won one of the most famous U.S. Opens in 1927, at merciless Oakmont, when he caught "Light Horse" Harry Cooper by rifling a three-iron to the final hole to set up a birdie and then winning the eighteen-hole play-off by three shots. In 1930, he defeated Gene Sarazen in the final of the PGA Championship at Fresh Meadow. He won his third major in 1931, taking the Claret Jug at Carnoustie when he nipped the Argentine José Jurado by a stroke. Armour was one of the game's most famed instructors, giving lessons while sitting under an umbrella at Boca Raton and Winged Foot. He wrote one of the all-time classic instructional books, *How to Play Your Best Golf All the Time.* **OPPOSITE:** Tommy Armour putting on the eighteenth hole in his victory at the 1927 U.S. Open at Oakmont. **BELOW:** Armour receives the silver cup after winning the 1929 Western Open at Milwaukee's Ozaukee Country Club.

Golf was introduced to Hungary by Baron Géza Andrássy in 1902, who played at the racetrack in Budapest. The first course followed in 1909 at Tátralomnic, founded by Dezso Lauber, the secretary of the Hungarian Olympic Committee and a future multiple Hungarian golf champion. The Budapest Golf Club was established in 1911. It became the Magyar Golf Club, with a course at Széchenyi Hill designed by Lauber, in the 1920s. Golf flourished in Hungary during the 1920s and 1930s, with Open, Amateur, and Ladies' Open championships all held at the Magyar Club. Another eighteen-hole course was built at Lillafüred, with a nine-hole course at Balatonfüred. Golf fell into disrepute during the Communist era but has enjoyed a strong resurgence in recent years. The Hungarian Golf Association was started in 1989, and courses have popped up through the country, including Birdland Golf & Country Club in Bürkfürdö, St. Lorence Golf & Country Club in Szentlörinc, Hencse National Golf & Country Club, Old Lake Golf Club in the Gerecse Foothills near Tata, Pannónia Golf & Country Club in Máriavölgy, and the Pólus Palace Golf Club near Göd. **OPPOSITE:** Travel poster for golf in Hungary.

Cobelbad

GYÓGYHELY GRÁC MELLETT SZANATORIUMMAL
DIÉTÁS, SPORT- és LAHMANN-KURÁK, RÁDIUMOS VIZŰ NYITOTT USZODA (1800 m²)

Golf in Czechoslovakia began at the famous Bohemian spa of Karlovy Vary (Carlsbad) in 1904, with a nine-hole course laid out in the Imperial Park in the valley of the Teplá River. The following year, a nine-hole course was completed at Marianské Lazné (Marienbad), another historic spa in western Bohemia, and officially opened by King Edward VII, a frequent guest. While those courses catered mainly to English visitors, Count Ringhoffer and his family, who were early proponents of the game, built a course in 1913 on their estate near the village of Volešovice, and, spurred on by the Ringhoffers, the Prague Golf Club opened in 1927. In 1935, Karlovy Vary opened its new eighteen-hole course with views over the Doupovské Hills and of the Krušne-Hory (Ore) Mountains. That same year, Marianské Lazné, which had been extended to eighteen holes in 1929, hosted the first Czechoslovakian Open, with Henry Cotton winning the title in 1937 and 1938. The Czech courses were destroyed or damaged during the war, with a few diehards restoring Karlovy Vary and the American army helping to reclaim Marianské Lazné. Golf was repressed during the Communist regime but is now thriving once again, with Karlovy Vary and Marianské Lazné leading the way. **OPPOSITE** and **BELOW:** Travel posters for golf in Czecholslovakia.

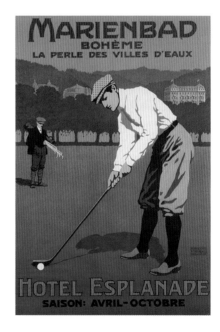

In 1926, Bobby Jones became the first man to win both the U.S. and British Opens in a single season. Jones qualified for the 1926 British Open at Lytham and St. Annes by shooting a sublime 66 at Sunningdale. In the championship, he found the green with his mashie, or four-iron, from the bunker to the left of the fairway on the seventeenth hole, a remarkable shot that is commemorated by a plaque, to win by two over Al Watrous. He returned home to a ticker tape parade down Broadway, and shortly thereafter won the U.S. Open at Scioto in Columbus, Ohio, birdying the last hole for a one-shot victory over Joe Turnesa. The following year, he defended his British Open title at St. Andrews, a victory that was especially meaningful to Jones. In the 1921 Open at St. Andrews, Jones had torn up his scorecard and stormed off the course in

disgust, much to his shame afterward, but he subsequently came to revere the Old Course, with its infinite subtleties, above all others. In 1928, Jones lost the U.S. Open in a thirty-six-hole play-off to Johnny Farrell at Olympia Fields. The following year, his game started to fall apart as he was coming down the stretch leading the U.S. Open at Winged Foot. Needing a par to tie Al Espinosa on the eighteenth, Jones holed the most storied putt in the annals of the Open, sinking a serpentine, downhill twelve-footer for par. The next day he won the thirty-six-hole play-off by twenty-three strokes! **OPPOSITE:** Bobby Jones tees off on the first hole of the Old Course in a practice round before his victory in the 1927 British Open at St. Andrews. **BELOW:** The program cover for the 1926 U.S. Open at Scioto in Columbus, Ohio, where Jones was the winner.

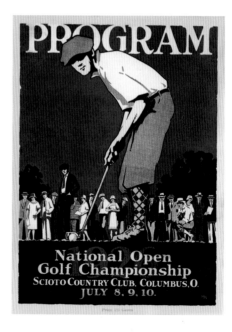

Golf in Tunisia dates from 1927, when the Carthage Golf Club was founded outside Tunis in La Soukra. A par-66 lined with century-old eucalyptus, the course lies near the ruins of ancient Carthage. Until the late 1970s, Carthage remained Tunisia's only course, but in recent years the country has become a golfing haven, with several courses designed by California-based Ronald Fream. Tabarka, Tunisia's answer to Cypress Point, is a Fream design laid out on the northwest coast near the Algerian border, with views of the sixteenth-century Genoese fort that guards the harbor. Hammamet, on the eastern coast, features three courses spread across six lakes and 430 acres of olive trees and pine forest, and there are courses at Monastir and Port El Kantoui.

Farther south, on Djerba, the largest island off the coast of North Africa—where Odysseus encountered the lotus-eaters—there is a twenty-seven-hole course encircled by date and sea palms designed by English architect Martin Hawtree. Tunisia's most recent layout is Fream's Oasis Course, located at the edge of the Sahara near the oasis village of Tozeur, with its distinctive yellow brick architecture and luxuriant palm grove, close to the vast salt lake of Chott el Jerid. **OPPOSITE:** French railway poster by Roger Broders for golf at Carthage Golf Club in La Soukra, outside Tunis. **BELOW:** The Tozeur Oasis course in southern Tunisia, at the edge of the Sahara.

GOLF de la Soukra TUNIS

Johnny Farrell, who was known as a natty dresser, started out as a caddy in Westchester. One of the leading pros of the 1920s, with six consecutive victories in 1927 and twenty-two during his career, he made up for his lack of length off the tee with an outstanding short game. In 1928, Farrell finished tied with Bobby Jones at the U.S. Open at Olympia Fields in Chicago, when Jones was at the zenith of the game, and then, in a shocking upset, beat Jones by one stroke in a thirty-six-hole play-off. Farrell was also runner-up in the British Open and PGA championships in 1929. From 1934 until 1972, he was the popular and much sought-after pro at Baltusrol, giving lessons to Presidents Eisenhower, Kennedy, Nixon, and Ford, and mixing with wealthy and well-known golfers on both sides of the Atlantic—including his friend the Duke of Windsor. Baltustrol's members dedicated a room filled with memorabilia relating to Farrell's career on the third floor of the clubhouse.

OPPOSITE: Johnny Farrell (right) and Bobby Jones during the 1928 U.S. Open at Chicago's Olympia Fields, where Farrell was the winner.

Joyce Wethered, who became Lady Heathcoat-Amory, was the supreme woman golfer of the 1920s, in a league of her own. Bobby Jones wrote after playing with her at St. Andrews that she was the finest golfer, man or woman, he had ever seen. Tall, elegant, and reserved, she came from a wealthy and intellectual family. Her father, H. N. Wethered, wrote about art history and golf course architecture with equal erudition, and her older brother Roger was a champion golfer, finishing runner-up in the British Open in 1921, winner of the British Amateur in 1923, and a five-time Walker Cup competitor. Joyce learned the game at the venerable links of Dornoch, in the Scottish highlands, where her family had their summer home. In 1920, when she was an unknown nineteen-year-old, she defeated Cecil Leitch in the final of the English Ladies' at Sheringham in Norfolk, beginning what was to be a fierce and closely followed rivalry. She went on to win the British Ladies' Championship four times—in 1922, 1924, 1925, and 1929. **OPPOSITE:** Joyce Wethered plays an escape shot during the Worplesdon Mixed Foursomes Tournament in 1926.

Marion Hollins, the daughter of a prominent investment banker and longtime partner of J. P. Morgan, was reared primarily in Islip on Long Island. The family's city residence at 12 West 56th Street, a Georgian mansion designed by Stanford White, is now the Consulate of Argentina. Born in 1893, Marion excelled in a wide range of sports, particularly polo, and was the first woman to enter an automobile in the Vanderbilt Cup road race on Long Island. She won the U.S. Women's Amateur in 1921, defeating Alexa Stirling in the final. While on a family vacation in California in the mid-1920s, Hollins met Samuel Morse, the developer of the Monterey Peninsula, who was struck by her forceful personality and hired her as athletic director for the property. Hollins took the lead in hiring the famed course architect Alister MacKenzie to design Cypress Point and worked with him on planning the layout. She then went on to develop her own estate and course at Pasatiempo, near Santa Cruz, working closely with MacKenzie on the course design; it is one of the finest courses open to the public in the United States. Pasatiempo Country Club opened in September 1929, with an exhibition match pairing Hollins and the English champion Cyril Tolley against Bobby Jones and Glenna Collett. In 1932, after being named "Outstanding Woman Athlete of the 1920s," Hollins was selected as captain of the inaugural U.S. Curtis Cup team, which defeated the team from Great Britain and Ireland captained by Joyce Wethered at Wentworth.

OPPOSITE: Pasatiempo Golf Club, first hole. **BELOW:** Marion Hollins (left) with Lillian Hyde during the Women's Metropolitan Golf Championship at Westchester's Sleepy Hollow Country Club in 1915.

Glenna Collett Vare, "The Great Glenna," was the titan of women's golf in America in the 1920s and 1930s. In charm and intelligence, she was the counterpart of the immortal Bobby Jones. She also came to symbolize the liberated American woman of the 1920s, together with her golfing rivals Virgina Van Wie and Edith Cummings (who was the 1923 Amateur champion and the model for Jordan Baker in *The Great Gatsby*). An all-around athlete, Collett learned the game at Metacomet in Rhode Island, where her father, who was the national cycling champion in 1899, introduced her to it. The young Glenna was inspired by the exploits of Alexa Stirling and took lessons from Alex Smith, the Scottish pro who also taught Jerry Travers. Collett went on to win six U.S. Women's Amateur Championships between 1922 and 1935, a record that has never been surpassed. She also played on four Curtis Cup teams, including the first match in 1932 at Wentworth, serving as team captain in 1934, 1936, 1948, and nonplaying captain in 1950. She became Mrs. Edwin Vare in 1931, and the Vare Trophy is awarded every year to the player on the LPGA Tour with the lowest stroke average per round. **OPPOSITE:** Glenna Collett (second from left) is congratulated after winning the 1922 U.S. Women's Amateur at the Greenbrier in West Virginia. **BELOW:** Collett in 1927.

Joyce Wethered was known for a perfectly balanced and rhythmical swing that unleashed considerable power. In 1922, she won the first of her four British Ladies' Championships, defeating Cecil Leitch, her great challenger, in the final at Prince's. She was the victor at Royal Portrush in 1924, and in 1925 she triumphed in her most epic match, prevailing over Leitch in the thirty-seven-hole final when the event was held at Royal Troon. After having retired for three years, she returned to the fray in 1929, a decision spurred by the playing of the championship over the Old Course at St. Andrews,

and defeated the U.S. Amateur champion Glenna Collett in a thrilling final match that came down to the thirty-fifth hole, being decided on the famous Road Hole. Wethered played in the first Curtis Cup Match in 1932, serving as captain of the British team, but thereafter retired from competitive golf, playing only in the Worplesdon Mixed Foursomes and devoting her energies to gardening. **OPPOSITE:** Joyce Wethered and Glenna Collett crossing the Swilcan Bridge during the final of the British Ladies' Championship at St. Andrews in 1929. **BELOW:** Travel poster for St. Andrews by Edward Higgins.

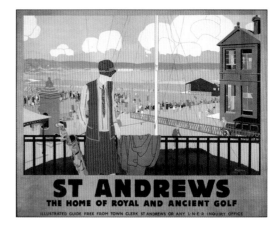

While Glenna Collett reigned supreme in women's golf in the 1920s in the United States, she was thwarted in her efforts to capture the British Ladies' Championship by her great transatlantic rival, Joyce Wethered. In 1925, she lost in the third round to Wethered, who went on to win the championship in her storied final match against Cecil Leitch. In 1929, when the tournament was played at St. Andrews, Collett and Wethered met in what proved to be one of the most memorable and exciting matches in the history of women's golf.

Playing inspired golf, Collett jumped out to a lead of five up after eleven holes, only to fall four down at the turn of the final eighteen. Collett fought back, carding 3s on the tenth and eleventh, before losing 3 and 1 on the thirty-fifth hole. In 1930, she was runner-up again, losing to Diana Fishwick in the final at Formby. **OPPOSITE:** Joyce Wethered and Glenna Collett on the eighteenth green during the final of the British Ladies' Championship at St. Andrews in 1929. **BELOW:** Collett (left) and Wethered before the big match.

The Ryder Cup, the biennial match between twelve-man teams from the United States and Europe, has grown into the most hotly contested and pressure-packed spectacle in golf. In 1926, an unofficial match was held at Wentworth outside London, with the British team walloping the Americans by a score of 13–1–1. Samuel Ryder, the British seed merchant who had invented the concept of selling seeds in small packets for a penny apiece, agreed to donate the trophy. Ryder had become obsessed with golf after taking up the game when he was already fifty, receiving lessons from the top English pro, Abe Mitchell, at his estate, Marlborough House in Hertfordshire. Mitchell became the model for the golfing figure that adorns the top of the Ryder Cup. The first official Ryder Cup Match took place at Worcester Country Club in Massachusetts in 1927, with the U.S. team captained by Walter Hagen dispatching the British squad led by Ted Ray by a score of 9 ½–2 ½. In 1979,

the British and Irish team was expanded to include players from the rest of Europe, ending the American domination of the competition and making for a series of dramatic matches. One of the most fabled contests in the history of the event came in 1999 at The Country Club, when the Americans under captain Ben Crenshaw trailed 10–6 going into the singles matches, but came storming back to victory by taking 8 ½ of the 12 points on Sunday. The Ryder Cup is now played in the September of even years, after the 2001 match was delayed for one year in the aftermath of the 9/11 attack on the World Trade Center in New York City. **OPPOSITE:** The victorious American team in the inaugural 1927 Ryder Cup (left to right) Al Watrous, "Wild" Bill Melhorn, Leo Diegel, Johnny Golden, team captain Walter Hagen, an unidentified non-competitor, Gene Sarazen, Johnny Farrell, and Jim Turnesa.

When Alister MacKenzie first surveyed the site of Cypress Point on California's Monterey Peninsula in 1926, he reported: "I am fully acquainted with the world's greatest golf courses and have no hesitation in saying that in the beauty of its surroundings, the magnificence of its sand dunes, its glorious Cypress trees—there is an opportunity of making [a golf course] which should be superior to any other." MacKenzie was introduced to the site and its possibilities by Robert Hunter, who became fascinated with golf course architecture during a trip to Great Britain in 1912 and in 1926 published *The Links*, one of the first and finest books about golf course architecture. Hunter was a leader of the American Socialist movement; his reputation as a social critic established by *Poverty*, published in 1904, he traveled internationally, meeting Lenin, Ramsey MacDonald, and Rosa Luxemburg. He had married an heiress, Caroline Phelps Stokes, leading his friend and golfing partner Finley Peter Dunne to describe him and his coterie as the "millionaire Socialists." In 1917, the Hunters moved from their Connecticut estate to Berkeley, where Hunter taught at the University of California. In the early 1920s they settled in Pebble Beach, where Hunter became partners with MacKenzie and worked with him on the design of the Valley Club of Montecito in Santa Barbara and the Meadow Club in Marin County. **OPPOSITE:** The Valley Club of Montecito, designed by Alister MacKenzie and Robert Hunter, fifteenth hole.

Golf in Australia was shaped in large part by a two-month sojourn in 1926 by the illustrious golf course architect Alister MacKenzie, who had been invited to make design suggestions for a new course at Royal Melbourne. The West Course, located on the southwest side of the famed "Sand Belt" around Melbourne, one of the world's mother lodes of great golf courses, is among MacKenzie's finest masterpieces. The course was conceived by MacKenzie, with broad fairways framed by ti trees and fluted bunkers carved into the sloping greens, but the actual realization of MacKenzie's vision after his departure was the work of Alex Russell, the 1924 Australian Open champion, and Royal Melbourne's superintendent, Mick Morcom. On his historic visit, MacKenzie also designed Yarra Yarra, another Sand Belt standout, and revised the bunkering of Kingston Heath in the scalloped, shrub-fringed style that is the hallmark of Royal Melbourne. MacKenzie also designed New South Wales, located south of Sydney in La Perouse, overlooking the shores of Botany Bay, another of Australia's best-known, world-class courses.

OPPOSITE: Royal Melbourne, West Course, sixteenth hole.

After returning to California from Australia, Alister MacKenzie began actual work on Cypress Point in the summer of 1927. O. B. Keeler famously described the course, with its dazzling landscape of wind-warped Monterey cypress, ice plant, and rocky coves lapped by the lapis lazuli waters of the Pacific, as "the crystallization of the dream of an artist who has been drinking gin and sobering up on absinthe." The par-3 sixteenth, with its 200-yard-plus carry over the Pacific to a green on a spit of rock with a solitary, sideways cypress, may well be the most famous and photographed hole in the world. The inspiration for the hole to be played as a one-shotter came from Amateur champion Marion Hollins. After teeing up a ball and hitting it onto what is now the green, she remarked that if she could make the carry, she was sure some men could as well. For many years Cypress Point was one of the courses, together with Pebble Beach and Spyglass, that hosted the Bing Crosby National Pro-Am. Crosby, who was a member of Cypress Point, once made a hole in one on the sixteenth. **OPPOSITE:** Cypress Point Golf Club, view of the fifteenth and sixteenth holes.

Leo Diegel had the reputation of being a perennial runner-up in the majors, despite his tremendously precise iron play. He was often undone by a nervous temperament down the stretch, but in 1928 and 1929 he won back-to-back PGA Championships, breaking the four-year winning streak of Walter Hagen in the event. In 1928 at the Baltimore Country Club, he avenged his loss to Hagen in the final in 1926, beating him in the quarter-finals and then defeating Al Espinosa in the final. The following year, he knocked Hagen out in the semifinals and defeated Johnny Farrell in the final at Hillcrest Country Club in Los Angeles. Diegel also played on four Ryder Cup teams, beginning with the inaugural match in 1927. He invented a particularly unorthodox putting style, known as "Diegeling," in which he kept his wrists stiff and bent his elbows so that his forearms were horizontal to the ground. In the 1940s, Diegel became the pro at the El Rio Golf Course in Tucson and was a founder of the Tucson Open. **OPPOSITE:** Leo Diegel putting during the second round of the 1929 British Open at Muirfield.

Cyril Tolley, together with Roger Wethered and Ernest Holderness, was one of the grand and elegant English amateurs of the 1920s. A long hitter, he cut a bold figure in his plus fours with his ever-present pipe, winning the British Amateur twice—in 1920 at Muirfield and 1929 at Royal St. George's. Tolley is actually best known for the match he lost to Bobby Jones in the fourth round of the 1930 British Amateur at St. Andrews. With Jones on the first leg of what would prove to be his Grand Slam year, the match seesawed back and forth, with the lead changing hands six times. Battling a fierce wind, Jones finally prevailed on the nineteenth hole, when his lag putt stymied Tolley, coming to rest directly in his line. After Jones won the British Open a few weeks later, Tolley accompanied him on the train ride to Southampton for his triumphant voyage back to the United States, and asked him in all seriousness: "Do you suppose you have ever played so badly for so long a period?" **OPPOSITE:** Cyril Tolley at Royal Liverpool Golf Club (Holylake) in April of 1925.

In 1930, Bobby Jones began his inexorable march to winning what his biographer O. B. Keeler called the "Grand Slam" or the "Impregnable Quadrilateral" by winning the British Amateur at St. Andrews, defeating Roger Wethered in the final. Next came the British Open, which he won at Hoylake, becoming the first player to hold both British titles in the same year since John Ball in 1890. Jones received his second ticker tape parade when he arrived back in New York on July 2, with the U.S. Open at Interlachen in Minneapolis just over a week away. In the morning round of the final day at Interlachen, he shot 68 for a five-stroke lead, and then shot 75 in the afternoon, holing a long birdie putt on the eighteenth to beat Macdonald Smith by two. In the U.S. Amateur at Merion, he routed his opponents, defeating Gene Homans by 8 and 7 in the final. Having climbed the Everest of the game, Jones retired at twenty-eight, escaping from the enormous physical and mental strain that competing at the highest level had placed on him. He turned his energies to creating the Augusta National Golf Club and also made a series of instructional films in Hollywood. Narrated by Jones in his deep Southern drawl, the *How I Play Golf* series remains just as informative as when it was made. It captures the wonderfully loose, flowing swing and absolutely modern technique displayed by Jones, which enabled him to drive the ball over 250 yards when he needed to, in the era of hickory-shafted clubs. **OPPOSITE:** Bobby Jones putts during the second round of the 1930 U.S. Open at Interlachen while Jock Hutchinson watches. Jones would win for the third leg of his historic Grand Slam. **BELOW:** Jones with the four trophies from his 1930 Grand Slam year.

After winning three majors early in his career, Gene Sarazen endured nine relatively lean years before winning the British Open at Prince's on the Channel Coast in 1932. By then, Sarazen had also invented the sand wedge to help him get out of the bunkers. Like Bobby Jones and Walter Hagen, Sarazen relished playing in the British Open, making the transatlantic voyage for the first time in 1923, when he missed the cut in the high winds at Troon. Fifty years later he would return to play in the 1973 Open at Troon and make a hole in one on the eighth with its tiny green, known as "The Postage Stamp." At Prince's in 1932, Sarazen finished five ahead of England's Arthur Havers, the winner at Troon in 1923, with a winning total of 283 that would stand as the record until 1950. The same year, Sarazen won his second U.S. Open, at the now defunct Fresh Meadow Country Club in Flushing, closing with a sizzling round of 66 to finish three ahead of Bobby Cruickshank. He added a third PGA Championship the following year at Milwaukee's Blue Mound Country Club. In 1940, he almost won the U.S. Open again, tying Lawson Little and losing in the eighteen-hole play-off. **OPPOSITE:** Gene Sarazen admires silent movie comedian Buster Keaton's driver while Jock Hutchinson looks on.

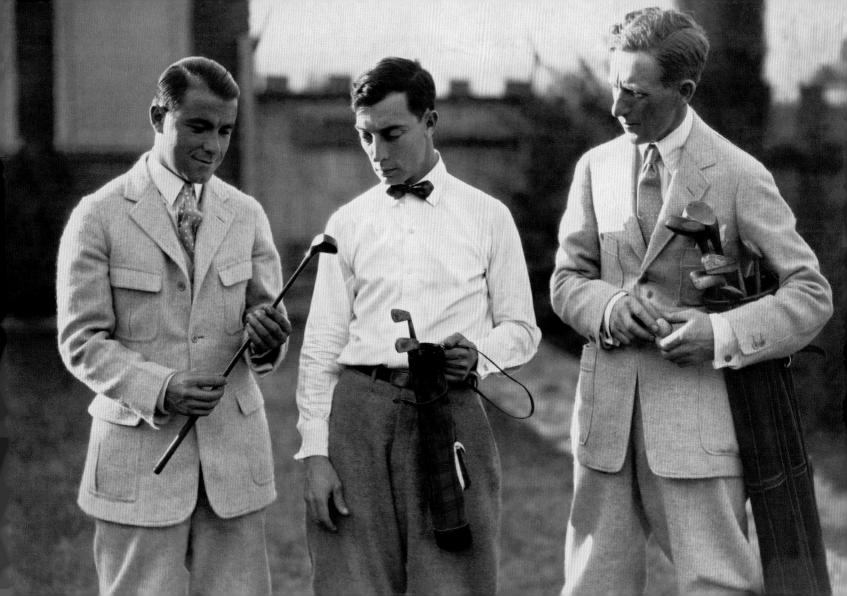

Maureen Orcutt, who cut a dashing figure in the golden era of women's golf, had a long and illustrious career as both a top amateur player and a golfing journalist. Brought up on Park Avenue, she and her twin brothers were introduced to golf by their mother in 1917, when Maureen was ten. Her father was the music critic for the *New York Tribune* and *The New York Times*. Orcutt won the first of her ten Women's Metropolitan Amateur titles in 1926 and the last forty-two years later, in 1968. Her big disappointment was never winning the U.S. Women's Amateur, losing in the finals in 1927 and 1936. In 1936, she was defeated at Canoe Brook in New Jersey by the great English amateur Pam Barton, who was killed when her plane crashed over the Atlantic in World War II. Orcutt did, however, win two U.S. Women's Senior Amateurs, in 1962 and 1966. She was a member of the inaugural U.S. Curtis Cup team in 1932 and competed in the 1934, 1936, and 1938 matches. Orcutt was also a pioneering woman sports reporter, writing about golf for the *New York World* and then *The New York Times*. She died in January of 2007 at age ninety-nine, the last surviving competitor in the 1932 Curtis Cup from either side. **OPPOSITE:** Maureen Orcutt, c. 1925, showing her twin brothers Benjamin and William how to do it at the White Beeches Country Club in New Jersey. **BELOW:** Two women ball markers holding the American and English flags to help the competitors in the 1936 Curtis Cup at Gleneagles identify their balls in the fog.

The Maidstone Club is one of three exceptional links courses on the East End of Long Island, together with Shinnecock Hills and the National Golf Links of America. In recent years, the original trio have been joined by such superb layouts as the Atlantic Golf Club, the Bridge, Friar's Head, and, in 2006, Sebonack. With several holes tucked away in the dunes along the Atlantic behind Hook Pond, Maidstone remains one the very few true seaside links in the United States. The club was started in 1891, but the present design is primarily the work of the old Scottish pro and pioneering course architect Willie Park, Jr., in the 1920s. Childe Hassam, the well-known American Impressionist, was a member of Maidstone, and his summer home was on Egypt Lane near the course. He painted numerous scenes of East Hampton, including some of golfers at Maidstone. **OPPOSITE:** *Morning on the Maidstone Links, the Fifteenth Green* by Childe Hassam, 1926.

"Lighthorse" Harry Cooper, who was given his nickname by Damon Runyon for his speed of play, was born in England but grew up in Texas, where his father was the professional at Cedar Crest Country Club in Dallas. Cooper is famed as one of the best players never to have won a major, having come excruciatingly close on several occasions. In the 1927 U.S. Open at Oakmont, he three-putted the final green, while Tommy Armour holed a birdie putt to force a play-off and went on to victory. In the 1936 Open at Baltusrol, he held a three-shot lead in the clubhouse but fell victim to a superlative closing-round 67 fired by Tony Manero. Cooper's thirty-one victories included the inaugural L.A. Open in 1926, two Canadian Opens, and the 1934 Western Open. He also made his mark as one of the game's finest teachers, giving lessons at Westchester Country Club well into his nineties. He died in 2000. **OPPOSITE:** Harry Cooper in 1932.

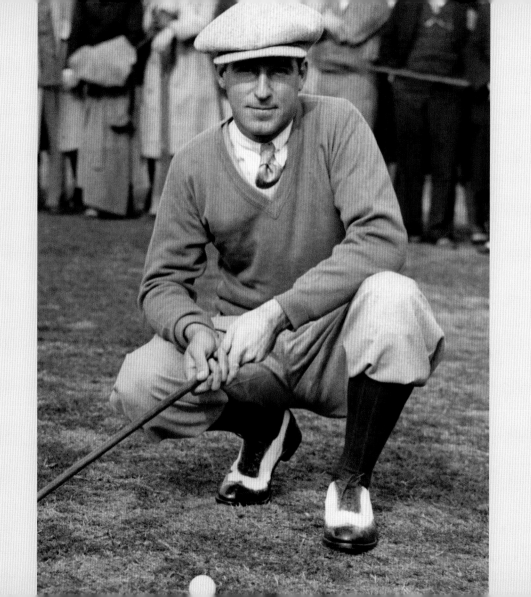

Medinah Country Club is an unlikely bastion of the Arabian in the Midwest, having been founded by a group of Shriners, from Chicago's Medinah Temple, who were members of the Arabian Order of Nobles of the Mystic Shrine. The members established three courses for their new country club, with Scottish-born architect Tom Bendelow completing Medinah No. 1 in 1925, followed by No. 2 the next year, and No. 3, which was originally the ladies' course, completed in 1928—with a major redesign in the 1930s. Course No. 2 fell victim to the Depression, but No. 3 emerged as a championship course, receiving face-lifts from Roger Packard in 1986 prior to the 1990 U.S. Open and from Rees Jones prior to the 2006 PGA. Medinah is famed for its redbrick Moorish clubhouse, complete with mosaic arches and minaret, designed by Chicago architect Richard G. Schmid, who specialized in designing Masonic temples. Member Gustav Brand, a German-born artist, was responsible for the rotunda and elaborate murals. The course's signature par-3s feature carries across Lake Kadijah, named after Mohammed's wife. "Lighthorse" Harry Cooper won the inaugural Medinah Open in 1930. The course hosted the 1949, 1975, and 1990 U.S. Opens, the 1988 U.S. Senior Open, and the 1999 and 2006 PGA Championships—both won by Tiger Woods. **OPPOSITE:** Tiger Woods gets in some putting practice under the gaze of his coach Hank Haney in front of the Medinah clubhouse before playing the final round to win the 2006 PGA Championship.

Stanley Thompson, known as "The Toronto Terror," is responsible for creating the enduring monuments of Canadian golf, sculpted on a massive scale from Brobdingnagian terrain. Thompson came to Toronto as a child when his family emigrated from England. After serving with the Canadian Expeditionary Force in France during World War I, he visited a number of the classic British links courses before starting out as a golf course architect in 1921. Thompson's twin Alberta masterpieces, both set in the splendor of the Candian Rockies, are Jasper Park, completed in 1926, followed two years later by Banff Springs, built for the Canadian Pacific Railway and opened by the Prince of Wales. Banff hugs the Bow River in a valley cradled by mountain peaks, making it one of golf's scenic wonders as well as a testament to Thompson's strate-

gic genius. His other national treasures include Nova Scotia's Cape Breton Highlands, Capilano outside Vancouver, St. George's in Toronto, and Green Gables on Prince Edward Island. A flamboyant figure with an arch sense of humor and known for spending freely, Thompson did not confine his work to Canada. He also created courses in South America, most notably the famed Gávea Golf and Country Club, completed in 1932, that runs through the hills of the Tijuca Forest and down to the seashore south of Rio de Janeiro, under the bulbous, stony Rock of Gávea. **OPPOSITE:** Banff Springs Golf Course, twelfth hole, designed by Stanley Thompson. **BELOW:** A postcard from 1931 for golf at Banff Springs, with the famed hotel in the background.

BRIGHT LIGHTS OF THE DEPRESSION ERA

139 | A DREAM COURSE COMES TO FRUITION

After Bobby Jones retired from competitive golf in 1930, he turned his attention to building his ideal course. In the spring of 1931, he drove down the long lane of magnolias that led to the antebellum manor house of the old Fruitlands Nursery in Augusta, Georgia, and knew as soon as he gazed out to the pine-covered slopes leading down to Rae's Creek that he had found the perfect site. Augusta was the hometown of Jones's wife, Mary, and he had played the Augusta Country Club many times, but he was shown the property that would become Augusta National by his friend Clifford Roberts, a New York investment banker who was part of a group of wealthy Northerners who retreated to Augusta for the winter. Roberts would become the chairman of Augusta National and the major domo of the Masters Tournament for more than forty years. The land, which had once been an indigo plantation, was purchased in 1857 by Louis Mathieu Edouard Berckmans, a Belgian baron, who together with his son Prosper established the foremost commercial nursery in the South, popularizing azaleas throughout the United States. After Prosper's death in 1910, his widow and sons sold their interests, and by the time Jones and his backers acquired the property, the nursery had been abandoned. Jones had distinct views about the type of course he wanted to create, and he selected Alister MacKenzie, the renowned architect whose work at Cypress Point he particularly admired, to collaborate with him on the design of Augusta National. Together they created an American St. Andrews set in the floral pageantry that is the legacy of Fruitlands. **OPPOSITE:** Bobby Jones testing shots at Augusta National while the course was under construction in 1932, as architect Alister MacKenzie in plus fours looks on.

The 1931 Ryder Cup Match was held at Scioto Country Club in Columbus, Ohio, best known today as the home course of Jack Nicklaus. The Americans were determined to avenge their loss at Moortown in 1929, with the PGA selecting Walter Hagen, Gene Sarazen, Horton Smith, Al Espinosa, Johnny Farrell, and Leo Diegel for the home team; the remaining four spots were filled, through a special qualifying event held at Scioto, by Billy Burke, Wiffy Cox, Craig Wood, and Denny Shute. Burke would go on to win the U.S. Open at Inverness in Toledo the following week, but only after two thirty-six-hole play-offs before outlasting amateur George von Elm by a single stroke. The British squad was led by Open champions Arthur Havers and George Duncan, with Henry Cotton sitting out the contest because he refused to accept the team rules requiring the sharing of exhibition revenues equally. The Americans came away the victors by a score of 9–3, including a win by Gene Sarazen over Fred Robson, the longtime pro at The Addington in London, in which Sarazen hit his tee shot on the par-3 fourth hole into the concession stand behind the green, and then chipped through a window onto the green. **OPPOSITE:** Scioto Country Club in Columbus, Ohio. **BELOW:** The par-3 tenth hole, known as "Gibralter," at Moortown Golf Club in Leeds, England, site of the 1929 Ryder Cup.

Bobby Jones and Alister MacKenzie designed Augusta National based on the strategic principles of the Old Course at St. Andrews. This approach manifested itself in expansive fairways that beckoned the average golfer while still demanding proper position from the pros in order to score well, and they used Rae's Creek to create risk/reward options, daring the golfer to make the long carries to the green on the par-5s. The Masters began in 1934 as a small informal tournament called the Augusta National Invitation Tournament, since Jones resisted using the title of the Masters as too pretentious. Horton Smith won the inaugural event, in which Jones also competed. The following year, Gene Sarazen made his famous double eagle on the fifteenth and won in the play-off over Craig Wood, giving the Masters real panache. By shortly after World War II, the tournament was accepted across the board as one of golf's four major championships. The Masters is the only major played at the same course each year, making Augusta National, with its emblematic greenery and exuberant splashes of foliage, the most exalted of American courses. **OPPOSITE:** Horton Smith putting on the final hole of the first Masters Tournament in 1934, which he won by a stroke over Craig Wood.

Herman Densmore "Denny" Shute was one of the top players of the 1930s, winning the British Open and a pair of PGA Championships between 1933 and 1937. In the 1933 Ryder Cup, Shute three-putted the eighteenth hole at Southport and Ainsdale to lose his match against Syd Easterbrook and plunge the American team to defeat. He then went to St. Andrews, where he rebounded from his crushing loss to win the British Open in a play-off over fellow American Craig Wood, who would eventually win the 1941 U.S. Open at Colonial with Shute finishing three shots back in second place. In the memorable U.S. Open of 1939 at Philadelphia Country Club, Shute's bogey on the seventeenth in the final round cost him victory, and he ended up tied with Wood and Byron Nelson, with Nelson claiming victory in a thirty-six-hole play-off after he and Wood were still tied after the first eighteen-hole play-off, Shute having been eliminated. Shute won back-to-back PGA Championships, in 1936 at Pinehurst and 1937 at Pittsburgh Country Club, the last man to repeat in the PGA until Tiger Woods in 1999 and 2000.

OPPOSITE: England's Syd Easterbrook putting on the eighteenth hole of his match against Denny Shute at Southport & Ainsdale, where his victory gave Great Britain and Ireland victory in the 1933 Ryder Cup. **BELOW:** Shute (left) with Craig Wood at the first Masters in 1934.

Olin Dutra came from Monterey, California, the home of Pebble Beach, and grew up playing golf with his neighbors Al and Abe Espinosa, who would both also go on to have successful pro careers. Dutra joined the PGA Tour in 1924, giving up a job in a hardware store, and went on to win nineteen tournaments and play on the 1933 and 1935 Ryder Cup teams. A hulking, powerful player, he won two major championships. In 1932, he cruised to victory in the PGA Championship held at the Keller Golf Club in St. Paul, Minnesota, the site of the St. Paul Open from 1930 to 1968. In 1934, he won the first U.S. Open to be played at Merion, outside Philadelphia, coming back from eight shots down after two rounds to defeat Gene Sarazen by one. Scotland's wee Bobby Cruickshank was in contention when he skulled his second shot on the eleventh, which bounced onto the putting surface after it hit a rock in the creek encircling the green. Cruickshank threw his club in the air and shouted, "Thank you, Lord," only to have it land on his head, leaving him dazed for the remainder of the round.

OPPOSITE: Olin Dutra stands at the center of the 1938 American Ryder Cup team at New Jersey's Ridgewood Golf Club. Left to right, Walter Hagen (captain), Sam Parks, Craig Wood, Gene Sarazen, Horton Smith, Dutra, Ky Laffoon, Henry Picard, Johnny Revolta, and Paul Runyan.

Gene Sarazen, who was still going strong as a knickered octogenarian kicking off the Masters in the 1980s, was one of the three incandescent golfing stars of the 1920s, together with Bobby Jones and Walter Hagen. The crescendo to Sarazen's career came at the 1935 Masters, the second year the tournament was played, when it was still known as the Augusta National Invitational. On the par-5 fifteenth, Sarazen hit what is assuredly the greatest shot seen by the fewest spectators in the history of the game—his famous four-wood that rolled in for double eagle. He parred in and then defeated Craig Wood, the seeming winner in the clubhouse, in the play-off the next day. The victory also gave Sarazen the distinction of being the first player to win each

of the modern majors. He would continue to be one of golf's most popular and engaging figures, serving as the host of *Shell's Wonderful World of Golf* television series. Sarazen was nicknamed "The Squire" because he owned a farm in New Hampshire before moving year-round to Florida's Marco Island. He was spry and quick-witted until the end, a link to the bygone sporting era of Babe Ruth, Jack Dempsey, and Bobby Jones. He died in 1999, not long after teeing off at the Masters, as the honorary starter, at age ninety-seven. **OPPOSITE:** Gene Sarazen putting on the final hole to win the 1935 Masters in a play-off over Craig Wood. **BELOW:** Sarazen interviewing Sam Snead (left) and Ben Hogan at Houston Country Club in 1964.

Perry Maxwell, born in 1879, brought the principles of classic links design to the American plains, designing Southern Hills in Tulsa and Prairie Dunes in Hutchinson, Kansas. Maxwell had moved to the Ardmore Indian Territory in Oklahoma in 1897 to recover from tuberculosis, becoming vice president of the local Ardmore bank. He took up golf around 1909 after reading an article by H. J. Whigham, and by 1925 was working full-time as a course architect. In the 1920s, he entered into a partnership with Alister MacKenzie, working with him on Crystal Downs in Michigan. In 1935, he designed Southern Hills, which has hosted three U.S. Opens and three PGA Championships. In 1937, he designed his masterpiece, Prairie Dunes, which meanders through the inland dunes and old cottonwood trees, and where Julie Inkster won the 2002 U.S. Women's Open. Only nine of the holes were actually built in the 1930s, with the second nine completed twenty years later by his son, J. Press Maxwell, who was also a successful course architect. Perry Maxwell was famed for his topsy-turvy greens, known as "the Maxwell rolls."**OPPOSITE:** Prairie Dunes Golf Club in Hutchinson, Kansas, designed by Perry Maxwell, second hole.

Lawson Little was the paragon of amateur golfers in the 1930s. The son of a colonel in the Army Medical Corps, Little grew up on military bases around the United States and in China. He was a sullen and introverted competitor who steamrolled his opponents. In 1934 and 1935, Little won back-to-back "Little Slams," taking both the U.S. and British Amateur championships when they were considered major tournaments. Following the 1934 Walker Cup, he won the British Amateur at Prestwick, crushing his opponent by 14 and 13 in the thirty-six-hole final, and then won the U.S. Amateur at Brookline. The following year he defended his respective titles at Royal Lytham and St. Annes and at the Cleveland Country Club. In 1936, Little turned pro, and although he won a handful of tournaments over the next few years, he was not the dominant presence in the pro ranks that he had been in the amateur. His curtain call in the majors came at the 1940 U.S. Open at Canterbury Golf Club, outside Cleveland, when he defeated Gene Sarazen in a play-off in Sarazen's last shot to win the Open. Described as bull-necked and barrel-chested, he was a strong driver with an adroit short game. He carried up to twenty-six clubs in his bag, including seven wedges, a bristling arsenal that led the USGA to introduce the rule in 1938 limiting players to fourteen clubs. **OPPOSITE:** Lawson Little teeing off during his victory at the 1935 U.S. Amateur at Cleveland Country Club. **BELOW:** Blasting out on the way to winning the 1940 U.S. Open at Canterbury Golf Club.

Henry Cotton, known as "Maestro," was the supreme British golfer of his era and the greatest English player in the long interval between Harry Vardon and Tony Jacklin. Cotton also broke the mold of the golf professional in Britain, coming from an upper middle-class background and having been educated at an English public school. Born in 1907 in Holmes Chapel, Cheshire, he played in his first British Open in 1927 and his last in 1977, winning the Claret Jug three times. His first Open win came in 1934 at Royal St. George's, when he opened with rounds of 67 and 65—a thirty-six-hole record only broken by Nick Faldo and Greg Norman in 1990 at St. Andrews—and eventually won by five shots. His second win came in 1937 at Carnoustie, when the field included Sam Snead, Byron Nelson, and all the other members of the U.S. Ryder Cup team, closing with a 71 in a downpour to finish two ahead of Reg Whitcombe. Cotton lost several of his prime years to World War II. He won his third and final Open in 1948 at Muirfield, breaking the course record with a second-round 66. Cotton and his independently wealthy Argentine-born wife, "Toots," lived in high style and hobnobbed with the rich and famous, residing in a grand house in Eaton Square in London and staying in five-star hotels on the Riviera, where Cotton ran a golf school in Monte Carlo. **OPPOSITE:** Henry Cotton tees off while Walter Hagen looks on during the 1929 British Open at Muirfield.

There are currently about three thousand golf courses in the golf-crazed nation of Japan, not to mention hundreds of multitiered driving ranges around Tokyo alone. The Tokyo Golf Club, founded in 1914, was the first Japanese club formed for Japanese members. In 1929, the Club decided to move to Asaka, twenty miles north of the city, and Komyo Otani, who had been exposed to the ravishing heathland courses outside London while a student in England, persuaded his fellow members that they should hire Harry Colt, the foremost English golf architect, to design the new course. Colt accepted the assignment but sent his associate, Charles Hugh Alison, who between his arrival via California on December 1, 1930, and his departure in late February, designed the courses that remain the shrines of Japanese golf. A top amateur golfer and leading crick-eteer, Alison had been the club secretary at London's Stoke Poges when it opened in 1907; there he met Colt, who had designed the course. Alison's course at Asaka, completed in 1932, was a project of Pharaonic proportions, built on a flat site by a workforce of sixty thousand laborers. Destroyed during the war, it was rebuilt afterward by Otani. Alison then went on to design the Fuji Course at the Kawana Resort on the Izu Peninsula, which opened in 1936. Next he traveled to Kobe and designed Hirono Golf Club on a lovely pastoral site of ponds, valleys, rivulets, and ravines. On the same trip, Alison consulted on the newly constructed Kasumiguseki, designed by Kinya Fujita, outside Tokyo, as well as Ibaraki Country Club near Kyoto and Naruo Golf Club near Osaka.

OPPOSITE: Hirono Golf Club, designed by C.H. Alison, thirteenth hole.

Like Ben Hogan and Byron Nelson, Ralph Guldahl was born in 1912 in Texas, but unlike them, he peaked early and then vanished from the golfing scene. From 1936 to 1939, Guldahl was the man out front. He won back-to-back U.S. Opens, finishing two shots ahead of Sam Snead at Oakland Hills in 1937, and then repeated at Cherry Hills in 1938. To top it off, he won the Masters in 1939. He also won the Western Open, the most important event on the Tour next to the majors, three times in a row starting in 1936 and was a member of the victorious U.S. team in the 1937 Ryder Cup at Southport and Ainsdale. Despite his success, he had an ungainly swing, with a fidgety setup and quick takeaway, and was a laborious putter. **OPPOSITE:** Ralph Guldahl waves to the crowd after winning the 1937 U.S. Open at Detroit's Oakland Hills.

Henry Picard was a bright light of the 1930s, a generally less luminous decade in the game's history between the glamorous era of Bobby Jones, Walter Hagen, and Gene Sarazen and the heydays of Ben Hogan, Byron Nelson, and Sam Snead. In 1935, he became the pro at Hershey Country Club in Pennsylvania, built in 1930 by Milton Hershey on the grounds surrounding his mansion— which earned Picard the nickname "The Chocolate Soldier." He won twenty-six tournaments, including the 1938 Masters and the 1939 PGA Championship, in which he defeated Nelson in extra holes. He also snagged other important titles of the era, including the North and South Open at Pinehurst and the exotic Agua Caliente Open, a big-money event held in Tijuana, Mexico. Picard encouraged and supported the young Hogan, recommending him for the job at Hershey when he moved on to Canterbury Golf Club in Cleveland in 1946. Designed by Maurice McCarthy, Hershey's West Course held the 1940 PGA won by Nelson, who defeated Snead in the final. **OPPOSITE:** Henry Picard (right) shakes hands with Byron Nelson at the 1939 PGA at Pomonok in Flushing, New York, after Picard defeated Dick Metz in their semifinal match and Nelson ousted Dutch Harrison in the other semifinal. Picard defeated Nelson in the final to win the championship the next day.

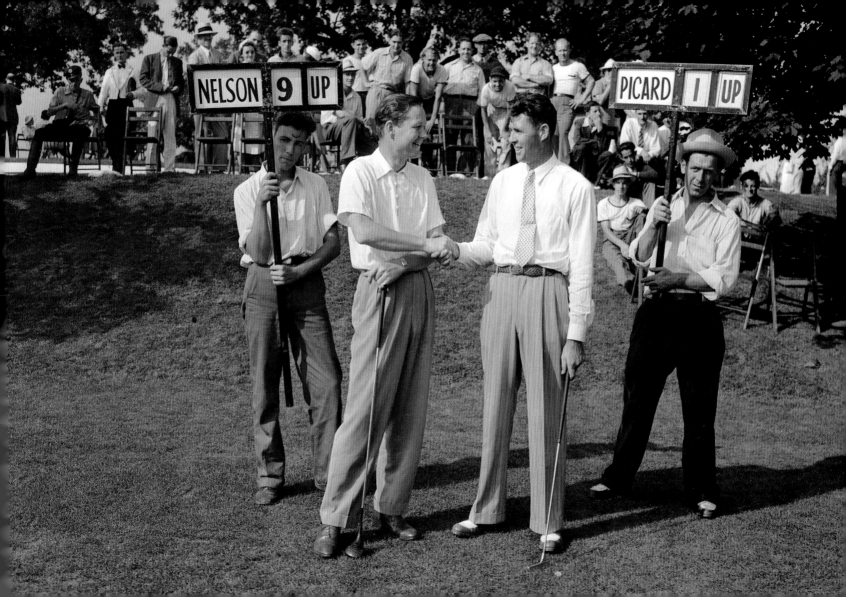

Paul Runyan, at five foot seven inches and 135 pounds, was an unlikely star of the 1930s, snagging twenty-nine PGA events, starting with the North and South Open in 1930. Born in Hot Springs, Arkansas, he turned pro at seventeen and worked as an assistant to Craig Wood at Westchester's now defunct Forest Hills Golf Course. He won nine events in 1933 and seven in 1934, when he won the PGA Championship at Buffalo's Park Country Club in a thirty-eight-hole final over none other than Wood. A notoriously short hitter with a superlative short game, "Little Poison," as he was popularly known, won his second major in 1938 at the PGA Championship held at Shawnee Country Club in Pennslyvania's Delaware Water Gap. Runyan dismantled Sam Snead by 8 and 7 in the final, despite being outdriven by forty yards on every hole by the young Snead. Runyan's short game wizardry never deserted him, and as late as 1951 he led the U.S. Open after three rounds. Runyan became one of the game's legendary instructors and could be seen on the Golf Channel expounding on the intricacies of the short game right up until his death from pneumonia at age ninety-four in 2002. **OPPOSITE:** A matchbook cover for Shawnee Country Club in Pennsylvania, the site of Paul Runyan's victory in the 1938 PGA. **BELOW:** Runyan displays the Wanamaker Trophy after defeating Sam Snead in the final at Shawnee to earn his second PGA Championship.

SHAWNEE COUNTRY CLUB

Byron Nelson was born in 1912 in Texas, the same year as that other golfing deity, Ben Hogan. Indeed, both Nelson and Hogan learned golf as caddies at Glen Garden Country Club, with Nelson besting Hogan in a play-off to take the 1927 Glen Garden caddie tournament. Yet their personalities and careers could hardly have been more dissimilar. Nelson won five majors and retired from competitive golf at the end of the 1946 season, when he was only thirty-four and still in his prime, just before Hogan won his first major. Nelson had a warm, generous personality, while Hogan was known on one side of the Atlantic as "The Hawk" and on the other as "The Wee Ice Mon," a reclusive and unyielding figure. In 1937, Nelson won the Masters for his first major victory, by two shots over fellow Texan Ralph Guldahl, with a birdie on the twelfth and an eagle on the par-5 thirteenth. His second Masters came in 1942, when he defeated Hogan in a potboiler of a play-off by a score of 69 to 70. **OPPOSITE:** Byron Nelson in 1936 before the L.A. Open at Los Angeles Country Club. **BELOW:** With Ben Hogan at the 1942 Masters. They finished tied after Hogan made up three strokes on Nelson in the final round, but Nelson won the play-off.

POST WORLD WAR II AND THE AGE OF BEN HOGAN

153 | THE HOGAN MYSTIQUE

Ben Hogan emerged as the indomitable figure in American golf in the decade after World War II, displaying a ruthless determination to succeed and an obsession with the inner secrets of the golf swing that have never been matched. His father, who was a blacksmith and car mechanic, committed suicide when Hogan was nine, leaving the family in distressed circumstances. In 1931, at age nineteen, Hogan turned pro. The 1930s were a period of trial for Hogan, who although a long driver, fought a hook, and he failed to enjoy the early success of fellow Texans Byron Nelson and Ralph Guldahl. In 1938, he won the Hershey Fourball partnered with Vic Ghezzi, the first of what would be sixty-four victories on the PGA Tour. In 1945, after he returned from war-time service in the air force, he won five tournaments. The next year he won thirteen times and broke through to win the first of his nine majors, the PGA Championship at Portland Golf Club in Washington State. By the summer of 1946, Hogan had conquered his hook, developing a fade through hitting hundreds of thousands of practice balls and discovering what he referred to as his "secret." This was the beginning of the Hogan mystique, and he would go on to win each of the majors, an achievement equaled only by Gene Sarazen, Gary Player, Jack Nicklaus, and Tiger Woods. **OPPOSITE:** Ben Hogan points to his winning score at the Chicago Open Championship in 1941. **BELOW:** Hogan meets the press at the 1967 U.S. Open at Baltusrol.

Sam Snead may not have been the greatest golfer of all time, based on his record in the majors, but there is little dispute that he had the most melodically mesmerizing swing of any golfer ever to play the game, and one that he took with him to the end of his days. Snead was a backwoods golfer who was born in 1912 in Ashwood, three miles from Hot Springs in the foothills of West Virginia, where his father worked maintaining boilers and also had a small farm. He learned about golf from his older brother Homer, who practiced his swing in the cow pasture; his first driver was carved out of a swamp maple root and he used it to hit acorns. Snead was an outstanding all-around athlete and extraordinarily limber, able to kick the top of a seven-foot-high door with either foot when he was in his seventies. He started caddying at the nearby Homestead Resort but had to quit after suffering frostbitten toes, since he only wore shoes to school and church. Snead got a job as the assistant pro at the Homestead when he was nineteen, and in 1935 became the pro at the Greenbrier Hotel in White Sulphur Springs, West Virginia. The Greenbrier, the golfing mecca in the Alleghenies, became Snead's base, where he honed his game. In 1936, he entered a PGA event at Hershey, Pennsylvania, finishing fifth. After that he began playing the Tour, and over the next twenty-nine years, he won a record eighty-two PGA tournaments. His last victory came in the 1965 Greater Greensboro Open, making him, at age fifty-two, the oldest player ever to win a PGA event. **OPPOSITE:** Sam Snead jumps over a hedge for good luck after the second round of the 1937 Metropolitan Open. **BELOW:** Playing in Nassau in the Bahamas in 1937.

Bing Crosby and Bob Hope not only teamed up on the big screen but were also golfing partners and closely associated with the game throughout their careers. Their respective pro-am tournaments, the Bing Crosby National Pro-Am and the Bob Hope Desert Classic, attracted movie stars and presidents alike and contributed much to the game's cachet. Both were dedicated and very fine golfers. Crosby in particular was a serious golfer who at his best was a two handicap; his youngest son, Nathaniel, won the 1981 U.S. Amateur. Crosby caddied as a boy at the Spokane Country Club, and by the 1930s, when he was the lead singer for the Paul Whiteman band, he was a member of Hollywood's Lakeside Country Club. The Crosby started as a weekend getaway for Bing and his golfing buddies at the Old Brockway Course in Lake Tahoe in 1934. In 1937, the first amateur-pro event was held at San Diego's Rancho Santa Fe, with the winner, Sam Snead, taking home $762.30, which he demanded in cash. Crosby became the official host in 1938 and threw a barbecue for the contestants at his home—and so the tournament became popularly known as "Bing's Clambake." In 1947, the tournament moved to the Monterey Peninsula and for many years was played at Pebble Beach, Cypress Point, and Del Monte, the three wonders of California seaside golf. Following Crosby's death in 1977, the event became known as the AT&T National Pro-Am and is currently played at Pebble Beach, Spyglass, and Poppy Hills. Given his devotion to the game, it seems fitting that Crosby died of a heart attack just after walking off the eighteenth green of La Moraleja Golf Club outside Madrid, after shooting a satisfying 85 in his final round. **OPPOSITE:** Cover of the program for the 1954 Crosby Pro-Am. **BELOW:** Crosby kids Ben Hogan about the rules before teeing off at the Pro-Am in 1956.

cypress point

monterey peninsula country club

pebble beach

january 15, 16, 17, 1954

national pro-amateur golf championship 13th

souvenir program .50

sponsored by

Bing Crosby

all proceeds for charity

Sam Snead cultivated a hayseed, hillbilly image in his early years on the Tour, which the press lapped up, but he was also a shrewd competitor. The ultimate natural, he, Ben Hogan, and Byron Nelson together formed the Great Triumvirate of the 1940s. With his graceful and ageless swing, Snead, unlike Nelson and Hogan, kept playing at the highest competitive level into his sixties, finishing second at the 1974 Los Angeles Open. He won a record eighty-two official PGA events and would undoubtedly have won even more had it not been for his putting jitters, which caused him to putt sidesaddle in his later years. He won six majors, but the great and well-known flaw in his career was that he never won the U.S. Open. Snead's missed chances are legendary. He was the favorite in 1937, the first year he played in the Open, but lost by two to Ralph Guldahl. The 1939 Open at Philadelphia Country Club is best remembered not for Byron Nelson's marathon play-off victory but for Snead coming to the final hole needing bogey to win and making an ignominious 8. In 1947, at the St. Louis Country Club, he birdied the final hole to force a play-off with Lew Worsham but lost on the eighteenth hole of the play-off when he missed a short putt after Worsham broke his concentration by asking for a measurement to see who was away. **OPPOSITE:** Sam Snead (left) shakes hands with Ben Hogan on the first tee of Riviera Country Club before their play-off in the 1950 Los Angeles Open, which Snead won. **BELOW:** Playing in the rain with President Eisenhower in 1956.

Byron Nelson won fifty-two PGA events in a career that was interrupted by World War II, when Nelson was at his peak, and cut short by his early retirement from competitive golf in 1946. He was naturally known as Lord Byron, a nickname the humble and upstanding Nelson did not particularly relish. In the 1940s, his earnings and those of the other leading PGA money winner of the day, Harold "Jug" McSpaden, led the press to dub them "The Gold Dust Twins." Nelson's most memorable victory came in the 1939 U.S. Open, the year he established himself as the game's top player. After finishing tied in regulation with Craig Wood and Denny Shute at Philadelphia Country Club's Spring Mill Course, Nelson was still tied with Wood after the eighteen-hole play-off, with Shute having been eliminated. In the second eighteen-hole play-off, Nelson holed his one-iron to the par-4 fourth hole for an eagle, which gave him a two-stroke lead that he never relinquished. In 1946, Nelson lost the U.S. Open at Canterbury Golf Club in another three-man, thirty-six-hole play-off. This time Nelson, Lloyd Mangrum, and Vic Ghezzi were all still tied after the first round of the play-off, with Mangrum ultimately prevailing. Nelson could have won in regulation had he not incurred a penalty when his caddie stepped on his ball in the rough. His caddie wept, but Nelson, an old caddie himself, put his arm around his shoulder and consoled him. **OPPOSITE:** Canterbury Golf Club in Cleveland, where Byron Nelson lost out in the play-off in the 1946 U.S. Open.

Jimmy Demaret was one of the wave of great golfers to come of age in Depression-era Texas. The son of a Houston housepainter, Demaret worked as a caddie before becoming an assistant pro under Jack Burke, Sr., at River Oaks Country Club and befriending as well as babysitting future two-time major winner Jack Burke, Jr. One of the game's most entertaining personalities, Demaret was a great storyteller and prankster, who was moonlighting as a singer in a Houston nightclub when he won the 1940 Masters. He was known for his colorful wardrobe, describing himself as "partial to brick red, mulberry, royal crimson, pale pink, hunter green, Nile green, heather green, and flaming scarlet." Demaret was one of the most accomplished players of the 1940s, who also won the Masters in 1947 and 1950, making him the first three-time winner. To earn the green jacket in 1950, he made up seven shots in the closing six holes to beat Australian Jim Ferrier by two. His friend Ben Hogan referred to him as "the most underrated golfer in history." **OPPOSITE:** Jimmy Demaret displays his wardrobe in 1950.

Lloyd Mangrum, born in Trenton, Texas, was known as a tough competitor and a steely putter under pressure. His budding career was interrupted by World War II, and he returned home a war hero after having been wounded at the Battle of the Bulge and receiving two Purple Hearts. His first postwar victory came in an epic contest at the 1946 U.S. Open over Cleveland's Canterbury Country Club. After he finished tied with Byron Nelson and Vic Ghezzi, the three remained tied after an eighteen-hole play-off. Mangrum then reeled off three late birdies in the second eighteen-hole play-off to edge both Nelson and Ghezzi by one stroke. Mangrum failed to win another major, but achieved much success on the Tour, winning thirty-six tournaments, including the Los Angeles Open four times, between 1949 and 1956, two Western Opens, two Bing Crosby Pro-Ams, and two Tucson Opens. He also won three All-American Opens and the 1948 World Championship of Golf, big-money events all held at Chicago's defunct Tam O'Shanter Golf Club, where Mangrum was also the club's touring pro. In the 1950 U.S. Open at Merion, he was part of the three-man play-off won by Ben Hogan in his historic comeback, with Mangrum incurring a two-shot penalty on the sixteenth hole because he picked up his ball to remove an insect. Altogether, he was runner-up in four majors and third in five more. Mangrum won six of his eight Ryder Cup Matches and was playing captain of the winning U.S. team in 1953 at Wentworth. **OPPOSITE:** Lloyd Mangrum sends up a cloud of dust while hitting out of the rough during the 1939 U.S. Open at Philadelphia Country Club.

Byron Nelson's 1945 season is the stuff of legend, when he won eleven consecutive tournaments, a record that, like Joe DiMaggio's fifty-six-game hitting streak, may never be broken. On March 11, 1945, he won the Miami Fourball, and he kept winning through early August. That year he also won the PGA Championship at Dayton's Moraine Country Club after having won his first PGA in 1940 at Hershey over Sam Snead in the final. Nelson won eighteen of the thirty-one tournaments he entered in 1945, and while detractors point out that the fields were relatively weak because of World War II, his scoring average was a phenomenal 68.3 per round. In 1946, Nelson won ten tournaments before retiring to fulfill his dream of owning a ranch in Texas. He continued to play in the Masters and occasional events and served as a TV commentator. In 1965, he captained the winning U.S. Ryder Cup team at Royal Birkdale. In 1968, he began hosting the Byron Nelson Classic on the PGA Tour, which was played for many years at Dallas's Preston Trail Golf Club and in more recent years at the Four Seasons Resort at Las Colinas. An exceptionally earnest and decent man, Nelson died in September 2006, at age ninety-four. **OPPOSITE:** Byron Nelson speaking to sportswriters during his remarkable 1945 season.

For sixty years, Fred Daly held the distinction of being the only Irishman ever to win the British Open—a feat he achieved at Hoylake in 1947—until Padraig Harrington won the Claret Jug at Carnoustie in 2007. Daly learned the game as a tiny caddie at Royal Portrush, the great links of Northern Ireland's Antrim Coast, near the Giant's Causeway, where he was born. The year after his Open victory he was runner-up to the renowned Henry Cotton, and finished third, fourth, and third from 1950 to 1952. Despite his slight build, Daly was a vaunted long-iron player, of whom Sam Snead said, "He could knock your hat off with a one-iron at 220 yards." He was also a clutch putter, despite taking innumerable waggles before striking the ball. A great storyteller and personality, he was a presence at Balmoral Golf Club, a parkland course just outside Belfast, for forty-five years, until his death in 1990. **OPPOSITE:** Fred Daly is held aloft at Hoylake after winning the 1947 Open by one stroke over American amateur Frank Stranahan.

The Turnesa brothers, like Johnny Farrell and Tony Manero, were products of the Fairview caddie pen in Westchester County, New York, where their father was the greenkeeper. Jim Turnesa, the sixth of seven golfing brothers, won the PGA Championship in 1952 at Big Spring in Louisville, coming from three down in the final to defeat Chick Harbert on the thirty-sixth hole. His brothers Joe and Mike each also came close to winning a major, but were never able to pull it off. Joe, the third oldest, had a four-stroke lead over Bobby Jones in the final round of the 1926 U.S. Open at Scioto, but slipped to finish one shot back. The following year, he had Walter Hagen on the ropes in the final of the PGA at Cedar Crest in Dallas but lost on the final hole. Mike Turnesa was also a regular on the PGA Tour, losing to Ben Hogan in the final of the 1948 PGA at

Norwood Hills in St. Louis. Willie "the Wedge" Turnesa, the youngest of the brothers, remained an amateur. He won the U.S. Amateur in 1938 at Oakmont and in 1948 at Memphis, and added the British Amateur title in 1947, defeating fellow American Dick Chapman in a dingdong final at Carnoustie. The Turnesa brothers also served as pros at some of Westchester's best-known clubs—Mike at Knollwood, Frank at Metropolis, and Doug at Briar Hall, the site of what is now Trump National. **OPPOSITE:** Willie Turnesa teeing off during the 1934 U.S. Amateur Champion at The Country Club in Brookline, Massachusetts. **BELOW:** Program cover for the 1948 U.S. Amateur at Memphis Country Club, which was won by Turnesa.

Sam Snead won the 1946 British Open at St. Andrews, a tournament that he only entered because the president of Wilson Sporting Goods, who wanted to boost sales of Snead's signature clubs in Great Britain, insisted that he play. When Snead first saw the Old Course out of the train window on the trip from London, he thought that it was an old abandoned course. Snead's initial reaction was not unlike that of other American golfers, including Bobby Jones, but unlike Snead, Jones came to treasure St. Andrews above all other courses. Snead's one prior British Open had been in 1937 at Carnoustie, a course that he despised, when all of the members of the American Ryder Cup team entered the championship. At St. Andrews, Snead not only was unimpressed by the course, but disliked the hotel, the food, and the caddies—his first choice to carry his bag having been jailed for drunkenness the night before play began. Nevertheless, Slammin' Sammy won by four over Bobby Locke and the American pro Johnny Bulla, whom Snead had brought over to Scotland with him so that he would have a friend on the journey. Snead did not play in the Open again until the 1960s, when he was well past his prime. He did, however, play in seven Ryder Cups and was the playing captain in 1959 at Eldorado Country Club in Palm Springs and the nonplaying captain in 1969, when the teams tied at Birkdale after Jack Nicklaus conceded a short putt to Tony Jacklin. **OPPOSITE:** Sam Snead outside the clubhouse at St. Andrews in 1946, where he won the British Open.

Mildred "Babe" Didrikson Zaharias was widely acclaimed as the greatest woman athlete of the twentieth century. Born in Port Arthur, Texas, in 1914, she earned her nickname as a slugger in baseball and also played professional basketball. In the 1932 Olympics held in Los Angeles, she won gold medals in the eighty-meter hurdles, javelin, and high jump, setting world records in each, but was later disqualified from the high jump for using the controversial Western Roll. The Babe came to golf relatively late in life, having been persuaded to turn to the game at the Olympics by the legendary sportswriter Grantland Rice, himself a scratch golfer. She quickly displayed the same athletic genius in golf, driving the ball enormous distances. In 1946, by which time she was married to the professional wrestler George Zaharias, she won the U.S. Amateur. The following year, she became the first American player to capture the British Ladies' Championship, winning at Gullane. When the LPGA was founded in 1950, she became the Tour's marquee player. **OPPOSITE:** Babe Didrikson Zaharias playing with Bing Crosby and Bob Hope at the Frank Condon Golf Tournament in Los Angeles in 1941, while starter Scotty Chisholm (in kilts) looks on.

With her competitive spirit, outgoing personality, and athletic fame, Babe Didrikson Zaharias played a key role in putting women's professional golf on the map and wowed galleries with her long drives. In 1948, the Babe won the U.S. Women's Open played at Atlantic City, and after her rival Louise Suggs took the title in 1949, she triumphed again in 1950. In 1953, she was diagnosed with the cancer that would claim her life three years later. She underwent surgery and then staged a valiant comeback, not only winning the 1955 Open at Salem Country Club in Massachusetts but demolishing the field with a winning margin of twelve strokes. She won five tournaments that season and thirty-one in her career before her untimely death the following year.

OPPOSITE: Salem Country Club, twelfth hole, the site of Babe Didrikson's 1955 U.S. Open victory. **BELOW:** The Babe (right) with Patty Berg at the Women's Western Open in Chicago in 1944.

Louise Suggs together with Babe Didrikson and Patty Berg made up the great troika in the early days of the LPGA Tour, of which she was a founder. She was born in Atlanta, where her grandfather owned the legendary Atlanta Crackers minor-league baseball team. Her father played pro baseball and built golf courses, including the Lithia Springs course, where she began playing at age ten. As an amateur, Suggs won the U.S. Women's Amateur Championship in 1947 and the British Ladies' Championship the following year at Royal Lytham. As a pro, she won fifty-eight tournaments between 1946 and 1962, fifth on the all-time list, including eleven majors. She won the 1949 U.S. Open by a record fourteen strokes and was the victor again in 1952. Bob Hope, who became a good friend of Suggs, dubbed her "Miss Sluggs." **OPPOSITE:** Louise Suggs driving during the Women's Western Open held at Des Moines, Iowa, in 1946. **BELOW:** Suggs (left) chats with playing partner Eileen Stulb at the 1955 Titleholders Tournament in Augusta, Georgia.

Patty Berg was "Little Patty Berg" when she was a teenage golfing phenomenon from Minneapolis. At age seventeen, she reached the final of the 1935 U.S. Amateur on her home course of Interlachen, losing 3 and 2 to Glenna Collett Vare in what would be Collett's sixth and last title. Berg went on to win the Amateur crown in 1938. In 1946, she won the inaugural U.S. Women's Open held at Spokane Country Club, the only time the tournament was played as a match-play event. Berg was a founding member of the LPGA, serving as its first president, and was the leading money winner on the Tour in 1954, 1955, and 1957. With her red hair, blue eyes, and oversize personality, Berg was a tireless promoter of the women's tour and estimated that she had given sixteen thousand clinics during her career.

OPPOSITE: Patty Berg is surrounded by caddies seeking her autograph at Westmoreland Country Club in Wilmette, Illinois, during the U.S. Women's Amateur in 1938, which she won.

Arthur D'Arcy "Bobby" Locke was the first of the great South African pros. Born in Germiston in the Transvaal in 1917, Locke went to work for the Rand Mining House, but luckily his employer sent him to London in 1936, where he entered the British Open and finished as low amateur, eighth overall. In a series of exhibition matches against Sam Snead back in South Africa, Locke shellacked Slammin' Sammy 12–2–2. Locke then went on to a wildly successful but short-lived stint on the PGA Tour, winning eleven times over a two-and-a-half-year period, including a torrid run in 1947 when he won four times in a five-week span. His sixteen-stroke win in the 1948 Chicago Victory National Championship remains a PGA record. A distinctive figure in puffy pearl-gray knickers and white shoes and stockings, the jowly Locke was known as "Old Muffin Face." After winning the Open at Royal St. George's in 1949, running away from Ireland's Harry Bradshaw in a thirty-six-hole play-off, Locke continued to give exhibitions and play in Britain. This led to his being banned from the PGA Tour, ostensibly on the grounds that he had broken commitments to sponsors in the United States. Locke was reinstated in 1951, but never played in the U.S. again. **OPPOSITE:** Bobby Locke keeps his plus fours and stockings dry in 1949 during the Harrogate Golf Tournament in North Yorkshire.

After having lost in the final to Paul Runyan in 1938 and to Byron Nelson in 1940, Sam Snead won the 1942 PGA Championship over Jim Turnesa at New Jersey's Seaview Country Club for his first major victory. He won two more PGA Championships, in 1949 at Richmond's Hermitage Country Club, which is now the publicly owned Belmont Park Golf Course, and in 1951 at Oakmont. Snead also won the first of his three Masters in 1949, finishing strong with back-to-back 67s. He won his second Masters in high winds in 1952, chipping in for bogey on the twelfth in the final round after dunking his tee shot in Rae's Creek. His third victory, in 1954, was far and away the most dramatic, for he came back to tie arch rival Ben Hogan in regulation and then won the eighteen-hole play-off. Snead had an unquenchable desire to play and compete in golf, serving as the honorary starter at the Masters with Gene Sarazen and Byron Nelson and taking on all comers for a wager at his home course at the Homestead. In 1994, Snead returned to the Greenbrier, where he had been the pro in the 1930s, as pro emeritus, continuing to play until his death in 2002, just four days short of his ninetieth birthday.

OPPOSITE: The Greenbrier Course, ninth hole, at the Greenbrier Resort in White Sulphur Springs, West Virginia.

In 1948, Ben Hogan won the U.S. Open at Riviera Country Club after having won the Los Angeles Open there in 1947 and 1948, and Riviera became known as "Hogan's Alley." That same year he won the PGA at Norwood Hills in St. Louis for his third major. After he got off to a good start in 1949, he and his wife, Valerie, were driving east of Pecos, Texas, on a foggy February morning when their car collided with an oncoming Greyhound bus. Hogan had leaned over to shield Valerie, which saved his life, but he was badly injured and near death. A return to championship golf seemed a pipe dream, and yet Hogan made a remarkable comeback that is at the heart of the Hogan legend. In January 1950, he fittingly began his comeback at Riviera in the L.A. Open, tying with Sam Snead before losing in a play-off. Then, at the U.S. Open at Merion, he climbed his way back to the summit of the game. On the third and final day of regulation play, which consisted of thirty-six holes, he parred the finishing hole to earn a tie with Lloyd Mangrum and George Fazio, hitting a one-iron to the green of the 460-yard eighteenth hole in that moment of supreme concentration that is captured in the timeless photograph by *Life*'s Hy Peskin. Hogan then won the eighteen-hole play-off the next day. In 1951, he won his first Masters, and that same year he won the U.S. Open at Oakland Hills, which had been beefed up for the championship by Robert Trent Jones. Hogan shot a final-round 67, and at the presentation ceremony he remarked: "I am glad that I finally was able to bring this monster to its knees." **OPPOSITE:** Ben Hogan hits the one-iron to the eighteenth green at Merion on June 10, 1950 in the final round of the U.S. Open. His par gave him a tie in regulation and he went on to win the play-off.

Dr. Cary Middlecoff was a sweet-swinging Tennessee dentist whose father and two uncles were also dentists. In 1943, while still an amateur, he won the North and South Open, a prominent PGA event, and in 1947 he gave up dentistry to turn pro. Middlecoff was one of the dominant players of the 1950s, winning forty PGA Tour events and earning more than any other player during that decade. Middlecoff's three major victories consisted of two U.S. Opens and one Masters. In the 1949 Open, he was the victor by one stroke over Sam Snead and Clayton Heafner at Medinah. In 1956 at Oak Hill in Rochester, New York, he finished one shot ahead of both Ben Hogan, who had won the Open in 1948, 1950, 1951, and 1953, and Julius Boros, the champion in 1952. In the 1955 Masters, Middlecoff walloped the field, finishing seven shots ahead of Hogan and Snead. Middlecoff was known as a painfully slow player who also had a pause at the top of his backswing. In the 1957 U.S. Open at Inverness, after shooting a pair of 68s, he lost in a play-off to Dick Mayer, who brought a camping stool with him to the first hole in a not so subtle reference to Middlecoff's snail-like pace of play. He appeared in two movies playing himself, *Follow the Sun* about Ben Hogan, and the 1960 Jerry Lewis comedy *The Bellboy*. **OPPOSITE:** Cary Middlecoff striding to victory at the 1955 Masters.

The name Robert Trent Jones became synonymous with American golf course architecture in the 1950s and 1960s. Born in Ince, England, in 1906, he grew up in Rochester, New York, where he caddied for Walter Hagen at the Rochester Country Club. Jones added his middle name, after the Trent River near where he was born, to avoid being confused with the great golfer. Jones set out at an early age to become a course architect, and to that end studied agronomy, engineering, and landscape design at Cornell. He worked with the legendary Canadian architect Stanley Thompson in the 1930s, a lean time for building courses, but gained international acclaim as the game boomed in the postwar years. Jones developed a particularly recognizable and enduring American style of design that featured long, multiple tees, fairways pinched in the landing areas by bunkers, and large greens with distinct quadrants, guarded in front by big, jigsaw puzzle–shaped sand traps. Jones described his style of design as "heroic" rather than penal, challenging the golfer to play a power game of forced carries over sand and stream but offering a safe layup. **OPPOSITE:** Peachtree Golf Club in Atlanta, one of Robert Trent Jones's early designs, sixteenth hole. **BELOW:** Jones at the 1965 U.S. Open at Bellerive, outside St. Louis, a course he designed.

Betsy Rawls, a native of South Carolina, won the U.S. Women's Open four times between 1951 and 1960, holding the record for most wins with Mickey Wright. In 1950, while still an amateur, she was runner-up to Babe Didrikson in the Open, finishing nine shots back. The next year, her first as a professional, she won the Open at Druid Hills Golf Club in Atlanta. She went on to win the championship in 1953, defeating Jackie Pung in an eighteen-hole play-off, and in 1957 at Winged Foot, when Pung actually finished one shot ahead but was disqualified for signing an incorrect scorecard. Rawls's fourth Open victory came in 1960 at Worcester Country Club. She led the Tour in victories in 1952, 1957, and in 1959—when she won ten tournaments—and was the leading money winner with a grand total of $27,000. Rawls majored in math and physics at the University of Texas and became an authority on the rules of golf. **OPPOSITE:** Betsy Rawls playing in the 1960 Women's Western Open in Chicago.

The year 1953 marked the highest trajectory of Ben Hogan's career and is the stuff of golfing legend. Hogan won all three majors that he entered: the Masters, the U.S. Open, and the British Open. At the Masters, for which he prepared annually at Seminole Golf Club in Florida, he won with a record low score for the tournament. Next came a record-tying fourth U.S. Open at Oakmont, with a winning score of five under par. That summer, Hogan made his only appearance in the British Open, arriving two weeks early at Carnoustie for meticulous preparation during which he charted his way around the course. When play began, Hogan was followed by an enormous and excited Scottish gallery that had come out to see "the Wee Ice Mon" with the cold glint in his eye and white cap. He lowered his score in each round, winning by four over Frank Stranahan, Dai Rees, Antonio Cerda, and Peter Thomson. The "Colossus at Carnoustie" returned home to a hero's welcome and a ticker tape parade in lower Manhattan. **OPPOSITE:** Ben Hogan on the green during his 1953 victory at the British Open at Carnoustie. **BELOW:** Hogan's swing in 1954.

South Africa's Bobby Locke won the British Open four times. After back-to-back triumphs in 1949 and 1950, he won again at Royal Lytham in 1952. Max Faulkner interrupted his streak in 1951, winning at Royal Portrush in Northern Ireland. (Faulkner was a popular character, known for his bright clothing, brio, and his collection of some three hundred putters, including one made from a piece of driftwood attached to a snooker cue.) An unorthodox player, Locke hit all his shots with a pronounced hook. One of the game's great, and possibly greatest, all-time putters, he also seemed to hook his putting stroke, bringing his hickory-shafted putting blade back well inside the line. It was Locke who came up with one of the game's punchiest one-liners: "You drive for show but putt for dough." Locke's fourth win came at St. Andrews in 1957, when he finished ahead of his great rival Peter Thomson. His career was cut short by a serious car accident in 1959, when his automobile was struck by a train. **OPPOSITE:** Bobby Locke surveys his putt on the last hole of the 1957 British Open at St. Andrews, the site of his fourth and final Open victory.

Peggy Kirk Bell was a leading amateur golfer in the 1950s and a member of the 1950 Curtis Cup team before becoming a founding member of the LPGA Tour. She competed on the Tour for ten years, marrying her high school sweetheart Warren "Bullitt" Bell, who had played pro basketball for the Fort Wayne Pistons, in 1953. That same year the Bells acquired the Pine Needles Lodge and Golf Course in the Sandhills of North Carolina, with its exquisite Donald Ross–designed course just down the road from Pinehurst. The Bells turned Pine Needles into a notably friendly, down-home resort, with Mrs. Bell a constant and charming presence. In 1991, Pine Needles played host to the U.S. Women's Open, won by Annika Sörenstam, and the event proved such a rip-roaring success that the tournament returned there in 2001, with Karrie Webb the winner, and in 2007, when Cristie Kerr headed the field. Peggy Bell made her mark as an outstanding instructor, and in 2002 she became the first woman to be voted into the World Golf Teachers Hall of Fame. **OPPOSITE:** Pine Needles Golf Club, sixth hole. **BELOW:** Peggy Kirk Bell.

Jack Burke, Jr., born in Houston in 1923, was one of the top pros of the 1950s, winning sixteen PGA events, including both the Masters and the PGA in 1956. His father, who had finished tied for second in the 1920 U.S. Open behind Ted Ray, was the pro at Houston's River Oaks Country Club, and young Jackie grew up steeped in the game, meeting and playing with many of the stars of the 1930s. Jack Burke, Sr., was a highly regarded teacher whose pupils included Babe Didrikson and Jimmy Demaret. Burke and Demaret, who worked as the assistant pro at River Oaks, became lifelong friends. In his glory year of 1956, Burke entered the final round of the Masters trailing Ken Venturi, who was still an amateur, by eight strokes. On a cold day in which Augusta National was raked by fierce winds, Burke shot a 71 to Venturi's 80 to win by one. In the PGA, he defeated Ted Kroll in the final at Massachusetts's Blue Hill Country Club. A popular player who placed a premium on golf's traditional values, Burke was the playing captain of the 1957 American team that went down to defeat at Lindrick, the first British and Irish victory since 1933. In 1957, he and Demaret bought land in a remote part of Houston and together developed Champions Golf Club, working with architect Ralph Plummer to design the course. Burke is still going strong at Champions, and over the years he has coached Steve Elkington and Hal Sutton. **OPPOSITE:** Jack Burke, Jr. plays out from under a dogwood on his way to winning the 1956 Masters.

Marlene Hagge, when she was Marlene Bauer, and her older sister Alice, were two of the thirteen founding members of the LPGA in 1950. At only fifteen years old, Hagge was the youngest of the charter members and remains the youngest ever member of the LPGA. Aged eighteen years, nine months, and fourteen days when she won the Sarasota Open in 1952, she also remains the youngest winner in LPGA history, three days younger than Paula Creamer. The first glamour girl on the LPGA Tour, she won twenty-six tournaments between 1952 and 1972. Her banner year was 1956, when she won the LPGA Championship and eight tournaments altogether, finishing first on the money list. She was married to the well-known golf course architect Robert von Hagge. **OPPOSITE:** Marlene Bauer swinging in 1950. **BELOW:** Left to right, Alice Bauer and Babe Zaharias paired against Patty Berg and Marlene Bauer in a 1951 exhibition match in San Francisco.

Welshman James David "Dai" Rees was an extremely engaging player with an unflagging enthusiasm for the game, whose career spanned from the late 1930s well into the 1960s. He won the British Match Play Championship, known as the *News of the World* after the sponsoring newspaper, four times, starting in 1936 when he was twenty-three. He reached the finals of the event in 1969, thirty-three years after his first win. His big disappointment was never winning the Open despite repeatedly coming close. In 1953, he tied for second when Ben Hogan dominated at Carnoustie. The following year, he lost by a stroke to Peter Thomson at Birkdale when he bogeyed the final hole. When the Open returned to Birkdale in 1962, he again fell one shot short, this time to Arnold Palmer. Rees's reputation rests foremost on his achievements in the Ryder Cup, in which he competed nine times, beginning in 1937, four times as playing captain. His crowning glory came in 1957, when he captained the British and Irish team to their historic comeback victory at Lindrick Golf Club, set in the midst of the heather and silver birch of the Yorkshire moorland. It was the only American defeat in the postwar era until 1985, by which time the event had been expanded to include Continental European players. Rees won his foursomes match and defeated Ed Furgol in the singles. He served for many years as the professional at South Herts Golf Club in London, following in the footsteps of the great Harry Vardon. **OPPOSITE:** Dai Rees gets a boost after winning the 1936 *News of the World* Tournament at Oxhey Golf Club in Hertfordshire. **BELOW:** Lindrick Golf Club, eighteenth hole, the site of Great Britain and Ireland's historic victory in the 1957 Ryder Cup.

The great Australian golfer Peter Thomson, who won the British Open five times, was born in Melbourne in 1929. He turned pro in 1949, having studied to be an industrial chemist. After finishing second to Bobby Locke in 1952, his leading rival on the international stage during the 1950s, and to Ben Hogan in 1953, Thomson reeled off three successive wins in the Open in 1954, 1955, and 1956. Thomson is the only golfer in the twentieth century to capture the Claret Jug three years in a row, a feat accomplished by Young Tom Morris, Jamie Anderson, and Bob Ferguson in the championship's primordial years. His fourth win was in 1958 at Royal Lytham, when he defeated Dave Thomas in a play-off. Thomson's crowning achievement came at Royal Birkdale in 1965, where he defeated defending champion Tony Lema, with whom he was paired in the final round, and a strong field that included the big guns of Arnold Palmer, Jack Nicklaus, and Gary Player in their golfing primes. **OPPOSITE:** Peter Thomson playing in the 1967 British Open. **BELOW:** Thomson's wife Lois admires the Claret Jug after his first Open victory in 1954 at Royal Birkdale.

Jimmy Demaret won thirty-one times on the PGA Tour, including his three Masters victories. He also came close to winning the U.S. Open more than once. He finished second to Ben Hogan in the 1948 U.S. Open at Riviera despite breaking the all-time Open scoring record, and in 1957 at Inverness he missed the Cary Middlecoff–Dick Mayer play-off, won by Mayer, by one stroke. In his three Ryder Cup appearances between 1947 and 1951, Demaret compiled a perfect 6–0 record in singles and foursomes. Demaret was also well known to TV audiences as the amiable cohost with Gene Sarazen of *Shell's Wonderful World of Golf,* a series featuring matches between two top pros held in exotic locales. Later in his career, until his death in 1983, he would hold forth in the clubhouse at Champions Golf Club, which he owned with Jack Burke, Jr. The Cypress Creek Course at Champions, which was carved through seventy thousand pines and includes a mimosa he planted in the greenside bunker on the seventeenth hole, hosted the 1967 Ryder Cup and the 1969 U.S. Open, won by Orville Moody. **OPPOSITE:** The Champions Golf Club, Cypress Creek Course, developed by Jimmy Demaret and Jack Burke, Jr., seventeenth hole. **BELOW:** Demaret (right) waits to tee off with Ben Hogan in Miami in 1948.

After his epic 1953 season, Ben Hogan never won another major. He seemed a shoo-in to become the first man ever to win five U.S. Opens in 1955 at San Francisco's Olympic, when the unknown Jack Fleck birdied the last hole by sinking an eight-foot putt to finish with a 67 that tied Hogan. The next day Fleck, who played out of the municipal course in Davenport, Iowa, jumped out to a three-shot lead in the play-off, but Hogan fought back to one stroke down going to the eighteenth hole. When Hogan made a six on the last hole, Fleck was the winner in the greatest upset in American golf since Francis Ouimet dethroned Harry Vardon and Ted Ray. Hogan's putting began to desert him in his later years but in 1960 at Cherry Hills, when he was forty-eight, he made a final run at the U.S. Open, falling short of Arnold Palmer when his wedge shot to the par-5 seventeenth spun back into the water. Hogan's final win came appropriately in his hometown of Fort Worth, at the Colonial Invitational in 1959. He retired to practice in solitude at Shady Oaks Golf Club in Fort Worth, built in the 1950s by his friend and sponsor J. Marvin Leonard, who had founded Colonial Country Club in 1936. Fleck continued to play the Tour into the 1960s, and he designed, owns, and operates Lil' Bit of Heaven Golf Club in Magazine, Arkansas, where he lives. **OPPOSITE:** Jack Fleck putts on the eighth green in the 1955 U.S. Open at Olympic, while Ben Hogan looks on. **BELOW:** Program cover for the 1955 U.S. Open.

Lionel and Junius Jay Hebert are the only American brothers ever to both win major championships. The great Scottish pro Sandy Herd, a native son of St. Andrews, won the 1902 British Open, while his younger brother Fred won the U.S. Open in 1898 at Myopia. Brought up in Louisiana, the Heberts both attended Louisiana State University. Lionel, five years younger than Jay, won his major first, capturing the PGA Championship in 1957 at Miami Valley Golf Club in Dayton, Ohio. In the last year the PGA was contested as a match-play event, Lionel defeated 1953 champion Walter Burkemo in the semifinal match and Dow Finsterwald in the final for his first Tour victory. Jay won seven tournaments between 1957 and 1961, taking the PGA Championship by one shot over Aussie Jim Ferrier in 1960 at Firestone. A popular player, Jay captained the winning American squad in the 1971 Ryder Cup at Old Warson Country Club in St. Louis. **OPPOSITE:** Lionel Hebert with the Wanamaker Trophy and his check after winning the 1957 PGA at Miami Valley Golf Club.

Oklahoma's Tommy Bolt was famed for his tempestuous temperament, earning him the nickname "Thunder Bolt." His reputation for throwing clubs tended to overshadow his superb ability as one of golf's finest shotmakers during the 1950s. He turned pro when he was thirty-four, after having served as head pro at a golf club in Rome when he was in the army during World War II. His major victory came in the 1958 U.S. Open in his home state, played in the steamy heat of Tulsa's Southern Hills, when he shot rounds of 69 and 72 on the final day to finish four shots ahead of Gary Player. Bolt's game held up well, and in 1971, when he was over fifty, he finished third behind Jack Nicklaus and Billy Casper in the PGA Championship at Palm Beach Gardens. A much more mellow and entertaining character later in his career, Bolt was one of the founders of the Senior or Champions Tour, teaming with Art Wall in the 1979 Legends of Golf, which they lost in a dramatic six-hole sudden-death play-off to Julius Boros and Roberto De Vicenzo.

OPPOSITE: Tommy Bolt reacts after sinking a putt for a 63 in the third round of the 1956 Los Angeles Open.

Herbert Warren Wind, the greatest of American golf writers, was born in Brockton, Massachusetts, in 1916, a town known for its shoe manufacturing industry. He was introduced to the game at the local Thorny Lea Golf Club, where his father had become a member in the 1920s. While attending Yale, he heard the song "Shouting in that Amen Corner" at a jazz concert that he covered for the *Yale Daily News,* and later bestowed the title of "Amen Corner" on the eleventh through thirteenth holes at Augusta National. After graduating, he studied at Cambridge, and while in England met the famed golf writer Bernard Darwin, who deeply influenced his career. After World War II, Wind went to work for *The New Yorker* and produced his timeless masterpiece, *The Story of American Golf,* which he updated over the years. He then joined *Sports Illustrated* as a founding editor in 1954, returning to *The New Yorker* in 1960. Wind covered all the majors, walking the courses to follow the action dressed like the British golfers of yesteryear, in a long-sleeved shirt, tie, and tweed jacket. His illuminating essays in *The New Yorker* combined historical insight with a conversational style. Wind liked to say that it took him ten thousand words to clear his throat. Later in life he edited the Classics of Golf series, which reprinted long-lost works by the game's finest writers with fresh and scholarly introductions by Wind. **OPPOSITE:** View of the sixteenth green at Augusta National during the 1973 Masters. **BELOW:** Herbert Warren Wind at the Masters.

Joe Carr was the greatest of Irish amateurs. One of seven children, he was adopted by his mother's sister and her husband, James Carr, who had just returned from India to become the steward and stewardess of Portmarnock Golf Club, enabling Carr to learn about the game at Dublin's legendary links. Carr would win each of Ireland's amateur events numerous times, beginning with the East of Ireland Amateur in 1941 when he was nineteen. Tall and wiry, with an idiosyncratic swing, Carr excelled in match play, winning the British Amateur Championship three times. His first victory came at Hoylake in 1953, defeating the American champion Harvie Ward in the final. In 1958, after intense preparation, he won his second Amateur title at St. Andrews, and two years later he was victorious again at Royal Portrush. In 1967, he became the first Irish player to be invited to compete in the Masters, and made the cut. He returned the next two years, eventually becoming an overseas member of Augusta National. A beloved figure, he was named captain of the Royal and Ancient Golf Club of St. Andrews, the first Irishman to receive the honor.

OPPOSITE: Joe Carr in 1967 at the British Open at Hoylake, where he had won the British Amateur in 1953.

Bob Rosburg, everybody's favorite on-course television commentator, started out as a golfing wunderkind from San Francisco. When he was twelve years old, he beat Ty Cobb in the first flight of the club championship at the storied Olympic Club, much to Cobb's chagrin. After graduating from Stanford in 1948, where he starred on the baseball team, Rosburg turned pro in 1953. His banner year was 1959, when he won the PGA Championship at Minneapolis Golf Club, his lone major, and finished runner-up to Billy Casper at the U.S. Open. A decade later, he had another close brush with winning the Open, missing a three-foot putt on the seventy-second hole that would have put him in a play-off with Orville "Sarge" Moody. Rosburg capped off his playing career with a win at the 1972 Bob Hope Desert Classic, when he was forty-five. Since the mid-1970s, "Rossie" has been the roving course reporter for ABC television, offering candid assessments of a players' prospects, particularly the phrase for which he is best known: "He's got no chance." **OPPOSITE:** Bob Rosburg playing in Miami in 1954.

Julius Boros, the son of Hungarian immigrants, did not take up golf until he was in his twenties, but went on to have a long and prosperous career on the PGA Tour, winning two U.S. Opens and the 1968 PGA Championship at age forty-eight, making him the oldest winner of a major. Boros grew up in Fairfield, Connecticut, and starred in baseball for the University of Bridgeport before working as an accountant. He got a job as the accountant for the Southern Pines Country Club in the North Carolina Sandhills in 1946, where he met Ann "Buttons" Cosgrove, whose family owned the nearby Mid Pines golf resort. At her urging he turned pro in 1949, and they were married the following year. Boros had a wonderfully languid, effortless swing, and his motto was "swing easy, hit it hard," which no doubt explains why his game

held up for so long. His first U.S. Open victory came in 1952 at Northwood in Dallas, besting Ed "Porky" Oliver by four shots. His second major win came at the 1963 Open, played at The Country Club in Brookline on the fiftieth anniversary of Francis Ouimet's historic victory, with Boros defeating Arnold Palmer and Jackie Cupit in an eighteen-hole play-off. His 1968 PGA win came at San Antonio's Pecan Valley, nipping Palmer and Bob Charles by a stroke. His son Guy Boros has also played on the PGA Tour, winning the 1996 Greater Vancouver Open. **OPPOSITE:** Julius Boros doffs his cap after winning the 1963 U.S. Open at The Country Club. **BELOW:** Cover of the program for the 1952 U.S. Open at the Northwood Club in Dallas, where Boros was the victor.

OFFICIAL PROGRAM—50 CENTS

USGA
52nd
Open
Championship

NORTHWOOD CLUB
DALLAS, TEXAS
JUNE 12, 13, 14

A robust natural golfer reared in Galway, Christy O'Connor is one of the all-time great Irish golfers. Known affectionately as "Himself," his hale personality made him a great fan favorite. O'Connor turned professional in 1951, when he was twenty-six, and went on to win the Irish Professional Championship ten times. He never won the British Open but came close a number of times, finishing tied for second in 1965 at Royal Birkdale behind Peter Thomson and one shot out of the 1958 play-off at Royal Lytham won by Thomson over Dave Thomas. O'Connor represented Ireland in the World Cup fifteen times, teaming with Harry Bradshaw to win the title in 1958 at Mexico City. He played in ten consecutive Ryder Cup matches between 1955 and 1973, a record only surpassed by Nick Faldo. It included a 7 and 6 victory over Dow Finsterwald in the British and Irish team's upset victory at Lindrick in 1957. From 1951 to 1957, he was the professional at Bundoran Golf Club in Donegal, and then was the pro for many years at Royal Dublin. **OPPOSITE:** Christy O'Connor teeing off in 1971.

Peter Thomson won five British Open Championships and the national championships of ten countries altogether, but rarely played in the United States. He also teamed with Kel Nagle, winner of the centenary Open at St. Andrews in 1960, to take home the World (Canada) Cup for Australia in 1954 at Royal Montreal and in 1959 at Royal Melbourne. Thomson captained the international team in the Presidents Cup in 1996 and 2000 at Robert Trent Jones Golf Club, and the winning squad in 1998 at Royal Melbourne. A great proponent of links golf and an astute analyst of the game, Thomson is also an accomplished course designer and golf author. In 1970, he founded a golf course architecture firm with Michael Wolveridge, John Harris, and later Californian Ron Fream that focused on designing courses in the Pacific Rim. One of his most recent designs is the Moonah Links on the Mornington Peninsula, the home course of the Australian Golf Union. **OPPOSITE:** The Moonah Links Open Course, designed by the firm of Thomson, Wolveridge & Perret, thirteenth hole.

Peter Allis was a leading English international player over a long and distinguished career before becoming the voice of golf on the BBC and a regular commentator on American telecasts of the British Open. Allis came from a strong golfing pedigree, his father, Percy, having a been a well-known professional and winner of five German Opens while serving as pro at Berlin's Wannsee Club. Allis is one of the rare breed of English golfing renaissance men who have combined successful playing careers with literary talents and work in course design. After having turned pro at the tender age of fifteen in 1946, his victories in Europe included the 1958 Spanish, Portuguese, and Italian Opens, which he won in successive weeks. He made eight appearances in the Ryder Cup between 1953 and 1969. His droll and urbane commentary has entertained television viewers for more than thirty years. Allis has also been a prolific author and has designed courses in Great Britain and Europe with Dave Thomas and Clive Clark, including The Belfry outside Birmingham. **OPPOSITE:** Peter Alliss at Wentworth for the 1953 Ryder Cup, the year he made his debut in the competition.

The Irish amateur Joe Carr, who played out of the nine-hole Sutton Golf Club, down the road from Portmarnock, where his father had been the club manager, was a member of a record eleven Walker Cup teams from 1947 to 1967. He was nonplaying captain in 1965 and playing captain in 1967. Despite his prowess in match play, Carr had a losing 5–14–1 record because he was invariably matched against the top U.S. players, including in 1961, when despite being moved down in the pairings, he ended up losing to Jack Nicklaus. In the 1990s, Carr consulted on the design of Old Head Golf Links, a thrilling course laid out on the headlands above the Atlantic at Kinsale in County Cork. Carr's son Roddy played in the 1971 Walker Cup Match only four years after his father's final appearance, winning 3½ out of 4 points in the Great Britain and Ireland team's victory over the Americans at St. Andrews. Roddy Carr owns and runs the Barbados Golf Club, a fine public course located in the island's Christ Church Parish, with fairways lined with casuarinas and an old bearded fig tree guarding the fifteenth green. **OPPOSITE:** Old Head Golf Club in Kinsale, Ireland, from the air. **BELOW:** Left to right, Joe Carr, Doug Sanders, and Roberto De Vicenzo in 1965.

THE SIXTIES AND THE ERA OF BIG THREE GOLF

193 | ARNIE USHERS IN A NEW ERA

Arnold Palmer's importance in the history of golf is hard to overstate, for more than any other person he was responsible for popularizing the game and giving it mass appeal as a televised sport at the dawn of the 1960s. Palmer attracted loyal legions of fans, known as "Arnie's Army," with his swashbuckling style of play, personal magnetism, and appealing, awshucks manner. Brought up in Latrobe, Pennsylvania, where his father, Deacon, was the golf pro and course superintendent, Palmer played college golf at Wake Forest and then went into the Coast Guard. He won the 1954 U.S. Amateur and then turned pro, but was a relatively late bloomer. He won his first Masters in 1958, the beginning of a barrage of seven majors between then and 1964—four Masters, the 1960 U.S. Open, and back-to-back British Opens in 1961 and 1962. In 1973, he won the Bob Hope Desert Classic for the last of his sixty-one PGA Tour victories, but he continued to give it his all on the course—with his unmistakable rip-it-and-recoil swing and with his popularity undiminished—for close to another three decades. **OPPOSITE:** Arnold Palmer during the 1966 U.S. Open at San Francisco's Olympic Club, which he let slip away to Billy Casper. **BELOW:** As an amateur, c.1953.

Gary Player seemingly willed himself to be one of the greatest golfers ever to play the game, winning nine majors in three different decades, which puts him fourth all-time. He was born in Johannesburg, South Africa, and learned the game at the Virginia Park course. His father was a gold mine captain; his mother died when he was only eight. He worked for the Johannesburg pro Jock Verwey, whose daughter Vivienne would become his wife, and in 1953, at age eighteen, he turned pro. Player, the ultimate globetrotting golfer, logged millions of miles in the air as he traveled the world in search of golfing glory. His first win outside South Africa came in 1955, at the Egyptian Match Play Championship held at the Gezira Sporting Club, which is located near the center of Cairo on an island in the Nile. In 1958, he finished second to Tommy Bolt in the U.S. Open. The next year he won his first major, the British Open at Muirfield, despite taking a double bogey that reduced him to tears on the final hole. Two years later, he won his first green jacket by a shot over Arnold Palmer and Charlie Coe, and the following year he won the PGA at Aronomink. Player won each of the four modern majors, a distinction that he shares with Gene Sarazen, Ben Hogan, Jack Nicklaus, and Tiger Woods.

OPPOSITE: Gary Player at the 1968 Masters. **BELOW:** Playing in the Daks Tournament at Wentworth, outside London, in 1956.

Jack Nicklaus, the greatest golfer of them all—at least during the century that preceded the arrival of Tiger Woods—was born in Columbus, Ohio, in 1940, where his great-grandfather had founded the Nicklaus Boiler Works. When he was ten, he started playing at Scioto Country Club, where his father, Charlie, a successful pharmacist who owned four drugstores, was a member. A fine all-around athlete who starred in high school basketball, young Jack broke 70 for the first time by age thirteen. His teacher, the club pro Jack Grout, had been an assistant to Henry Picard early in his career. By his late teens, Nicklaus emerged as the most outstanding amateur golfer since Bobby Jones. He attended Ohio State, where he met his wife, Barbara, and won the NCAA individual championship in 1961 and the U.S. Amateur in 1959 and 1961.

Nicklaus, like Vardon and Jones before him and Woods afterward, changed the fundamental conception of how golf could be played, lifting the game to a higher level. He attacked the ball with brutal force, hitting it unprecedented distances but also displaying nerves of steel over short putts. His record of eighteen major professional victories is monumental, with Woods, the next closest, having thirteen to date. The arc of Nicklaus's career is also defined by his mythic encounters with heroic rivals, from Arnold Palmer and Gary Player to Lee Trevino, Johnny Miller, and Tom Watson—all of whom rank high in the pantheon of the game. **OPPOSITE:** Jack Nicklaus lashing his drive at the 1973 U.S. Open at Oakmont. **BELOW:** At the World Series of Golf in 1962.

The year 1960 defined Arnold Palmer's career, with victories in the Masters and the U.S. Open that are indelibly etched in the game's lore. In 1958, Palmer had won the Masters in controversial fashion when he invoked the imbedded ball rule on the par-3 twelfth, playing a second ball to make a par after taking a five with his first. In 1960, he won the Masters with a closing birdie-birdie salvo. In the U.S. Open at Denver's Cherry Hills, he entered the final round trailing Mike Souchak by seven strokes. Palmer confided to sportswriters Bob Drum and Dan Jenkins during the lunch break between rounds that he thought he could shoot a 65, which might just be good enough to win. He famously proceeded to drive the green of the opening par-4 for a two-putt

birdie, then birdied the next three holes to shoot 30 on the front nine, and finished with a winning 65. Jack Nicklaus, then a twenty-year-old amateur, finished second, while Ben Hogan saw his final run at the U.S. Open fade away when he found the water on the seventeenth green. **OPPOSITE:** Arnold Palmer consulting with Bobby Jones (in dark glasses) and Clifford Roberts about the imbedded ball rule while Ken Venturi looks on at the 1958 Masters. Palmer played a second ball on the twelfth hole, and went on to defeat Venturi. **BELOW:** Arnie tosses his hat skyward on the final hole after charging to victory in the 1960 U.S. Open at Cherry Hills.

Golf in the 1960s was dominated by the "Big Three" of Arnold Palmer, Jack Nicklaus, and Gary Player, with the rivalry between Nicklaus and Palmer defining much of the decade. When Nicklaus arrived on the scene as a stocky young amateur in the 1960 U.S. Open, and for a few years thereafter, he was perceived as an upstart seeking to usurp Palmer's crown. After finishing second to Palmer in the 1960 Open, Nicklaus turned the tables in 1962, winning in an eighteen-hole play-off at Oakmont that was to signal his emergence as the game's supreme player. In 1966, Palmer appeared to have the Open firmly in his grasp at Olympic, with a seven-stroke cushion with nine to play over Billy Casper, but squandered the lead and lost to Casper in a play-off. Palmer continued to win on Tour and to enjoy an immense popularity with golfing fans around the world that has never waned. Palmer also established a successful international design business and hosts the Arnold Palmer Invitational on the PGA Tour at the Bay Hill Club in Orlando, which he purchased in the late 1960s. **OPPOSITE:** The pairing of Arnold Palmer and Jack Nicklaus at the start of the second round of the 1962 U.S. Open at Oakmont, where Nicklaus defeated Palmer after an eighteen-hole play-off. **BELOW:** The Big Three at the inaugural World Series of Golf held at Akron's Firestone Country Club in 1962.

In an era of sixties superstars, Billy Casper made a fourth to the "Big Three" of Arnold Palmer, Jack Nicklaus, and Gary Player. The San Diego native turned pro in 1954 and collected a haul of fifty-one Tour victories over his career, with his twenty-seven wins between 1964 and 1970 surpassing all of the "Big Three." Casper won the first of his three majors in 1959, finishing one shot ahead of Bob Rosburg in the U.S. Open at Winged Foot. Seven years later, he won the Open again. Suffering from food allergies, he had by then slimmed down on an unusual high-protein diet consisting of bear, caribou, venison, hippo, elk, moose, and, in particular, buffalo meat. An underrated player nowadays, Casper logged victories all over the globe, winning the Trophée Lancôme, the Italian, Mexican, and Brazilian Opens; and the Havana Invitational. Later on in his career, he became good friends with and the personal instructor to King Hassan of Morocco, who built many fine courses in Morocco, including Royal Dar es Salam. **OPPOSITE:** Billy Casper holes a bunker shot in the second round en route to winning the 1966 U.S. Open at San Francisco's Olympic Club.

Ken Venturi grew up in San Francisco, where his father managed the Harding Park pro shop. He was sponsored on the pro Tour by Eddie Lowery, Francis Ouimet's little caddie at the 1913 U.S. Open, who grew up to be a successful car dealer in the Bay Area. One of the game's great ball strikers but a sometimes shaky putter, in 1956 Venturi came ever so close to becoming the only amateur ever to win the Masters when he held a four-stroke lead after three rounds, only to shoot an 80 in bad weather in the final round to lose to Jack Burke, Jr. Venturi appeared to have the tournament sewn up in 1960 when Arnold Palmer's birdie-birdie finish gave him a one-shot victory. Venturi's shining hour came in the 1964 U.S. Open at a stifling Congressional, the last year the tournament was played as thirty-six holes on the final day. Wan and exhausted, he played the final eighteen suffering from heat prostration, holding on for a four-stroke victory in one of the game's great acts of courage. Venturi is one of golf's most respected and well-liked figures as a result of his work as the lead analyst on CBS's golf broadcasts from the late 1960s until his retirement from the booth in 2002. **OPPOSITE:** Ken Venturi on the way to winning the 1964 U.S. Open at Congressional Country Club. **BELOW:** A dazed Venturi smiles after winning the 1964 U.S. Open.

Mary Kathryn "Mickey" Wright was by far the greatest woman golfer of her era, and is widely regarded by her contemporaries as the greatest woman golfer of all time. Her record in modern times is rivaled only by Annika Sörenstam. A native of Southern California, Wright attended Stanford before turning pro in 1957. She won eighty-two tournaments on the LPGA Tour (second only to Kathy Whitworth's eighty-eight) during a relatively short career, retiring from full-time play in 1969, at age thirty-four. During her peak years of 1958 to 1966, she won twelve majors, and added a thirteenth in 1973, downing a twenty-five-foot putt on the last hole of the Colgate Dinah Shore. Between 1961 and 1964, she topped the money list each year, racking up ten, ten, thirteen, and eleven wins respectively. During the same four-year span, she won seven majors. **OPPOSITE:** Mickey Wright (right) with Barbara Romack before their match in the final of the 1954 U.S. Women's Amateur, which Romack won at Pittsburgh's Allegheny Country Club. **BELOW:** Wright at the trophy presentation ceremony after winning the 1961 U.S. Women's Open at Baltusrol.

Mickey Wright was shy and introverted but had a tremendous drive to be the best at the game and worked obsessively to perfect her swing. She was a very big hitter, but even more impressive was her ability to shape towering long-iron shots, which she could draw and fade on command. Of the four major events during her career, Wright won the LPGA Championship three times, the U.S. Women's Open four times, the Titleholders Championship twice, and the Western Open three times. She won her first U.S. Open in 1958 and repeated the next year at Pittsburgh's Churchill Valley, captured her third Open crown in 1961 at Baltusrol, and then won in 1964 at San Diego Country Club in a play-off over Ruth Jessen. **OPPOSITE:** The cover of the program for the 1959 U.S. Women's Open at Churchill Valley Country Club, won by Mickey Wright (inset).

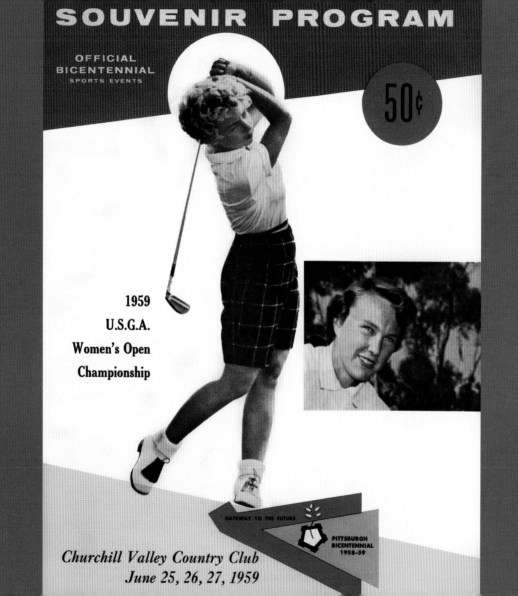

Arnold Palmer recognized the importance of the British Open in the canon of golf's major championships at a time when few American pros made the long overseas trip for what was a small purse. Palmer's appearances in the early 1960s restored the international luster that the tournament had held in the days of Hagen, Jones, and Sarazen. In his maiden appearance in 1960, Palmer finished one back of Australia's Kel Nagle in the centenary Open at St. Andrews. In 1961, he returned to win the Claret Jug at Birkdale, withstanding a great gale on the second day. After play was suspended for a day owing to flooded greens, he defeated Dai Rees by a stroke in the traditional thirty-six-hole final. The next year, he successfully defended his title at a dusty Troon, running away from the field to finish six ahead of Nagle, with Nicklaus, who had beaten him in the U.S. Open play-off that year at Oakmont, twenty-nine shots back. Palmer also won his third Masters in 1962, in a play-off over Gary Player and Dow Finsterwald. His final major win would come at Augusta in 1964, making him the first four-time Masters winner and giving him victories in seven of the twenty-five majors held from 1958 through the 1964 Masters. **OPPOSITE:** Arnold Palmer in 1970 at home in his workshop in Latrobe, Pennsylvania. **BELOW:** Teeing off at the 1962 World Series of Golf.

When his competitive playing career ended, Henry Cotton and his wife settled in Penina, near the fishing village of Portimão, on the Algarve Coast of southern Portugal. Cotton grew to love the Algarve and focused his energies on designing courses, establishing his own firm in the late 1950s, giving lessons, and writing about golf. Cotton was a driving force in bringing golf to the region, which is now one of the world's major golf destinations, with a diadem of outstanding courses—including San Lorenzo, Vilamoura Old, and Palmares—strung along the coast all the way to Sagres. While he designed several courses in England, his most cherished creation was the Penina Golf Club, the first of the Algarve's great courses. Completed in 1964, it was laid out in what had been rice paddies, with Cotton planting thousands of eucalyptus, cypress, orange, lemon, and loquat trees to absorb and drain the water from the course. Cotton continued to give lessons at Penina while living in the Penina Golf Hotel, with a donkey named Pacifico serving as his caddie. He died in 1987, just after having received a knighthood. He and his wife are buried in the churchyard of the small village of Mexilhoeira Grande, overlooking Penina. **OPPOSITE:** Penina Golf Club in Portugal's Algarve, designed by Henry Cotton, thirteenth hole. **BELOW:** Cotton (right) with his brother at a Boys' Golf Championship in 1921.

"Champagne" Tony Lema was one of golf's effervescent stars of the early 1960s, with a game that combined power and grace. Lema grew up in a working class neighborhood of San Francisco, becoming the assistant pro at San Francisco Golf Club before joining the Tour in 1958. He earned his nickname by buying bubbly for the members of the press after his victories and living large. He narrowly lost out to Jack Nicklaus in the 1963 Masters, his first appearance in the tournament, after Nicklaus holed a long putt on the final hole. His major win came in the 1964 Open Championship at St. Andrews, where he uncorked a five-stroke victory over Nicklaus. He had never played a links course before, but was guided around the nooks and crannies of the Old Course by legendary local caddie Tip Anderson. Lema and his wife died tragically young in a small plane crash in 1966. **OPPOSITE:** "Champagne" Tony Lema living up to his nickname in 1964. **BELOW:** Cradling the Claret Jug after his victory in the 1964 Open at St. Andrews.

Bob Charles once had the dual distinction of being New Zealand's greatest golfer and the best left-hander ever to play the game. Michael Campbell can challenge him for the first honor, while the success of Mike Weir's and Phil Mickelson's run of major victories have cost him his claim to the latter. Born in Carterton, on New Zealand's North Island, he won a stunning victory in the New Zealand Open in 1954 against a strong international field when he was an eighteen-year-old amateur. Despite his success, he continued to work as a bank teller for another six years before turning pro in 1960. Charles became a top-flight international player, winning all around the world; his biggest victory came in 1963, when he won the Claret Jug at Royal Lytham.

After finishing tied in regulation with American Phil Rodgers, Charles won the thirty-six-hole play-off—the last in the history of the Open—by eight strokes. In 1968, Charles tied for second in both the Open at Carnoustie and the PGA Championship at Pecan Valley in Texas; the following year, he was sole second in the Open behind Tony Jacklin. Charles also won the British Senior Open in 1989 and 1993. Throughout his career, he was known for his unflappable demeanor and superb putting stroke, which were the keys to his success. In 1999, he was knighted by Queen Elizabeth. **OPPOSITE:** Bob Charles in the 1980s. **BELOW:** Charles on his way to winning the British Open at Royal Lytham & St. Annes in 1963.

Gene Littler was an outstanding amateur in the golfing hotbed of San Diego, and seemed destined for greatness at an early age. He won the U.S. Amateur in 1953 and the San Diego Open while still an amateur. His rapturously rhythmic swing earned him the nickname "Gene the Machine." A quiet, unassuming man, he enjoyed a long and successful career on the PGA Tour, winning twenty-nine events but never achieving the commanding heights that were expected of him early in his career. His lone major came at the 1961 U.S. Open at Oakland Hills, when he held off Bob Goalby and Doug Sanders by one stroke. In 1970, he lost the Masters to Billy Casper in an eighteen-hole play-off. He was diagnosed with lymphatic cancer in 1972, but recovered and continued to win on Tour. In 1977, he was on the verge of winning the PGA at Pebble Beach but let a four-stroke lead slip away, and lost to Lanny Wadkins in a sudden-death play-off. **OPPOSITE:** Gene Littler playing the seventh hole at Pebble Beach during the 1977 PGA, which he lost to Lanny Wadkins. **BELOW:** Littler (right) and Billy Joe Patton at the 1955 Masters.

Jack Nicklaus debated remaining an amateur in the tradition of Bobby Jones, his role model, but turned pro in 1961 and joined the Tour in 1962. He had already challenged Arnold Palmer in the 1960 U.S. Open, finishing two shots back, and in 1962 he defeated Palmer in a play-off at Oakmont, making the U.S. Open his first professional victory—much to the chagrin of Arnie's Army, which had mobilized in full force on Palmer's home turf. The next year he won the first of his six Masters, by one over Tony Lema, and his first PGA at Dallas Athletic Club in stifling heat. In 1965, his superiority became manifest when he left the field in his wake, winning by nine strokes and manhandling Augusta National, prompting Bobby Jones's famous remark that Nicklaus "played a game I'm not even familiar with." In 1966, he became the first player to win consecutive Masters, prevailing in a play-off over Gay Brewer and Tommy Jacobs. That same year, he won the British Open at Muirfield, rarely using his driver on the narrow fairways, and relying instead on his stupendous long-iron game. Nicklaus, more than any other player before him, defined his career by focusing on the majors, an approach that Tiger Woods has emulated, sharing Nicklaus's historic perspective on the game. With his name on the Claret Jug at Muirfield, Nicklaus achieved the career Grand Slam at age twenty-eight.

OPPOSITE: Playing a practice round with Arnold Palmer before the 1965 British Open at Royal Birkdale, where Peter Thomson was the winner.

Gary Player, a small, wiry man at five foot seven inches and 150 pounds, lacked the brawn of his rivals but more than compensated with a relentless determination to succeed and supreme self-confidence. He devoted himself to physical fitness and followed a carefully regimented diet, long before that was the norm. He wore mostly black on the course, earning him the moniker "The Black Knight," because he believed that he would then absorb the strength of the sun. In 1965, he won the U.S. Open at Bellerive in St. Louis, giving him at that point one victory in each of the four majors. Player finished tied with Australia's Kel Nagle in regulation, winning the play-off the next day to make him the first overseas player to win the U.S. Open since England's Ted Ray in 1920. Player's second Claret Jug came at Carnoustie in 1968, when he finished two ahead of Jack Nicklaus in his prime. Player named his horse ranch in the Magoebaskloof Mountains, 250 miles from Johannesburg, Bellerive to commemorate his U.S. Open victory. **OPPOSITE:** Gary Player after holing the final putt to win the 1974 Masters. **BELOW:** Player with Arnold Palmer on his way to winning the 1965 U.S. Open at Bellerive, outside St. Louis.

Dave Marr grew up in Houston, the son of a golf pro and the cousin of Jack Burke, Jr. While he never lost his Texas roots, Marr worked as an assistant pro for the legendary instructor and 1948 Masters champion Claude Harmon at Winged Foot in Westchester County, near New York City, in the 1950s. Golf writer Dan Jenkins dubbed him "The Pro from 52nd Street," a reference to the nightclubs that lined the street. After going out on the PGA Tour in 1960, Marr's big win came in the 1965 PGA Championship at Laurel Valley in Ligonier, Pennsylvania, when he defeated the Goliaths Jack Nicklaus and Billy Casper by two shots. Marr went on to become a tremendously popular commentator for ABC TV, combining a folksy sense of humor with deep insight into the game, and also later became the American voice of the BBC golf telecasts. He died of stomach cancer in 1997, and his five children scattered his ashes around Royal Birkdale, where he played in the 1965 Ryder Cup match; Walton Heath, where he captained the 1981 Ryder Cup team; and the eighteenth hole at Laurel Valley. **OPPOSITE:** Dave Marr plays his bunker shot during the 1965 Ryder Cup at Royal Birkdale while teammate Arnold Palmer looks on.

The 1966 U.S. Open at San Francisco's Olympic Club, one of the most memorable, is recalled more for Arnold Palmer's last-round meltdown than Billy Casper's second Open crown. Palmer squandered a seven-shot lead with nine holes to play, while Casper kept holing putts to finish in a tie, and then beat Palmer 69–73 in the play-off. One of the game's all-time great putters, with a distinctive pigeon-toed stance, Casper needed only 117 putts over the ninety holes of the tournament. In his 1959 U.S. Open victory at Winged Foot, Casper one-putted thirty-one of the seventy-two holes, wielding a mallet-head putter that he had never used before. Casper capped off his career with a green jacket at the 1970 Masters, this time defeating Gene Littler in an eighteen-hole play-off after one-putting six of the first seven play-off holes. Casper also won the 1983 U.S. Senior Open and captained the winning 1979 U.S. Ryder Cup team at the Greenbrier. He continues to play at the San Diego Country Club, where he learned the game across the way from his boyhood home.

OPPOSITE: Billy Casper misses a putt to win the 1970 Masters on the eighteenth hole in regulation, but went on to defeat Gene Littler in the play-off.

Roberto De Vicenzo, the greatest of Argentine golfers, was born in 1923 in Buenos Aires, the son of a house painter. His mother died in childbirth when he was eight. The fifth of seven children, he started out in golf at the Migueletes Course across the street from his home, where he worked as a pond boy, retrieving balls. Soon thereafter, in 1931, he began to caddie. A powerful man with massive hands, De Vicenzo was a prodigious ball striker over a long career, who struggled with his putting. He made his debut on the world stage in the 1948 British Open at Muirfield, finishing third. Two years later, he was runner-up to Bobby Locke at Troon, and he finished second or third six times going into the 1967 Open at Hoylake. That was the year when he finally put his name on the Claret Jug. His third-round 67 gave him the lead over Jack Nicklaus and Gary Player, and a closing 70 left him two clear of Nicklaus, the defending champion. In 1953, he teamed with Antonio Cerda to lead Argentina to victory in the first ever Canada (World) Cup, played at Royal Montreal. **OPPOSITE:** Roberto De Vicenzo relaxes before playing the first round of the 1968 British Open at Carnoustie.

Catherine LaCoste stunned the golf world in 1967, at age twenty-two, when she became the first and only amateur to win the U.S. Women's Open, vaulting to a two-shot victory at the Cascades Course at the Homestead Resort in Hot Springs, Virginia. LaCoste is the daughter of René "the Crocodile" LaCoste, the great French tennis star of the 1920s and founder of the sportswear company that bears the famous crocodile logo. Her mother, competing as Simone Thion de la Chaume, was the leading French woman golfer of the 1920s and 1930s, in 1927 becoming the first French woman to win the British Ladies' Championship. An exceptionally long driver, renowned for her ability to hit a one-iron, Catherine learned the game at the pastoral woodland course of Chantaco, founded by her maternal grandfather, René Thion de la Chaume, in 1928 at St. Jean de Luz near the Basque Coast. In 1969, she won the British Ladies' Championship at Royal Portrush in Northern Ireland, up the coastline from Royal County Down, where her mother had won the same title. That same year, she won the U.S. Amateur Championship at Las Colinas Country Club in Texas. In 1974, she succeeded her mother as president of Golf de Chantaco. **OPPOSITE:** The Cascades Course, eleventh hole, at the Homestead Resort in Hot Springs, Virginia, site of Catherine LaCoste's 1967 U.S. Women's Open victory. **BELOW:** LaCoste with the championship trophy.

In the 1967 U.S. Open at Baltusrol, the battle lines were drawn between Jack Nicklaus and Arnold Palmer. By now they were entrenched rivals, with Nicklaus gradually overcoming the hostility he encountered early on as the challenger to Palmer's golfing sovereignty. Palmer came into the Open seeking to redeem himself from his bitter loss to Billy Casper the year before, and after three rounds, Nicklaus, Palmer, and Casper stood tied. In the final round, Nicklaus shot a 65 to finish four ahead of Palmer, giving him a four-round total of 275 that eclipsed Hogan's record low total at Riviera in 1948. When Nicklaus first came on the scene, he was a burly young man in bulky clothes with a blond crewcut. By the early 1970s he had transformed himself into "The Golden Bear," slimming down, growing his hair, and sprucing up his wardrobe. In 1970, he won the British Open at St. Andrews after Doug Sanders missed little more than a tap-in on the eighteenth hole to end up in a tie, with Nicklaus taking the play-off the next day and hurling his putter skyward at the end. In 1971, he completed his second career Grand Slam when he captured the PGA at Florida's PGA National. **OPPOSITE:** Arnold Palmer congratulates Jack Nicklaus after his victory in the 1967 U.S. Open at Baltusrol, where Nicklaus pulled away from Palmer in the final round. **BELOW:** The Golden Bear in 1970.

Carol Mann was one of the top players on the LPGA Tour during the 1960s and early 1970s, as well as a keen student of the golf swing and an independent spirit. In 1965, she won the U.S. Women's Open at Atlantic City Country Club. In 1968, she dominated the Tour, winning ten times and earning the Vare Trophy for lowest stroke average. She also served as the LPGA's president from 1973 to 1976. At six foot three inches, Mann was a commanding presence on the course, with a strong sense of style. She currently plays a leading role in organizing exhibits for the World Golf Hall of Fame in St. Augustine, Florida, into which she was inducted in 1977. **OPPOSITE:** Carol Mann in action in 1974.

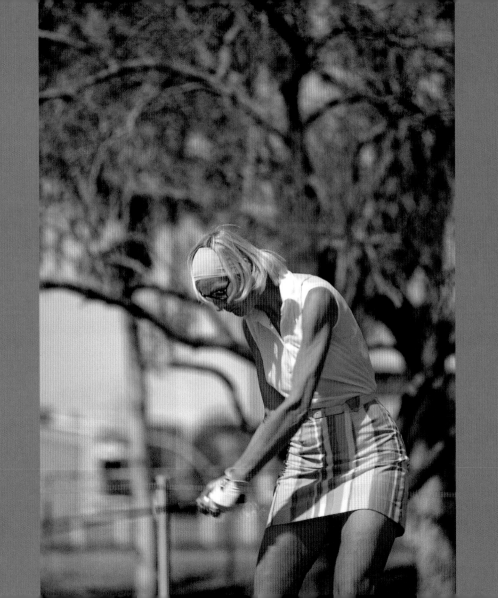

Argentina's Roberto De Vicenzo won 231 professional tournaments around the world, including nine victories in the Argentine Open, the last coming in 1985, when he was sixty-two. In the mid-1950s, he played the PGA Tour, basing himself in Mexico City to be closer to the United States, but for most of his career he competed mainly in South America. In 1968, nine months after his triumph in the 1967 British Open, De Vicenzo was the subject of the most infamous and painful incident in the history of the Masters. He fired a final-round 65 at Augusta, but his playing partner Tommy Aaron mistakenly marked him down for a 4 instead of a birdie 3 on the seventeenth hole. After De Vicenzo signed the incorrect scorecard, he was penalized one stroke, leaving him one behind the winner Bob Goalby and out of what would have been an eighteen-hole play-off. He famously remarked of his scorecard snafu: "What a stupid I am." Augusta National's chairman Clifford Roberts sent De Vicenzo a sterling silver cigarette box engraved with the signatures of the previous winners, the only time up to that point that the prize had been given to anyone other than the winner. A genial man, De Vicenzo continues to hold forth at Ranelagh Golf Club in Buenos Aires, his home course of many years.

OPPOSITE: A disconsolate Roberto De Vicenzo sits at right at the scorer's table after learning that he signed an incorrect scorecard at the 1968 Masters to cost him a tie for first. Winner Bob Goalby is seated at the scorer's table center left with Ray Floyd next to him, while Tommy Aaron, De Vicenzo's playing partner, speaks with an official on the upper left.

Pete Dye revolutionized golf course architecture, starting in the late 1960s, with a series of groundbreaking courses. Born in Urbana, Ohio, where his father was the postmaster and built the local course, Dye became a top amateur golfer in Indiana. His wife, Alice, who plays an important advisory role in his designs, was herself a multiple Indiana State Amateur champion. After giving up a successful career selling insurance to design courses in the Midwest, Dye traveled to Scotland in 1963 and toured the great courses, which profoundly influenced his approach. He realized that by using modern earth-moving equipment, he could replicate and enhance elements of classic links golf, and began creating a sort of nouvelle Scottish design. These features are displayed at Harbour Town on Hilton Head Island, one of Dye's seminal courses from the late 1960s, in which he created large waste areas, pot bunkers, and small greens. Its famous eighteenth hole runs along Calibogue Sound and toward the cherry-striped lighthouse. In particular, he incorporated railroad ties and wood planks, modeled after the "sleepers" at Prestwick, into his courses and they became his design trademark. Dye also experimented with different types of grasses and used indigenous elements in his designs. In the 1970s and 1980s, his courses became increasingly more sculpted, with very sharp lines, earning him the nickname "Marquis de Sod." This angular style is exemplified by the TPC at Sawgrass with its iconic island green, opened in 1980 as the first stadium course, and PGA West in Palm Springs. **OPPOSITE:** Harbour Town, seventeenth hole. **BELOW:** Pete Dye.

Lee Buck Trevino's is one of the greatest success stories in the history of the game. He rose from extreme poverty to become one of the game's most impressive and radiant stars, winning six majors and emerging as a rival of Jack Nicklaus in some of golf's most storied showdowns. Trevino was born in Dallas of Mexican descent, and was brought up by his mother and his grandfather, who was a gravedigger. He began helping out at a local driving range as a boy and received his first set of clubs from the owner, Hardy Greenwood. After enlisting in the Marines on his seventeenth birthday, he returned four years later to work as an assistant pro in El Paso, while hustling all comers, including playing a par-3 course with a Dr Pepper bottle. In 1967, he entered the U.S. Open at Baltusrol, finishing fourth, and started playing the Tour, becoming Rookie of the Year at age twenty-eight. The following year, he began his march to the forefront of the game in earnest, winning the U.S. Open at Oak Hill in Rochester by five over Jack Nicklaus and becoming the first man ever to break 70 in all four rounds of the Open. **OPPOSITE:** Lee Trevino doffs his cap on the way to winning the 1968 U.S. Open at Oak Hill in Rochester, New York. **BELOW:** The Merry Mex in 1978.

Tony Jacklin restored the luster of British golf after many lean years, scaling the heights of the game between 1969 and 1972. Born in Scunthorpe in 1944, the son of a truck driver, Jacklin turned pro when he was seventeen. In 1968, he became the first British player to win on the PGA Tour when he claimed the Greater Jacksonville Open. Then, in 1969, in a momentous triumph at Royal Lytham, he became the first Englishman to win the Open since Max Faulkner in 1951. The following year, he played inspired golf at the U.S. Open at Hazeltine. He led from wire to wire and was the only player to break par, with his seven-stroke victory the largest winning margin in forty-nine years. Jacklin's victory in the U.S. Open was the first by a British player since Ted Ray's in 1920, and he became the first man since Ben Hogan to hold both the British and U.S. open titles at the same time. In 1972, Jacklin was on the verge of winning his second Open, this time at Muirfield, when he and Lee Trevino reached the par-5 seventeenth hole tied for the lead. Trevino, off the back of the green in three, proceeded to chip in for an improbable birdie, while Jacklin, comfortably on the green in three, three-putted from short range for a bogey. Trevino went on to par the final hole for victory, and a devastated Jacklin was never to contend again in a major.

OPPOSITE: Tony Jacklin in action on his way to winning the 1970 U.S. Open at Hazeltine, outside Minneapolis.

Juan "Chi Chi" Rodriguez has played the game with his own inimitable flair, working his way up from his caddie days in his native Puerto Rico to become a star and showman on the PGA Tour. Born in Rio Piedras in 1935, he started out as a seven-year-old using a guava tree branch as a makeshift club and a metal can for a ball. By the time he was twelve, he shot a round of 67. He made up for his slight stature with remarkable dexterity, able to maneuver the ball at will—and he could drive more than two hundred yards with a putter. He won eight times on Tour from 1963 through 1979, including the 1964 Western Open and the 1972 Byron Nelson Classic. He was even more successful on the Senior Tour, racking up twenty-two victories, including two majors. Rodriguez was known for his "sword" dance after making a birdie, waving his putter toreador style to slay the bull. A philosophical and good-humored man with a deep appreciation for how golf enabled him to succeed from humble origins, he established the Chi Chi Rodriguez Youth Foundation to help young people who have suffered hardships.

OPPOSITE: Chi Chi Rodriguez playing in the Tradition on the Champions Tour in 1997 at the Desert Mountain Resort's Cochise Course in Arizona. **BELOW:** With Lee Trevino (center) in the 1960s.

Doug Sanders, born in 1933, grew up in a poor family in Cedartown, Georgia, where he caddied at the nine-hole golf course. On the PGA Tour, he won twenty tournaments but was better known for his well-deserved reputation as a playboy, partygoer, and fashion plate, whose social circle included Frank Sinatra and Evel Knievel. Sanders blended the colors of his golfing clothes, in shades of chartreuse and mauve, by matching them to medicine capsules, and dyed his underwear and socks to match. He had a famously flat, short swing, of the kind, as they say, that you can fit in a telephone booth. Sanders finished second in four majors—the 1957 PGA, the 1961 U.S. Open, and the 1966 and 1970 British Opens. He will forever be remembered for the one that got away from him at St. Andrews in 1970, when his two-and-a-half-foot putt to win on the final hole drifted off to the right and he lost in a play-off the next day to Jack Nicklaus. **OPPOSITE:** Doug Sanders (right) walking with Jack Nicklaus at the 1970 British Open at St. Andrews, where Sanders missed the short putt on the seventy-second hole that would have given him victory. **BELOW:** Sanders with Gene Sarazen in 1987.

Michael Bonallack is best known to golfers around the world for his role as the secretary of the Royal and Ancient Golf Club of St. Andrews from 1983 to 1999, golf's official rule-making body outside the United States, but he is also hands-down the finest amateur golfer produced by England in the modern era. Relying on an uncanny short game and a knack for holing key putts, he won the British Amateur five times, starting in 1961 at Turnberry. Three of his victories came in succession, when he defeated Ireland's Joe Carr in the final at Troon in 1968 and then won back-to-back over American Bill Hyndman in 1969 and 1970. Bonallack played in every Walker Cup from 1957 through 1973, including captaining the victorious British and Irish team in 1971 at St. Andrews, which took back the Cup by a margin of 13–11 after having last prevailed in 1938, when the match was also played at the Old Course. He was knighted in 1998. The Sir Michael Bonallack Trophy is an event held every two years between teams of twelve amateurs from Europe and the Pacific Rim.

OPPOSITE: Michael Bonallack in 1971, the year he captained the British and Irish squad to victory in the Walker Cup at St. Andrews.

Robert Trent Jones designed hundreds of courses in the United States and all around the world over a long career, assisted by his sons Robert Trent Jones, Jr., and Rees Jones, both of whom have flourished as course architects in their own right. In the United States some of his better-known layouts include Peachtree Golf Club outside Atlanta, which he worked on with Bobby Jones; Spyglass Hill on the Monterey Peninsula; Mauna Kea, built over the lava fields of Hawaii; Hazeltine outside Minneapolis; and Firestone's South Course. Jones was also brought in to toughen up and revamp a number of U.S. Open courses, including Oakland Hills before Ben Hogan's victory in 1951, at which he tamed the "Monster," and Baltusrol in advance of the 1954 Open. It was Jones who turned the creek into the large pond that now defines the sixteenth hole at Augusta National, and who created the putting green at the White House for President Eisenhower, an avid golfer and Augusta National member. A consummate marketer who designed on a bold scale, Jones was also much in demand abroad, where his notable designs included Ballybunion's Cashen Course, Valderrama and Sotogrande on Spain's Costa del Sol, Troia in Portugal, Pevero on Sardinia's Costa Smeralda, and El Rincón outside Bogotá, Colombia. In the late 1980s, working with his right-hand man, Roger Rulewich, he was lured out of semiretirement to design the eight courses, now expanded to ten, that comprise Alabama's Robert Trent Jones Golf Trail, a massive public golf project funded by the Retirement Systems of Alabama.

OPPOSITE: Oxmoor Valley Golf Course in Birmingham, Alabama, one of the courses on the Robert Trent Jones Golf Trail.

Kathy Whitworth, a lanky and low-key Texan, achieved a record of success on the LPGA Tour that has never been equaled, winning eighty-eight tournaments—the most victories by a professional golfer, man or woman. Her long career spanned the heydays of Mickey Wright and Nancy Lopez. Whitworth turned pro in 1959 and notched her first win in 1962 at the Kelly Girl Open; her last victory came in 1985. She won six majors during her career and was LPGA Player of the Year seven times between 1966 and 1973, but, like Lopez, she never won the U.S. Women's Open. **OPPOSITE:** Kathy Whitworth playing in the 1969 U.S. Women's Open at Scenic Hills Country Club in Pensacola, Florida. **BELOW:** Whitworth in 1974.

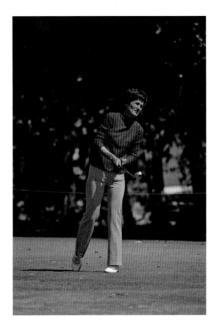

Deane Beman is best known as the innovative and ambitious Commissioner of the PGA Tour, succeeding Joe Dey in 1974. During his twenty-year tenure, he presided over a period of phenomenal Tour growth, with increased television coverage resulting in skyrocketing purses and unprecedented popularity for the game. As Commissioner, Beman launched both the highly successful Senior Tour, now known as the Champions Tour, and a junior circuit, initially known as the Ben Hogan Tour and now the Nationwide Tour. He also pioneered the concept of stadium golf, building Tournament Players Clubs designed with grass amphitheaters and spectator mounds. Beman hired Pete Dye to design the first TPC Stadium Course at Sawgrass, built on an inhospitable swamp in Ponte Vedra Beach, Florida, near the Tour's headquarters, which became the site of the annual Players Championship. A contemporary of Jack Nicklaus, Beman had been a leading amateur golfer early in his career, winning the 1959 British Amateur at Royal St. George's in an all-American final over Bill Hyndman, and both the 1960 and 1963 U.S. Amateurs. A short-hitting but scrappy competitor, he won four times on the PGA Tour after turning pro, finishing one shot behind Orville Moody in the 1969 U.S. Open. **OPPOSITE:** A welcoming party for Deane Beman at the airport after his victory in the 1959 British Amateur.

Lee Trevino, who won twenty-nine PGA Tour events, was entirely self-taught, using an open stance and flat swing to produce a low, boring fade that made him one of the most accurate drivers in the history of the game. In the summer of 1971, "The Merry Mex" produced one of golf's epic seasons, winning the U.S., Canadian, and British Opens in the span of a month. At the U.S. Open at Merion, he finished tied with Jack Nicklaus and then won the eighteen-hole play-off by three shots, after taking a rubber snake from his golf bag and tossing it at a startled Nicklaus on the first tee. His victory in the Open Championship came at Royal Birkdale, when he was coasting home with a four-stroke lead over his playing partner, Taiwan's Lu Liang Huan, known as "Mr. Lu," and made it interesting by taking a 7 on the seventeenth hole, parring the final hole to win by one. The following year, he won the Claret Jug at Muirfield in one of the championship's most startling finishes. Trevino began the final round one shot ahead of his playing partner, Tony Jacklin, England's golfing hero. Trevino was still clinging to a one-shot lead coming to the par-5 seventeenth hole, when he seemingly frittered away his chance for victory, lying four off the back of the green while Jacklin had a fifteen-foot birdie putt. Trevino then chipped in for par, while a dispirited Jacklin three-putted for bogey, and Trevino parred the last hole to finish one shot ahead of Nicklaus, who had charged in with a closing 66. **OPPOSITE:** Lee Trevino flings his hat after winning the 1971 British Open at Royal Birkdale.

JACK NICKLAUS AND HIS RIVALS IN THE SEVENTIES

226 | THE GOLDEN BEAR IN THE HUNT

In 1972, Jack Nicklaus mounted a furious charge at winning all four majors in a quest to claim the grail of the single-season Grand Slam. He started out by winning the Masters by three shots. Next came the U.S. Open at Pebble Beach, when he struck what is the most famous single shot of his career, a titanic one-iron into a stiff breeze that clattered off the flagstick on the par-3 seventeenth that runs out to the Pacific, setting up the birdie putt that secured victory. At the British Open at Muirfield, Nicklaus entered the final round trailing Lee Trevino by six, but came barreling back with a 32 on the front nine to close with a 66. It left him just one stroke shy of Trevino, and the dream was dashed. The Golden Bear continued his majestic play in the mid-1970s, winning the PGA at Canterbury in 1973 to break Bobby Jones's record of thirteen major victories. In 1975, he won a rip-roaring Masters, edging Tom Weiskopf and Johnny Miller by a stroke after holing a forty-five-foot crescent moon of a putt on the par-3 sixteenth. That same year he won the PGA at Firestone Country Club's South Course in Akron, Ohio. **OPPOSITE:** Jack Nicklaus driving during the 1978 British Open at St. Andrews, where he earned his third Open championship.

Raymond Floyd was one of the premier players of the modern era, winning major championships in three different decades. Floyd grew up in Fort Bragg, North Carolina, where his father was stationed in the army and also served as the base's golf pro. As a competitor, Floyd was known for his baleful stare and deadeye short game. After joining the Tour in 1963, he won the first of his four majors in 1969, nipping Gary Player by one in the PGA Championship at Dayton's National Cash Register Course. Floyd came into his own after he tied the knot in 1974 and left behind his playboy lifestyle, earning seventeen of his twenty-two Tour titles between 1975 and 1992. In 1976, he won the Masters in convincing fashion by eight strokes. He came within a whisker of winning at Augusta again in 1990, when he finished tied with Nick Faldo in regulation but lost on the second hole of sudden death when he pulled his second shot into the pond guarding the eleventh green. His first major win in the 1980s came at the 1982 PGA at Southern Hills, when he opened with a 63 and never looked back, finishing three clear of Lanny Wadkins. Floyd saved the best for last, taking center stage at the 1986 U.S. Open at Shinnecock.

OPPOSITE: Raymond Floyd holds the trophy after winning the 1986 U.S. Open at Shinnecock. **BELOW:** Floyd being interviewed by Jim McKay after winning the 1969 PGA while runner-up Gary Player looks on.

Tom Weiskopf, who grew up in Massillon, Ohio, had the difficult burden early in his career of being compared to his contemporary Jack Nicklaus, whom he followed by two years at Ohio State. At six foot three inches, Weiskopf had a regal, upright swing that was beautiful to behold, and he carried high expectations with him when he turned pro in 1964. He had a successful career, winning sixteen times on Tour starting in 1968, but he only won one major, and, by his own account, he should have won more. His banner season came in 1973, when his game peaked and he won seven events worldwide. That year saw his greatest triumph when he took the British Open at Royal Troon by three strokes over Johnny Miller and Neil Coles, with the outcome never in doubt. Weiskopf finished second in the Masters four times, including a particularly demoralizing loss to Nicklaus in 1975. In one of the greatest battles in Augusta history, Weiskopf, Miller, and Nicklaus stood tied when Nicklaus, playing one group ahead of Weiskopf and Miller, holed a long birdie putt on the sixteenth to carry him to victory. **OPPOSITE:** Tom Weiskopf with Jack Nicklaus at the 1972 Masters won by Nicklaus. **BELOW:** Thumbs up at the 1973 British Open at Royal Troon.

Isabella "Belle" McCorkindale Robertson, born in Campbeltown in 1936, where her father was a farmer, has the finest amateur record of any Scottish woman golfer. She won seven Scottish Ladies Close Amateur Championships during her career. After many near misses, including losing in the final in 1959, she won the British Ladies' Amateur title in 1981 at Conwy Golf Club in Wales. She was a mainstay of the British Curtis Cup team, competing in her seventh and final match in 1986, after having captained the team in 1974 and 1976. Robertson learned the game at Machrihanish, the remote championship links that saunters through the dunes on the Mull of Kintyre, with picturesque views across the sea to Gigha ("God's Island") and Islay and Jura in the faraway Hebrides. **OPPOSITE:** Machrihanish Golf Club on the Mull of Kintyre, third hole.

Johnny Miller, with his blond California good looks, wide belts, and rainbow-colored trousers, epitomized golf in the 1970s. His blazingly accurate iron game ignited one of the most glorious and glorified rounds in history when he fired a final-round 63 at Oakmont, a course synonymous with severity, to win the 1973 U.S. Open. Miller's 63 remains tied for the lowest round ever recorded in the U.S. Open, enabling him to leapfrog over a dozen players for a one-stroke edge over John Schlee. For the next couple of years, Miller continued to set a torrid pace, with his second and final major coming in the 1976 British Open at Royal Birkdale. His final-round 66 easily outdistanced Jack Nicklaus and a teenage Seve Ballesteros, who finished tied for second, seven shots back. Just as Miller seemed poised to assume the mantle of the next Nicklaus, his game slipped and he was never again the dominant force he had been in the mid-1970s. Theories abounded as to Miller's loss of peak form, ranging from minor injuries to having become too muscular from doing heavy yardwork. **OPPOSITE:** Johnny Miller on his way to winning the 1973 U.S. Open at Oakmont. **BELOW:** Miller's scorecard from the 1973 U.S. Open.

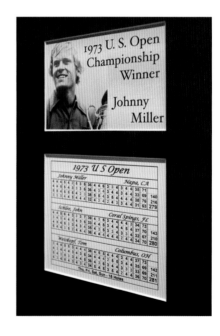

Golf flourished in Morocco under the royal patronage of the late King Hassan II, an ardent golfer. There were already well-established eighteen-hole courses at Tangier, Marrakesh, and Mohammedia, as well as nine-hole courses at Meknes, set in the walled garden of the Royal Palace with its stone ramparts; Anfa, surrounded by a racetrack in Casablanca; Royal Agadir; and Ben Slimane, between Rabat and Casablanca. The king commissioned Robert Trent Jones, the monarch of American golf course architects, to design Royal Dar es Salam, also known as Royal Rabat, in a cork oak forest, with the championship Red Course completed in 1971. That same year, the course hosted the inaugural tournament for the Hassan II Trophy, a jewel-encrusted dagger made of gold. The first winner was 1969 U.S. Open champ Orville Moody, and over the years the tournament has attracted top players from around the world, with the roster of winners including Billy Casper, Lee Trevino, Payne Stewart, Vijay Singh, and Nick Price. King Hassan enlisted Cabell Robinson, a protégé of Jones who had attended Yale with Jones's son Rees, to design the Royal Links at Agadir. Robinson's work in Morocco also includes the Dunes Course at Agadir; El Jadida, an hour south of Casablanca; and Amelkis, near Marrakesh, while Houston-based Robert von Hagge created a new eighteen-hole course at Ben Slimane. **OPPOSITE:** Royal Mohammedia Golf Club, near Casablanca.

JoAnne Gunderson Carner was one of the most colorful and dynamic personalities on the LPGA Tour during a long and superlative career. As "The Great Gundy," she was the outstanding amateur of her era, a big hitter who won the U.S. Women's Amateur five times between 1957 and 1968, a record surpassed only by Glenna Collett Vare's six championships. She is the only woman to have won the USGA Girls' Junior, U.S. Women's Amateur, and U.S. Women's Open titles. Carner turned pro in 1970, when she was already thirty, morphing into "Big Mama," and won a total of forty-three LPGA events. She won the U.S. Women's Open in 1971 at the Kahkwa Club in Erie, Pennsylvania, a vintage Donald Ross layout, and again in 1976, this time at Rolling Green Golf Club outside Philadelphia. After finishing second to Sandra Palmer in the 1975 U.S. Open, Carner turned the tables, defeating Palmer in an eighteen-hole play-off by two shots. In 1987, she lost the championship in a play-off to England's Laura Davies. Carner was Player of the Year in 1974, 1975, 1981, 1982, and 1983, winning the Vare Trophy for lowest scoring average each of those years. **OPPOSITE:** JoAnne Gunderson Carner on the way to victory at the U.S. Women's Open in 1971 at the Kahkwa Club. **BELOW:** The Great Gundy in 1963.

Donna Caponi was one of the top players on the LPGA Tour during the 1970s, winning twenty-four tournaments, including four majors, between 1969 and 1981. Caponi became the first woman since the incomparable Mickey Wright to win consecutive U.S. Women's Opens. In 1969, she birdied the final hole to win the Open by a stroke at Scenic Hills in Pensacola, the only time a U.S. Open has been held in Florida. The following year she was the victor at Muskogee Country Club in Oklahoma, designed in 1924 by the legendary architect Perry Maxwell. Caponi has made a second career as a popular on-course announcer for the Golf Channel. **OPPOSITE:** Donna Caponi in full swing in 1974.

The Kraft Nabisco Championship, the first of the four majors on the LPGA schedule, started out in 1971 as the Colgate Dinah Shore Tournament and is still popularly known as the Dinah Shore or "The Dinah." Shore, who achieved fame as a songstress in the 1940s, was better known by the 1970s as a television talk show host. She became hooked on golf through her association with the tournament and was a very active participant in the event until her death in 1994. The tournament is held each year at the Mission Hills Country Club in the Coachella Valley in Palm Springs, at the course named after Shore, with the winner traditionally taking a victory dunk in the lake that guards the eighteenth green. The event became recognized as a major in 1983.

OPPOSITE: Mission Hills Country Club, Dinah Shore Course, eighteenth hole.

A no-nonsense player with a reservoir of resolve, Hale Irwin was one of the top players on Tour throughout the 1970s and 1980s. Born in Joplin, Missouri, Irwin was actually better known for his feats on the gridiron than on the golf course at the University of Colorado. He was a two-time All–Big Eight defensive back, while also winning the NCAA golf championship in 1967. On the way to posting twenty victories on the PGA Tour, his defining achievements were winning the U.S. Open in 1974, 1979, and 1990. The 1974 Open will always be remembered as "The Massacre at Winged Foot," when the pros were humbled and humiliated by the fiendish course setup. In the midst of the carnage all around him, Irwin hung on to win with a score of seven over par. In 1979, he won by two over Gary Player and Jerry Pate at Inverness in Toledo, Ohio. Irwin also enjoyed considerable success on the international stage, winning the Picadilly World Match Play event back-to-back in 1974 and 1975, and teaming with John Mahaffey to win the World Cup in 1979 at Glyfada in Athens, with Irwin taking the individual honors. **OPPOSITE:** Hale Irwin and his caddie after winning the 1979 U.S. Open at Inverness.

Graham Marsh, who was born in Kalgoorlie, Australia, in 1944, was a truly international star, winning events on five continents. After turning pro in 1969 on the advice of Peter Thomson, he racked up more than sixty wins around the globe, including the 1971 and 1973 Indian Opens, the 1973 Thailand Open, the Scottish Open at St. Andrews in 1973, the 1977 Trophée Lancôme in France, the 1977 Picadilly World Match Play Championship at Wentworth, where he defeated Ray Floyd in the final, and the 1977 Heritage Classic at Harbour Town on Hilton Head Island. In Japan, he won three Suntory Opens and two Chunichi Crowns. More recently, he enjoyed great success on the U.S. Champions Tour, winning the 1997 U.S. Senior Open. During the past few years, Marsh has turned his energies to golf course design, focusing on Australasia, where he has designed several courses. In the United States, he has drawn rave reviews for his work at Sutton Bay Golf Club in South Dakota, a rugged links laid out on the Sutton Ranch overlooking Lake Oahe, forty-five miles north of Pierre. **OPPOSITE:** Graham Marsh eyes a shot in 1977.

One of the pioneering black golfers on the PGA Tour along with Charlie Sifford and Pete Brown, Lee Elder made history when he became the first African-American to play in the Masters in 1975. Born in Dallas in 1934, Elder grew up in poverty and under difficult circumstances, losing both his parents when he was young. He began caddying at Dallas's Tennison Park Golf Club when he was nine, and teamed up in the early 1960s with the legendary hustler Titanic Thompson in high-stakes matches. In 1961, he joined the all-black United Golf Association Tour, winning five UGA national championships, and then became one of the first black golfers on the PGA Tour in 1967.

Elder earned his invitation to the Masters by winning the 1974 Monsanto Open at Pensacola Country Club in a sudden-death play-off, six years after he and his fellow African-American tour members had been refused entrance to the clubhouse. He returned to Augusta in 1977 by virtue of winning the 1976 Houston Open and played in six Masters during his career. Elder was invited by Gary Player to play in the 1971 South African PGA Tournament, the first desegregated tournament in that country's history. In 1979, he also became the first black golfer to play in a Ryder Cup Match. **OPPOSITE:** Lee Elder hits his tee shot on the first hole at the 1975 Masters.

The affable Al Geiberger will forever be known as "Mr. 59," having blazed to the first sub-60 round in the history of the PGA Tour in the second round of the 1977 Danny Thomas Memphis Classic at the Colonial Country Club, going on to win the tournament. Geiberger's competitive first has subsequently been equaled by Chip Beck, David Duval, and Annika Sörenstam. After graduating from USC in 1959, Geiberger had a long and successful career on the Tour, winning eleven tournaments, including the 1966 PGA Championship at Firestone Country Club. Geiberger's son Brent is a two-time winner on the PGA Tour, while his son John coaches the Pepperdine University Waves golf team. Geiberger, who is now the pro emeritus at Stone Eagle Golf Club in Palm Springs, had a penchant for munching peanut butter sandwiches during rounds, earning him a longtime endorsement from Skippy. **OPPOSITE:** Stone Eagle Golf Club in Southern California, the golfing home of Al Geiberger. **BELOW:** Geiberger being interviewed after winning the 1966 PGA at Firestone.

Hubert Green, a native of Birmingham, Alabama, was a top-flight pro during the 1970s despite a twitchy, hunched-over swing and a knock-kneed style of putting. Green won nineteen tournaments between 1971 and 1985, with the exclamation point of his career coming in 1977, when he won the U.S. Open at Southern Hills in Tulsa. Green will always be remembered for ignoring a death threat that was phoned to the course during his final round, continuing to play steady golf down the stretch to hold on to a one-stroke victory over Lou Graham. He also won the 1985 PGA Championship at Cherry Hills over Lee Trevino. Green enjoyed success on the Champions Tour before being diagnosed with throat cancer in 2003, which he has fought courageously.

OPPOSITE: Hubert Green with Jack Nicklaus at the 1974 British Open at Royal Lytham & St. Annes.

After attending the University of Alabama and winning the 1974 U.S. Amateur, Jerry Pate joined the PGA Tour in 1975 as a cocky and copiously talented young player. He quickly made good on his great promise, winning the 1976 U.S. Open at Atlanta Athletic Club when he was only twenty-two with one of the most memorable shots in the history of the tournament. Standing in the right rough on the eighteenth hole with a dangerous 194-yard shot to a green fronted by a pond, and clinging to a one-shot lead over John Mahaffey, Pate rocketed a five-iron that touched down two feet from the pin to ensure victory. Pate won seven more times on Tour, crowned by his 1982 victory in the first Players Championship, held at the TPC at Sawgrass, when he famously tossed PGA Commissioner Deane Beman and course architect Pete Dye into the lake beside the eighteenth green and then dove in after them. Pate's career was cut short by a series of shoulder injuries, after which he developed a homespun image as a television announcer. He has been active in course design, working with Tom Fazio and Bob Cupp, and designed The Preserve in Vancleave, Mississippi, adjoining a nature preserve of cypress swamps and pitcher plant bogs. **OPPOSITE:** Jerry Pate dives in after throwing PGA Commissioner Deane Beman and course architect Pete Dye in the water after winning the 1982 Players Championship at the newly minted TPC at Sawgrass. **BELOW:** On the way to winning the 1976 U.S. Open at the Atlanta Athletic Club.

After winning one major in the 1950s and four in the next decade, Gary Player won four more in the 1970s, starting with the 1972 PGA at a tough Oakland Hills outside Detroit. Player's best year was yet to come, when he won both the Masters and the British Open in 1974. At the Masters, his victory charge was propelled by a third-round 66, in which he ran off five straight birdies on the twelfth through sixteenth. In the Open a he chipped back left-handed with his putter to win by four over Peter Oosterhuis. Perhaps his most memorable win of all came at the 1978 Masters, when he started the final round seven strokes off the lead of Hubert Green, shooting 64 with a blistering closing nine of 30 to overtake Green, Rod Funseth, and Tom Watson by one stroke, receiving an embrace at the end from playing partner Seve Ballesteros. Player remained keenly competitive and in fighting trim well into his sixties, winning two U.S. Senior Opens and three Senior British Opens, the last in 1997 when he was sixty-one. **OPPOSITE:** A fired-up Gary Player after winning the 1978 Masters, paired with Seve Ballesteros.

Tony Jacklin played a role of immeasurable importance in revitalizing the Ryder Cup Match, captaining the European teams that shattered the American side's postwar domination of the competition after the event was expanded to include players from the Continent in 1979. As a player, Jacklin played in seven successive Ryder Cup Matches from 1967 to 1979. The Americans won outright each time, except in 1969 at Royal Birkdale, when the event came down to the final singles match between Jacklin and Jack Nicklaus. Jacklin canned a fifty-foot putt for eagle on the seventeenth hole to pull to even. On the final hole, in one of the game's most enduring gestures of sportsmanship, Nicklaus conceded a short putt to Jacklin, allowing the British side to tie the match for the first time in history, with the U.S. retaining the Cup. Nicklaus and Jacklin recently teamed up to design a course together, fittingly named the Concession Golf Club, on Florida's Gulf Coast. In 1983, Jacklin served as nonplaying captain, the first of his four consecutive tours of duty, with the European squad narrowly succumbing at PGA National. In 1985 at The Belfry, Jacklin's infectious optimism led his team to Europe's first Ryder Cup win since 1957 at Lindrick. In 1987, the Europeans struck an even greater blow, winning for the first time ever on American soil at Muirfield Village. In his fourth appearance at the helm, the Europeans tied the favored American team at The Belfry to retain the Cup, with Christy O'Connor lashing a two-iron to the eighteenth green for a one-up win over Fred Couples.

OPPOSITE: Tony Jacklin (right) celebrating with Seve Ballesteros and Sam Torrance after Europe's win in the 1985 Ryder Cup at The Belfry.

Hollis Stacy's star shone brightest in the USGA's big events. After winning three consecutive USGA Junior Girls' Championships between 1969 and 1971, she captured three U.S. Women's Opens during her twenty-six-year pro career. Stacy grew up in Savannah, Georgia, one of ten children from an athletic family—her father was an all-Conference running back at Clemson in 1941. She was motivated to succeed in golf by attending the 1966 Masters at Augusta. In 1977, she out-dueled Nancy Lopez by two shots at Hazeltine, out-side Minneapolis, to win her first U.S. Open, and repeated the following year at the Country Club of Indianapolis. In 1984, she won at Salem Country Club, where Babe Didrikson Zaharias had been the champion thirty years earlier. **OPPOSITE:** Hazeltine Golf Club, sixteenth hole, where Hollis Stacy won the 1977 U.S. Women's Open. **BELOW:** Holding the trophy after winning at Salem Country Club in 1984.

Dave Stockton, who grew up in San Bernardino, California, and attended the University of Southern California (USC), turned pro in 1964. He was never a big hitter, but was known as a superb putter and a gritty competitor. Stockton won the PGA Championship twice. In 1970, he was the winner at a sweltering Southern Hills in Tulsa over Arnold Palmer and Bob Murphy. In 1976, he holed a clutch thirteen-foot putt on the final hole to nip Don January and Ray Floyd by a shot at Congressional. Stockton was also a world-beater on the Senior Tour, winning fourteen events, including the 1996 U.S. Senior Open at Canterbury. He was the captain of the 1991 Ryder Cup team that won the Cup by a score of 14 ½–13 ½ against the European side at the Ocean Course on Kiawah Island, in one of the most memorable and bitterly contested matches ever. **OPPOSITE:** Team captain Dave Stockton (center) pushes Corey Pavin into the water while Mark O'Meara (left) and Payne Stewart join in celebrating the U.S. victory in the 1991 Ryder Cup at South Carolina's Kiawah Island.

With her ebullient smile and natural warmth, Nancy Lopez captivated the golf world and became an overnight sensation in 1978, winning nine tournaments, including a record five in a row during her first full season on the LPGA Tour. Lopez learned to play at the municipal course in Roswell, New Mexico, where she was introduced to the game and encouraged by her father, Domingo, who owned an automobile body repair shop. A junior star, she won the New Mexico Women's Amateur when she was only twelve years old and the USGA Girls' title in 1972, when she was fifteen. As a professional, Lopez was the dominant player of her era, with a power game despite a deceptively slow and looping takeaway. She won forty-eight times on Tour between 1978 and 1997, and was voted LPGA Player of the Year in 1978, 1979, 1985, and 1988. In 1982, she married Cincinnati Reds baseball star Ray Knight. **OPPOSITE:** Nancy Lopez in 1979.

Johnny Miller is best known to today's golf audiences for his no-punches-pulled and insightful commentary as lead analyst for NBC's golf telecasts. Miller, more than any other announcer, focuses on the golfer's vulnerable psyche and has never shied away from using the word "choke" to explain a bad shot. During his playing career, Miller won twenty-five times on the PGA Tour. In addition to his two majors, he was particularly in his element playing in the desert on the Tour's West Coast swing, earning him the title "King of the Desert." He won four Tucson Opens as well as a pair of Phoenix Opens and the 1976 Bob Hope Desert Classic. In 1994, by which time he was affected by a severe case of the putting "yips," the forty-six-year-old Miller experienced a totally out-of-the-blue return to winning form at the AT&T National Pro-Am, the former Crosby Pro-Am, an event that he had won back in 1974 and 1987.

OPPOSITE and **BELOW:** Johnny Miller in his heyday during the 1970s.

One of the greatest of Australian golfers, David Graham left school when he was fourteen to become an assistant professional. In 1970, he teamed with Bruce Devlin to win the World Cup for Australia at Buenos Aires, and in 1976 he won the Piccadilly World Match Play Championship at Wentworth in a thirty-eight-hole donnybrook with Hale Irwin. Graham's first major victory came in the 1979 PGA Championship at Oakland Hills, outside Detroit, when he had a two-shot lead over Ben Crenshaw coming to the final hole, needing par to shoot a 63 and break the PGA seventy-two-hole scoring record.

Instead, he stumbled to a double bogey after miscalculating the yardage and airmailed his six-iron approach over the green. He held on to win the ensuing sudden-death play-off over Crenshaw, birdying the third play-off hole. Graham crowned his career by winning the 1981 U.S. Open, the last to be held at Merion, hitting all eighteen greens in regulation to win by three strokes.

OPPOSITE: David Graham marching to victory at the 1981 U.S. Open at Merion.
BELOW: Winning the 1979 PGA at Oakland Hills.

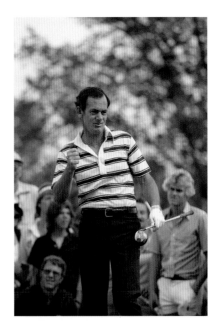

From 1976 to 1983, Tom Watson was golf's crown prince, eclipsing even the great Jack Nicklaus, who finished second to Watson in four of his major victories. Despite learning golf in the heart of the Midwest at Kansas City Country Club, Watson achieved golfing immortality on the billowy seaside courses of Great Britain, winning the British Open five times to tie Peter Thomson's modern record and just one shy of Harry Vardon's all-time record of six victories. After graduating from Stanford, Watson turned pro in 1971. With his strawberry-blond hair and Missouri upbringing, he was portrayed as a golfing Tom Sawyer early in his career, and had a reputation for not closing tournaments. In 1975, playing in his first British Open, he won at Carnoustie for the first of his eight career majors. In what would become a typically clutch performance, he defeated Jack Newton in an eighteen-hole play-off, his par on the final hole earning him a one-stroke victory. Watson won thirty-nine times on the PGA Tour, his final victory coming at the 1998 Colonial, and has won nine times on the Champions Tour, including two Senior British Opens. **OPPOSITE:** Tom Watson on the way to winning the 1977 Masters. **BELOW:** Playing in the 1978 PGA at Oakmont, where Watson and Jerry Pate lost out in a play-off to John Mahaffey.

Lanny Wadkins, a streaky player who played fast and swung quickly, bagged twenty-one wins on the PGA Tour. After playing at Wake Forest and winning the U.S. Amateur in 1970, he turned pro in 1971. Wadkins's sole major victory was a memorable one, knocking off Gene Littler on the third hole of a sudden-death play-off in the 1977 PGA Championship at Pebble Beach. In 1987, the tables were turned when Wadkins lost the PGA to Larry Nelson in sudden death at PGA National in Palm Beach Gardens. Wadkins played on eight Ryder Cup teams between 1977 and 1993, slaying Seve Ballesteros in singles with a record of 4–0 against the Spaniard. He captained the losing U.S. Ryder Cup team in 1995 at Rochester's Oak Hill. **OPPOSITE:** Lanny Wadkins at the 1989 Ryder Cup at The Belfry, where he defeated Nick Faldo in their singles match but Europe retained the Cup after a 14–14 tie. **BELOW:** Holing the winning putt to take the 1977 PGA in sudden death at Pebble Beach.

In 1974, Lee Trevino won the PGA Championship at Tanglewood, in North Carolina, giving him victories in every major except the Masters—Augusta National did not set up well for his patented fade. In 1975, Trevino was struck by lightning at the Western Open and subsequently had back surgery, which slowed him down but did not keep him from continuing to win. In 1984, when he was forty-four, he had his final hurrah in the majors, winning the PGA at Birmingham, Alabama's Shoal Creek over Gary Player and Lanny Wadkins. Trevino also enjoyed success in the Ryder Cup, compiling a record of 17–7–6, and was captain of the losing American team in 1985 at The Belfry. Known as a talkative player on the course, he has fired off some of golf's best one-liners. Accompanied by his longtime caddie and friend, the late Herman Mitchell, Trevino was a big hit on the Champions Tour, winning twenty-nine events, including four senior majors. **OPPOSITE:** Lee Trevino (right) with Jack Nicklaus and Hubert Green at the 1974 PGA at Tanglewood Park in Winston-Salem, North Carolina, which Trevino won. **BELOW:** Holding the Wanamaker Trophy after winning the 1984 PGA at Shoal Creek Country Club.

In 1977, Tom Watson won his second British Open in the famous "Duel in the Sun" with Jack Nicklaus, beneath the lighthouse at Turnberry overlooking Ailsa Craig. It was the first Open ever played on the famous Ailsa links, which had been restored to splendor by Philip Mackenzie Ross after World War II, during which the fairways had been turned into concrete runways for the RAF. In what may very well have been the greatest head-to-head matchup in the history of the game, Watson and Nicklaus played scorching golf in the Scottish sunshine, pulling away from the field after both shot 65 paired together in the third round. In the barn-burner of the final eighteen, Nicklaus staked out a one-stroke lead going to the sixteenth hole. Watson came back, dropping a bombshell of a putt to pull even on sixteen and a birdie on the seventeenth to give him the lead by one. When Nicklaus drove into the knee-deep marram grass on the eighteenth and Watson hit his approach from the fairway next to the flag, it seemed all over except the shouting, but Nicklaus refused to give up. He knocked his second on the green with a herculean effort and made the thirty-five-foot birdie putt. Watson was forced to make his short putt for birdie, which he holed for a 65 and a one-shot triumph. Watson's third Open victory came at Muirfield in 1980, by four over Lee Trevino. He then won back-to-back Opens, in 1982 at Troon by one over Nick Price and Peter Oosterhuis, and in 1983 at Birkdale by one over Hale Irwin and Andy Bean. A deeply principled player and a great proponent of links golf, Watson warmed up for the Open by playing in Ireland, particularly at Ballybunion, his favorite course. **OPPOSITE:** Tom Watson and Jack Nicklaus square off at Turnberry in their classic duel.

Isao Aoki has achieved more success at the international level than any other Japanese golfer. Born in Abiko, Chiba, Japan in 1942, Aoki learned the game as a caddie at Abiko Golf Club, and went on to win over fifty events on the Japan Golf Tour between 1972 and 1990, second only to baseball-pitcher-turned-pro-golfer Masashi "Jumbo" Ozaki. While Ozaki and Tsuneyuki "Tommy" Nakajima, another star of the Japanese Tour, were well known to the American golf audience from their frequent appearances in the Masters, Aoki played the U.S. Tour on a more regular basis. He is remembered for hanging tough with Jack Nicklaus at the 1980 U.S. Open at Baltusrol, finishing two shots back despite breaking the Open scoring record. In 1983,

he became the first Japanese player to win a U.S. Tour event, holing a full wedge shot for an eagle on the final hole of the Hawaiian Open. Aoki also captured the 1978 World Match Play Championship at Wentworth, defeating New Zealand's Simon Owen in the final, and the 1983 European Open. He enjoyed considerable success on the Champions Tour, winning nine events between 1992 and 2003. Tall and slender, Aoki is best known for his sleight of hand around and on the greens, and for a unique putting style in which he tilts the blade so that the toe is angled sharply upward. **OPPOSITE:** Isao Aoki in his match against Simon Owen to win the 1978 World Match Play Championship at Wentworth.

In the late 1970s, Spain's Severiano Ballesteros singlehandedly put European golf on the map with his smoldering bravado and magical powers of recovery. Ballesteros, whose uncle Ramón Sota was a leading Spanish pro who finished sixth in the 1965 Masters, grew up next to the Pedreña Golf Club in Cantabria in northern Spain, where his father was a greenkeeper. He started out as a caddie, honing his game by hitting pebbles on the beach with a sawed-down three-iron handed down by one of his brothers. After turning pro in 1974, Ballesteros burst onto the scene in 1976, when at age nineteen he led the British Open at Birkdale after three rounds, finishing tied for second with Jack Nicklaus, behind Johnny Miller. The Open would prove to be the stage for Seve's most memorable triumphs. His name was inscribed on the Claret Jug for the first time in 1979 at Royal Lytham & St. Annes. He won despite his wayward driving, famously making a birdie on the sixteenth hole after his tee shot finished in the parking lot to the right of the fairway. His second Open victory came at the Old Course in 1984, when he birdied the final hole to finish two ahead of Tom Watson, who had bogeyed the Road Hole, and Bernhard Langer. He repeated at Lytham in 1988, when his sizzling final-round 65 outpaced Nick Price by two strokes. **OPPOSITE:** A young Seve Ballesteros raises his arms in triumph at the 1979 Open at Royal Lytham & St. Annes. **BELOW:** On his way to his third Open victory and second at Royal Lytham, in 1988.

In addition to winning more majors than any other golfer in history, Jack Nicklaus had a remarkable nineteen second-place finishes, one of the most memorable being his battle royal with Tom Watson at Turnberry in 1977. The next year, he came back to win his third Open Championship at St. Andrews. After a slump in 1979, he captured the U.S. Open at Baltusrol in 1980, where he had won in 1967, beating his own record low total for the championship with a total of 272. Nicklaus played all four rounds with Isao Aoki, who challenged him throughout until Nicklaus prevailed at the end by two, with the gallery providing a rousing chorus of "Jack Is Back." He *was* back, and won the PGA that August at Rochester's Oak Hill. In 1986, having already won a record five green jackets, the forty-six-year-old Nicklaus thundered to glory one final time.

He played his most transcendent round of all, a closing 65 with a back nine of 30 that featured a starburst of a birdie putt on the seventeenth, to finish one ahead of Greg Norman and Tom Kite. It was his last PGA victory, with his farewell to competitive golf coming at the 2005 British Open at St. Andrews, where he had won in 1970 and 1978. Over his long career, Nicklaus had three assets that no other player could come close to matching in combination: raw power when needed, a cerebral approach that enabled him to plot his way around a course better than anyone, and an uncanny ability to cocoon himself in concentration when it mattered most. **OPPOSITE:** Jack Nicklaus holes the putt on the seventeenth hole at the 1986 Masters that would carry him to his storybook victory. **BELOW:** On the way to winning the 1980 U.S. Open at Baltusrol.

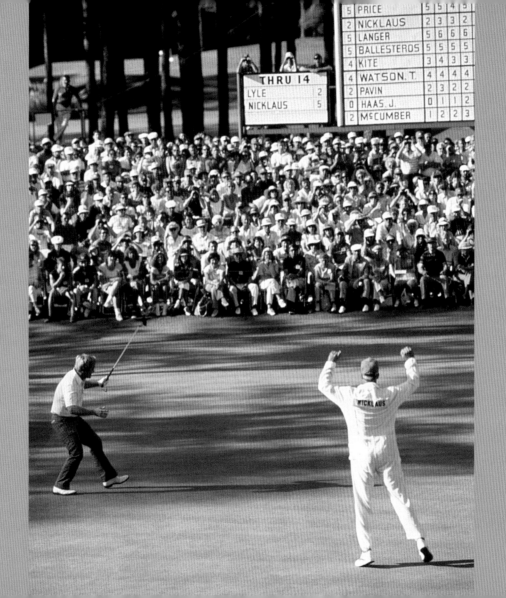

Besides his five British Open championships, Tom Watson notched two victories in the Masters. In 1977, he won the Masters by two over Jack Nicklaus, foreshadowing their showdown at Turnberry in July of that year. In 1982, Watson won his second green jacket by two over Nicklaus and Johnny Miller. The most enduring image of Watson, and the shot that will forever remain his career highlight, is when he chipped in from off the seventeenth green for birdie in the 1982 U.S. Open at Pebble Beach. Lying in thick rough with little green to work with, his chip jackrabbited into the hole, and Watson went on to upend Nicklaus, who was already in the clubhouse, by one. In his halcyon days, Watson was a bold and fearless putter, particularly sure from short range. But after winning seven majors between 1977 and 1983, short putts became his bane, even as his ball-striking became better than ever. His final chance at a major victory came at Olympic in 1987, when he finished one shot back of Scott Simpson. Bruce Edwards, Watson's caddie through thick and thin, was afflicted with Lou Gehrig's disease in 2003, from which he died in 2004, and Watson dedicated himself to raising funds to find a cure. **OPPOSITE:** Tom Watson chips in for birdie on the seventeenth hole in the 1982 U.S. Open at Pebble Beach, the shot that would catapult him to victory over Jack Nicklaus.

As his playing career wound down, Jack Nicklaus increasingly concentrated his ambition on golf course architecture, having first been introduced to the field as a consultant to Pete Dye at Harbour Town in the late 1960s. In the 1980s and 1990s, he established himself as the leading international architect, with more than two hundred courses around the world, in thirty countries and thirty-eight U.S. states. Nicklaus invariably designs robust, well-bunkered courses with strong lines and a distinct sensitivity to preserving native trees and plants. Over the years he has worked with a number of talented assistants, including Bob Cupp and Jay Morrish, Jim Lipe and Scott Miller, and he currently works with his sons Jackie, Steve, Gary, and Michael, and his son-in-law, Bill O'Leary. His designs range from the Sebonack Golf Club, in conjunction with Tom Doak, on the old Bayberry Estate overlooking Peconic Bay in Southampton, which opened in 2006, to Old Works in Montana; from Lake Las Vegas in Nevada to Cabo del Sol in Baja; and from Royal Springfield in Thailand to Le Robinie outside Milan. The nearest and dearest to his heart is Muirfield Village in his hometown of Columbus, Ohio, designed with the late Desmond Muirhead, which opened on Memorial Day of 1974. Modeled on Augusta National, the course has the same sense of serene grandeur, its plush fairways lined with streams on eleven holes. Muirfield Village has been the home of Nicklaus's tournament, the Memorial, since 1976. One of the Tour's most prestigious events, each year the Memorial honors a legend of the game.

OPPOSITE: Muirfield Village Golf Club in Columbus, Ohio, home of the Memorial Tournament, ninth hole.

THE RISE OF THE EUROPEANS

257 | SEVE AND THE RISE OF THE EUROPEANS

Seve Ballesteros was at the vanguard of the wave of European players who made their mark on the game in the 1980s and into the 1990s, ending the long dominance of American players. Between 1980 and 1999, Ballesteros, Germany's Bernhard Langer, England's Nick Faldo, Scotland's Sandy Lyle, Wales's Ian Woosnam, and Seve's fellow Spaniard José Maria Olazábal would win the Masters eleven times between them. Ballesteros won his first Masters in 1980, when he built up a ten-shot lead; his second green jacket came in 1983. He was in position to win again in 1986 when a pulled four-iron on the sixteenth hole found the drink, allowing Jack Nicklaus to meet his date with destiny. Seve also enjoyed success on the U.S. Tour, but had a stormy relationship with PGA Commissioner Deane Beman, who insisted that he play a minimum of fifteen PGA events a year, which he refused to do, opting to play in Europe instead. Ballesteros built a grand house overlooking the Pedreña Golf Club, where he had caddied as a small boy and taught himself to play by sneaking onto the course at dusk. **OPPOSITE:** Seve Ballesteros exults after winning the Open at St. Andrews in 1984.

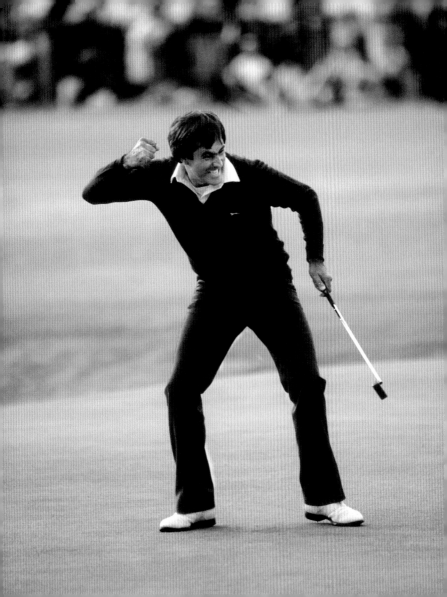

Ben Crenshaw was golf's golden boy, widely heralded as the next Nicklaus while still a collegiate golfer at the University of Texas, where he won the NCAA championship three times in succession between 1971 and 1973 (tying with teammate Tom Kite in 1972). Although he never quite achieved the Olympian heights for which he seemed destined as an amateur, Crenshaw had a very successful pro career that started with winning his first professional tournament, the Texas Open, in 1973. He won nineteen tournaments over twenty-three years, and was in the thick of many a major. He finally broke through in 1984, winning the Masters by holing two outrageously long putts in the final round. Although a somewhat wayward driver, Crenshaw was a preternaturally great putter, perhaps the greatest ever, making his game well suited for Augusta at the time—with its lack of rough and exceptionally slick, treacherous greens. **OPPOSITE:** Ben Crenshaw watches his long birdie putt go in on the way to victory at the 1984 Masters.

Australia's Jan Stephenson became the LPGA's sex symbol in the late 1970s, causing considerable controversy by posing for photographs in revealing outfits and appearing in a bathtub full of golf balls in 1986. Stephenson was also a top-notch player, whose name was frequently atop the leader board after she joined the LPGA Tour in 1974. She won the U.S. Women's Open at Cedar Ridge Country Club in Broken Arrow, Oklahoma, in 1983, one shot ahead of JoAnne Carner and Patty Sheehan. She won a dozen tournaments on the Tour between 1981 and 1987, including the 1981 du Maurier Classic and the 1982 LPGA Championship, for a total of three major championships.

OPPOSITE: Jan Stephenson playing in 1976.

Frank Urban "Fuzzy" Zoeller, who got his nickname from his initials, was one of the most popular players on the PGA Tour during the 1980s. Outgoing and good-humored, Zoeller grew up in Indiana and played at the University of Houston before turning pro in 1973. He won ten PGA tournaments, including the Colonial, the Heritage, and the Bing Crosby National Pro-Am, and two very memorable majors. In 1979, he won the Masters in his first appearance, beating Ed Sneed and Tom Watson in a sudden-death play-off after Sneed agonizingly missed a three-foot putt coming down the stretch. In 1984, he won the U.S. Open at Winged Foot, famously waving a white towel in capitulation on the eighteenth fairway after Greg Norman, playing in the group ahead of him, rolled in a monster putt that Zoeller believed was for birdie. Unbeknownst to Zoeller, the putt was for a par, Norman having pushed his second shot into the grandstand thirty yards right of the green. In the eighteen-hole play-off with Norman the next day, Zoeller carved out a 67 to win convincingly. **OPPOSITE:** Fuzzy Zoeller shouts for joy after winning the 1979 Masters in sudden death while a forlorn Ed Sneed looks away.

Craig Stadler was a crowd favorite and an instantly recognizable player on the PGA Tour throughout the 1980s. Known as "The Walrus" for his portly physique and drooping mustache, Stadler grew up in San Diego, playing at La Jolla Country Club, the home course of Mickey Wright and Gene Littler. While playing golf at USC, where he was an all-American, he won the 1973 U.S. Amateur at Inverness. In the early 1980s, Stadler was at the very top of the pro ranks, winning four times in 1982—including the Masters in sudden death over Dan Pohl, which gave him his lone major title. Stadler enjoyed continuing success, winning a total of thirteen events on the PGA Tour, including the 2003 B.C. Open, after he had already turned fifty and was playing on the Champions Tour. A down-to-earth man who readily registers his disgust with a bad shot, Stadler has also done well on the Champions Tour, winning eight times to date. **OPPOSITE:** Craig Stadler escaping from trouble on his way to winning the 1982 Masters.

Greg Norman is golf's Sampson, a blond giant of a player endowed with enormous talent who suffered a series of agonizing losses in the majors. He repeatedly fell victim to either a miracle shot by an opponent or an ill-timed slip in the final moment. Born in Mount Isa in Queensland, Australia, Norman turned pro in 1974 and, like earlier Australian pros, became an international player, making his debut in the United States in the early 1980s. He finished fourth in the 1981 Masters. With his gleaming game, sharp features, and tales of underwater diving off the Great Barrier Reef, he was soon dubbed "The Great White Shark." Norman won two British Opens in majestic fashion, but holds the unfortunate distinction, with Craig Wood, of having lost each of the majors in a play-off. **OPPOSITE:** Greg Norman beseeches the golfing gods during the 1981 Suntory World Matchplay Championship at Wentworth.

Greg Norman was the longest, straightest driver of his generation, with a bravura style of play that matched his personality. In 1986, he led every major after three rounds, although victory eluded him in each except the British Open. In the Masters that year, Norman's blocked four-iron into the gallery on the final hole enabled Jack Nicklaus to achieve his stirring finale in the majors, while Ray Floyd was another sentimental winner at the U.S. Open at Shinnecock. It was that year's PGA, however, that gave the first intimation of Norman's reputation as a snakebitten player. Bob Tway, who had trailed by four going into the final round at Inverness, holed his bunker shot on the seventy-second hole, leaping skyward as a stunned Shark finished one shot back. Norman won the British Open comfortably at Turnberry that year, riding a scintillating second-round 63 to victory. Three years later, he was on the cusp of winning the Claret Jug again in a play-off with Mark Calcavecchia and Wayne Grady at Troon, but a three-wood belted down the right side of the fairway on the eighteenth hole bobbled into a pot bunker more than three hundred yards away, allowing Calcavecchia to seize the victory. **OPPOSITE:** Greg Norman unleashes a drive on the ninth hole during the final round of the 1986 British Open at Turnberry, where he won the first of his two Open championships.

Bernhard Langer, together with Seve Ballesteros, was one of the twin pillars of European golf in the 1980s, ending the long-standing dominance of American players in the major events. Born in Anhausen in Bavaria, the son of a bricklayer, he was introduced to the game at age eight after his older brother started to caddy. His rise to the very top coming from modest circumstances in a country without a golfing tradition, required single-minded dedication and perseverance. In 1974, he won the German National Open Championship as an amateur, and in 1976 he turned pro at age eighteen. Langer has won forty events on the European Tour, including the 1981 German Open, making him the first German to win his country's national championship since the inception of the event in 1911. His two majors both came at Augusta. In 1985, he became the second European after Ballesteros to win the Masters, besting Curtis Strange, Ray Floyd, and Ballesteros by two shots. His second green jacket came in 1993, this time finishing four clear of Chip Beck. In 2007, when he was forty-nine, he almost won at Colonial, losing in a three-man sudden-death play-off to Rory Sabbatini. **OPPOSITE:** Bernhard Langer genuflects after a near miss on his way to winning the 1985 Masters. **BELOW:** Playing in the 1987 U.S. Open at Olympic.

Robert Trent Jones, Jr., and his younger brother Rees both followed their illustrious father into the world of golf course architecture, and all three enjoyed a competitive rivalry. Trent Jr. graduated from Yale, and not long after joined his father's firm in 1960, heading the West Coast office in Palo Alto, California. He went out on his own in 1972 and, like his father, became an international architect of the first rank, designing courses all around the world. His courses combine a strong sense of drama with an emphasis on highlighting natural beauty. This is evident at the Links at Spanish Bay on the Monterey Peninsula, completed in 1987, with its delicate ecosystem protected by man-made dunes. Other notable courses around the globe include the rugged Wild Coast in South Africa; Penha Longa outside Lisbon, with its views of the hills of Sintra; the Four Seasons Nevis Resort in the Caribbean; The Mines in Kuala Lumpur, built on the site of the Hong Fatt Tin Mine; Spring City's Lake Course in China's Yunnan Province; Miklagard Golf Club in Oslo; and Moscow Country Club, Russia's first eighteen-hole golf course. Chambers Bay, his links-style course in University Place, Washington, has been selected to host the 2015 U.S. Open. **OPPOSITE:** The Old Course at the National Golf Club in Cape Schanck, Australia, designed by Robert Trent Jones, Jr., first hole.

Calvin Peete, who won a dozen PGA events between 1979 and 1986, most notably the 1985 Players Championship, had one of the unlikeliest ascents to the top of the game. One of nine children, he was born in Detroit, and after his parents separated, he went to live with his grandmother in rural Hayti, Missouri. When he was twelve, he fell out of a cherry tree and shattered his left elbow, which was surgically fused. Some swing analysts claim that Peete's permanently bent elbow was actually an advantage when it came to maintaining a perfectly square swing plane, although Peete disputes this. What is undisputed is that he became one of the straightest drivers in the history of the game, perennially leading the Tour in driving accuracy. When he was twenty-three, Peete, who was making a living selling goods to migrant workers, discovered golf by playing a round at Genesee Valley Golf Club in upstate New York. He began practicing relentlessly and, inspired by watching Lee Elder narrowly lose to Jack Nicklaus in the 1968 American Golf Classic, devoted himself to making it to the PGA Tour. He finally earned his card in 1975. With his uncanny accuracy, Peete was expected to make a big mark on the Champions Tour, but was held back by his battle against Tourette's syndrome, which was only diagnosed in 1999. Peete became the second black player after Elder to play in the Ryder Cup, earning a spot on the 1983 and 1985 teams. **OPPOSITE:** Calvin Peete at the Players Championship in 1982.

Sam Torrance, born in Largs on the west coast of Scotland, grew up playing golf. His father is the well-known instructor Bob Torrance, who coached some of Europe's biggest names—including Seve Ballesteros, Padraig Harrington, and Ian Woosnam. Sam turned professional when he was sixteen, and joined the European Tour the following year, in 1970. He won twenty-one events on the European Tour from 1976 to 1998, including the Irish, Spanish, Portuguese, Scandinavian, Tunisian, Italian, and French Opens. The gregarious and straight-talking Torrance is best known for his role as a leader of Europe's Ryder Cup forces, competing in eight consecutive matches between 1981 and 1995. In the historic 1985 match, he clinched the Ryder Cup for the Europeans by beating Andy North one up, giving the Americans their first taste of defeat since 1957. Torrance returned to captain the Europeans to victory at The Belfry in 2002, and was awarded an OBE (Order of the British Empire) the following year. He is one of the top players on the European senior circuit. **OPPOSITE:** Europe captain Sam Torrance reflects on his team's victory in the 2002 Ryder Cup at The Belfry in Sutton Coldfield, England.

Pat Bradley grew up in Westford, Massachusetts, and was a competitive skier and ski instructor before attending Florida International University and setting her sights on golf. She has the distinction of becoming the third player in history to win all four women's majors as they existed at the time, following in the footsteps of Louise Suggs and Mickey Wright. Her first major was the Peter Jackson Classic in 1980 (subsequently the du Maurier Classic). The following year, she won the U.S. Open at LaGrange Country Club in Illinois.

In 1986, her record-smashing season, she won the Nabisco Dinah Shore, the LPGA Championship, and the du Maurier Classic, giving her six career majors; won the Vare Trophy for lowest stroke average; and became the first woman golfer to eclipse the $2 million mark in career earnings. In 2000, Bradley served as captain of the U.S. Solheim Cup team that was defeated by the European squad at Loch Lomond. **OPPOSITE:** Pat Bradley in 1986 posing with her trophies from each of the four majors.

Ray Floyd capped his career in grand fashion by winning the U.S. Open at Shinnecock Hills in 1986, when he was forty-three, making him the oldest man at the time to win golf's most grueling test. His birdie at the par-5 sixteenth en route to a final-round 68 gave him a two-shot cushion over Chip Beck and Lanny Wadkins. The tournament also showcased the linksland splendor of Shinnecock, a long-lost champion venue that had last hosted the Open a century before, in 1896. Shinnecock in its present incarnation was laid out in 1930 by the Philadelphia-based partnership of William Flynn and Howard Toomey, with Dick Wilson, who would go on to a career as Robert Trent Jones's design rival of the 1950s and early 1960s, serving as the construction supervisor. Floyd was subsequently selected to captain the 1989 Ryder Cup squad that finished in a tie at The Belfry outside Birmingham. He then reappeared as a player in the 1991 Ryder Cup and was one of Tom Watson's captain's picks in 1993, when the Americans won at The Belfry. At age fifty-one, Floyd won both his matches that year paired with Payne Stewart, and then defeated José Maria Olazábal in their singles match. Floyd is a member of Shinnecock, the site of his greatest triumph. **OPPOSITE:** Ray Floyd at home in his office in 1981.

Larry Nelson, from Fort Payne, Alabama, won ten tournaments on the PGA Tour, three of them majors. A soft-spoken and devout man, who let his sticks do the talking, Nelson did not take up golf until he was twenty-one, after returning from military service in Vietnam. Armed with nothing but Ben Hogan's *The Five Fundamentals of Golf,* he proved a natural. Nelson turned pro in 1971, serving as the assistant at Pine Tree Country Club in Kennesaw, Georgia, before qualifying for the Tour in 1974 at age twenty-seven. In 1981, he won his first major, the PGA Championship held at Atlanta Athletic Club. In 1987, he won his second PGA at a steamy PGA National in Palm Beach Gardens, beating Lanny Wadkins on the first hole of sudden death. In between, in 1983, he achieved his greatest triumph, winning the U.S. Open at Oakmont by one shot over Tom Watson after firing a third-round 65 and draining a sixty-foot putt on the sixteenth in the final round. Nelson also had a superlative Ryder Cup record of 9–3–1 and continues to shine on the Champions Tour, winning nineteen events between 1998 and 2004. **OPPOSITE:** Larry Nelson on his way to winning the 1981 PGA at the Atlanta Athletic Club.

Nick Faldo became the top player in the world in the decade between his first major win, at the British Open in 1987, and his sixth, at the Masters in 1996, taking English golf to heights that it had not seen since the days of Harry Vardon. Born in Welwyn Garden City in 1957, he turned his attention to golf and away from cycling, his first sporting interest, after watching Jack Nicklaus on television in the 1971 Masters. He won the English Amateur in 1975, and the following year turned pro. Early in his career he was a top British player, but Sandy Lyle outshone him and the English press gave him a rough time, dubbing him "Fold-o" after he collapsed in the 1983 British Open.

Faldo then worked with David Leadbetter to develop a perfectly balanced swing that could hold up under pressure, even if it cost him some length, and emerged as the modern-day ice man of golf. In 1987, he won the first of his three Open championships, methodically making eighteen pars in the final round at Muirfield to edge Paul Azinger by one. Faldo also won the Masters three times and came close to winning the U.S. Open, losing in a play-off to Curtis Strange in 1988. **OPPOSITE:** Nick Faldo sinks a twenty-five-foot putt to win the 1989 Masters in a sudden-death play-off over Scott Hoch. **BELOW:** Faldo at the 1992 Masters.

Larry Mize will long be remembered for his storybook victory in the 1987 Masters. A native of Augusta, Mize had worked the scoreboard on the third hole at the Masters as a teenager, going on to attend Georgia Tech and turning pro in 1980. In 1987, Mize was the soft-spoken underdog when he finished tied with international superstars Seve Ballesteros and Greg Norman. After Ballesteros stumbled on the first play-off hole and was eliminated, it came down to Norman and Mize on the eleventh hole. Mize, well off the green and facing a seemingly impossibly slick approach to the downslope, chipped in with a sand wedge for his seismic sudden-death win. Mize was hardly a flash in the pan. He won two regular events on the PGA Tour in 1993 and also ran away with the Johnny Walker World Championship at Tryall on Jamaica, but he was later unable to sustain the world-class form that he displayed at Augusta. **OPPOSITE:** Larry Mize leaps after chipping in to win the 1987 Masters in sudden death.

Curtis Strange was an intense and determined competitor who surmounted the summit of golf when he won back-to-back U.S. Opens in 1988 and 1989. One of the top players throughout the 1980s, Strange grew up in Virginia Beach, the son of a golf pro. In 1974 he won the individual NCAA Championship while playing at Wake Forest, under legendary coach Jesse Haddock. He was on one of the greatest teams in the history of collegiate golf, its members including future Tour players Jay Haas and Bob Byman. After turning pro in 1976, Strange was in contention to win the 1985 Masters, but stumbled when his second shot at the thirteenth found Rae's Creek and he failed to extricate himself. In 1988, Strange won the U.S. Open at The Country Club in Brookline, seventy-five years after Francis Ouimet's epic victory,

coolly getting up and down from the deep bunker in front of the eighteenth green to force a play-off with Nick Faldo that he won by four strokes. The next year, Strange ground out par after par on the back nine of a brutal Oak Hill in Rochester, becoming the first player to defend his title successfully since Ben Hogan in 1951, prompting him to exclaim afterward: "Move over, Ben Hogan." After his second U.S. Open win, Strange's form slipped, and it proved to be the last of his seventeen Tour victories. He played on five Ryder Cup teams and captained the losing U.S. team in 2002 at The Belfry.

OPPOSITE: Curtis Strange pumps his fist on the way to winning the 1988 U.S. Open at The Country Club in Brookline, Massachusetts.

Hale Irwin's most memorable victory came in the 1990 U.S. Open at Medinah when, as a veteran forty-five-year-old star, he shot a final-round 67 to tie journeyman Mike Donald. Both shot 74 in the eighteen-hole play-off, with Irwin then birdying the first hole of sudden death to deprive the hard-luck Donald of his only chance for golfing immortality. An overjoyed Irwin sprinted around the eighteenth green glad-handing the gallery, shedding his image as one of golf's most stoic players. Since then, he has been the Ponce de León of the Champions Tour, enjoying phenomenal success since he turned fifty in 1995. Irwin has won a record forty-five events on the Senior Circuit, including the 1998 U.S. Senior Open at Riviera and the 2000 Senior Open at Saucon Valley. He amassed a stellar 13–5–2 record in his five Ryder Cup appearances. In one of the most gut-wrenching battles in the event's history, Irwin halved his decisive match with Bernhard Langer in 1991 at Kiawah Island when Langer missed an eight-foot putt on the eighteenth hole, resulting in victory for the United States. **OPPOSITE:** Hale Irwin on his victory lap after winning the 1990 U.S. Open at Medinah.

Tom Kite was one of the most consistent and successful players on the PGA Tour from the mid-seventies through the mid-1990s, and has continued to have success on the Senior Tour. Growing up in Austin, Texas, he was a boyhood rival of Ben Crenshaw and their careers are inexorably linked. Like Crenshaw, Kite was a pupil of the great golfing guru Harvey Penick at Austin Country Club and starred with Crenshaw on the University of Texas golf team that won the National Championship in 1971 and 1972. While Crenshaw was the golden boy whose stardom never seemed in doubt, it was the unassuming and hardworking Kite, known for his impeccable wedge game, who amassed nineteen Tour victories and always seemed to be near the lead. Kite was a moneymaking machine, the first player to reach $9 million in career earnings. Kite's breakthrough in a major, after many near misses, came at the 1992 U.S. Open at Pebble Beach. While the rest of the field struggled in the final round against high winds that made the slick greens virtually unplayable, Kite calmly carded a 72 to win by two. He played on seven Ryder Cup teams and was captain in 1997, when the U.S. team went down to defeat at Valderrama.

OPPOSITE: Tom Kite chipping in on the seventh hole on his way to victory in the 1992 U.S. Open at Pebble Beach. **BELOW:** Kite during the 1998 PGA at Sahalee Country Club.

Tom Fazio learned the ropes of the golf course architecture business starting as a teenager in 1962, working for his uncle George Fazio, who had been a top player during the 1930s and 1940s, losing to Ben Hogan in a play-off in the 1950 Open. Beginning in the early 1980s, Fazio began designing the type of visually striking and architectonic courses that have come to define contemporary design, making him the most sought-after name in the field. Fazio shaped and molded the landscape on an overarching scale to create lavishly framed golf holes that often look more difficult than they actually play. Fazio's courses have many different looks, but all of them place an emphasis on aesthetic shaping and proper proportions. His designs include Wade Hampton, laid out through rushing streams at the base of the Blue Ridge Mountains in Cashiers, North Carolina; Karsten Creek, the Oklahoma State University course that wanders through bucolic meadows; the World Woods Club's Pine Barrens Course, an homage to Pine Valley on the west coast of Florida; Galloway National near the seashore of Atlantic City; and Shadow Creek, completed in 1990 for casino magnate Steve Wynn in Las Vegas, where Fazio planted thousands of mature maples, pines, tamaracks, and willows and created waterfalls and ponds to transform a patch of bare desert floor into a verdant, forested course. Outside the United States, his Green Monkey in Barbados was painstakingly sculpted from an old coral rock quarry, while Querencia perches above the Sea of Cortez in Mexico's Los Cabos. **OPPOSITE:** The Green Monkey Course at the Sandy Lane Resort in Barbados, designed by Tom Fazio.

Betsy King was a member of the Furman University team that captured the national collegiate title in 1976, and she then joined the Tour in 1977. She won twenty tournaments from 1984 through 1989, the most victories by a man or woman during that time span. In 1989 and 1990, King won back-to-back U.S. Opens. In 1989, she was the winner at the Old Course at Indianwood Golf and Country Club, a vintage layout from the 1920s designed by Wilfried Reid in Lake Orion, Michigan. The following year, at the Atlanta Athletic Club, she steadily whittled away at a ten-stroke lead held by Patty Sheehan in the third round to win by one shot in a thirty-six-hole final on Sunday necessitated by bad weather earlier in the week. King was captain of the victorious U.S. Solheim Cup team in 2007 at Halmstad Golf Club in Sweden. **OPPOSITE:** Betsy King in 1979.

Mark Calcavecchia learned to play on a nine-hole course built on an old cornfield in Laurel, Nebraska, before his family moved to southern Florida when he was thirteen. He has had a long and successful career on the PGA Tour. He currently has thirteen career Tour victories, as well as wins in the 1998 Australian Open and the 1993 and 1995 Argentine Open. In the late 1980s, Calcavecchia was a force to be reckoned with, winning six times between 1986 and 1989, including the 1989 British Open at Troon for his lone major, while finishing one shot behind Sandy Lyle in the 1988 Masters. Calc's Open victory was chock full of drama, coming in a three-way, four-hole play-off with Greg Norman and Wayne Grady, the first time that the championship was ever decided using the four-hole play-off format. In the play-off,

Norman's drive on the eighteenth hole ran too far down the baked fairway and finished in the right-hand bunker, while Calcavecchia closed with a magnificent five-iron shot to seven feet to seal the win. He is also remembered for his meltdown at the epic 1991 Ryder Cup battle at Kiawah Island. Although the U.S. team managed to eke out a victory, it appeared that all might be lost when Calcavecchia blew a four-up lead over Colin Montgomerie with only four to play, after fanning his two-iron on the par-3 seventeenth hole into the water, and had to settle for a halve. Calcavecchia's most recent win came at the 2007 PODS Championship at Tampa's Innisbrook Resort, using the claw putting grip that has served him well in recent years. **OPPOSITE:** Mark Calcavecchia has a photo op after his victory at the 1989 British Open.

Ian Woosnam, the greatest of Welsh golfers, was actually born on the English side of the border in Owestry in Shropshire, where he grew up working on his family's dairy farm. He learned the game at Llanymynech Golf Club, which straddles the border with three holes in England and fifteen in Wales. Woosnam came of age at the same time as Nick Faldo, Sandy Lyle, Bernhard Langer, and Seve Ballesteros, in a golden era for European golf. Like them, he has won the Masters. Although standing barely over five feet four inches, Woosie is a phenomenally powerful player, driving the ball prodigious distances. He has won twenty-eight European Tour events and tournaments all over the world, ranging from the Zambian to the Hong Kong Opens. He has also repeatedly represented Wales in the World Cup, taking the team and individual titles in 1987 at Kapalua on Maui. In 1991, he became the fourth straight British player to win the Masters, succeeding Lyle and Faldo. Woosnam made par on the eighteenth hole by deliberately poking his drive well out to the left of the fairway, finishing one ahead of José Maria Olazábal and Tom Watson. In 2006, Woosnam captained the victorious European team at the Ryder Cup, and he was awarded an Order of the British Empire in 2007. **OPPOSITE:** Ian Woosnam after holing the final putt to win the 1991 Masters.

Nick Faldo was born in 1957, like Seve Ballesteros and Bernhard Langer, and the trio's rise to the pinnacle of the game propelled European golf to a level in the 1980s and 1990s not seen since the early days of the game. In 1989, Faldo won the first of his three green jackets at Augusta, beating Scott Hoch on the second hole of sudden death after Hoch missed a short putt on the first play-off hole. Faldo would repeat at Augusta the following year, again winning on the second hole of sudden death, this time when Ray Floyd faltered. That same year, he convincingly won the British Open at St. Andrews. Faldo was paired with Greg Norman in the third round, after both had gotten off to a blazing start over the first thirty-six holes, with Faldo pulling away from Norman in a matchup that would presage their final-round pairing in the 1996 Masters. In 1992, Faldo won his third Open, and second at Muirfield, again refusing to succumb to pressure in an intense finish. Two shots back with four holes to play, he steeled himself with two birdies and two pars, while John Cook, on the verge of victory in the group ahead, missed a three-foot birdie putt on the seventeenth and then bogeyed the final hole to lose by one. **OPPOSITE:** Nick Faldo during the final round of his clutch victory in the 1992 Open at Muirfield.

The Solheim Cup was founded by Karsten and Louise Solheim in 1990 as the biennial match between the top American pros and their European counterparts, modeled after the Ryder Cup. The late Karsten Solheim, who had emigrated from Bergen, Norway, as a child, became an engineer for General Electric and designed his famous PING putter in his spare time. Solheim then established the PING golf equipment company, which gained enormous success by making investment-cast, perimeter-weighted irons. The new type of irons was more forgiving than traditional forged irons, enabling the average golfer to achieve a higher trajectory. The inaugural Solheim Cup match took place at Lake Nona Golf Club in Orlando, with the U.S. team prevailing 11½–4½ under captain Kathy Whitworth. In 2007, the U.S. team captained by Betsy King came from behind in the final day's singles matches to defeat the Europeans at Halmstad Golf Club in Sweden, giving the American side an overall record of six wins to Europe's three. **OPPOSITE:** U.S. team captain Patty Sheehan (center) punches the air after Rosie Jones's win gave the Americans victory in the 2002 Solheim Cup at Interlachen Golf Club outside Minneapolis. **BELOW:** Meg Mallon gets ready for her match in the 2002 Solheim Cup.

STARS OF THE NINETIES

282 | BOOM BOOM AT THE MASTERS

Fred Couples is known for his laid-back personality and a long, languid swing that unleashes enormous power, earning him the nickname "Boom Boom." An exciting, streaky player, with matinee idol good looks, Couples has long been a gallery favorite. He grew up in Seattle, learning the game from his father, who worked for the Seattle Parks and Recreation Department. Couples played on the University of Houston golf team with future Tour pro Blaine McAllister and CBS broadcaster Jim Nantz, who were his roommates. Couples turned pro in 1980, and was considered somewhat of an underachiever in his early years on Tour. His grandstand year came in 1992, when he became the number one ranked player in the world, winning the Los Angeles Open for the second time, the Nestlé Invitational, and the Masters—his lone major. Couples's fifteen PGA titles include the 1984 and 1996 Players Championships and the 1998 Memorial. In recent years his career has been hampered by severe back problems. **OPPOSITE:** Fred Couples gets his green jacket from Ian Woosnam after winning the 1992 Masters.

Payne Stewart, whose father won the Missouri State Amateur and missed the cut in the 1955 U.S. Open, was born in Springfield, Missouri, and played his college golf at Southern Methodist University. After failing to earn his Tour card, he played for a couple of years in Asia, where he saw Australian players Rodger Davis and Stewart Ginn wearing plus fours. When he made it to the PGA Tour in 1982, Stewart started making his own fashion statement by wearing color-coordinated knickers and a tam-o'-shanter cap. In his early years, he was best known for his haberdashery and as a hard-luck player, losing four sudden-death play-offs. Then, in 1989, he broke through, brashly winning the first of his three majors at the PGA at Kemper Lakes Golf Club outside Chicago. Stewart fired a 31 on the back nine that included five straight closing birdies, overtaking frontrunner Mike "Radar" Reid, who faltered on the sixteenth hole when his tee shot found the lake to the right of the fairway.

OPPOSITE: Payne Stewart teeing off at the 1990 British Open at St. Andrews.

Pete and Alice Dye were hired to build the Ocean Course on the long sand barrier reef of Kiawah Island, South Carolina, with the express purpose of hosting the 1991 Ryder Cup Match. The fruit of their labors is one of the most tantalizing, tough, and authentic links courses in the United States, with unmanicured beauty at every turn. Laid out in a loose figure eight, a routing that is a favorite of Dye's, the course wends its way along the dunes and marshland, with the last few holes tacking along the Atlantic. Alice Dye insisted that the level of the holes away from the shoreline be raised several feet, so that every hole would offer views of the sea. At Whistling Straits, part of the Kohler Resort in Wisconsin, Dye cooked up a links course along Lake Michigan from scratch, creating the dunes and sprinkling them with cranberry-colored grasses at what had previously been Camp Haven, a flat, abandoned airfield. Whistling Straits was the site of Vijay Singh's 2004 PGA win and Brad Bryant's victory in the 2007 U.S. Senior Open, and will host the 2010 and 2015 PGAs. Dye's favorite of all his concoctions is the Teeth of the Dog at the Casa de Campo Resort, in the southeast corner of the Dominican Republic. With fairways chiseled from the sharp coral rock known as *dientes del perro*—from which the course takes its name—caressing the cornflower-blue Caribbean, and inland holes bedecked with flowering cashew trees, it is hard to dispute the creator's assessment. **OPPOSITE:** Teeth of the Dog at the Casa de Campo Resort in the Dominican Republic, seventh hole.

Bernhard Langer's rise to the highest echelons of the game came at the same time as Nick Faldo and Seve Ballesteros transformed the Ryder Cup competition and ushered in a new era of intense rivalry. Langer was a formidable competitor, combining a stoic temperament with a deep Christian faith. A razor-sharp long-iron player, he had to overcome several bouts with the dreaded yips, resorting to a number of highly inventive putting styles. Langer will always be remembered for his decisive role in the "War by the Shore," the 1991 Ryder Cup Match at Kiawah Island. He agonizingly missed an eight-foot putt on the eighteenth green of the Ocean Course and halved his match with Hale Irwin, thereby allowing the United States to take back the Cup with a 14½–13½ victory. Langer played on ten Ryder Cup teams starting in 1981, compiling an overall fine record of 21–15–6, and captained the victorious European team in 2004 at Oakland Hills. **OPPOSITE:** Bernhard Langer in a serene moment during the final round of his 1993 Masters victory. **BELOW:** The moment of agony as Langer misses the putt on the eighteenth hole to give the United States victory in the 1991 Ryder Cup at the Ocean Course.

Laura Davies has been a major force in women's golf for twenty years, starting in the mid-1980s and so far winning sixty-seven times playing in the United States and internationally. By far the greatest English woman professional, she started out playing on the Ladies' European Tour in 1985. Arriving in the United States in 1987, she won the U.S. Women's Open over JoAnne Carner and Ayako Okamoto in an eighteen-hole play-off at Plainfield Country Club in New Jersey, the first of her four career majors. Davies continued to play in both the United States and Europe, dominating the Ladies' European Tour and topping the money list or Order of Merit seven times between 1985 and 2006. A big woman and natural athlete, Davies rockets the ball huge distances with her freewheeling swing and go-for-broke style. She is the only player, European or American, to have played in all ten Solheim Cup matches between 1990 and 2007. Davies has a reputation as a fun-loving free spirit, who on one occasion flew to Las Vegas to gamble all night in between rounds of a tournament in San Diego. **OPPOSITE:** England's Laura Davies playing in the 2005 Solheim Cup match at Crooked Stick in Indiana.

Greg Norman's finest hour came at the 1992 British Open at Royal St. George's, when on a sun-drenched day on the great links that puffs its chest out as it parades through the dunes of the Channel Coast, he shot a flawless final-round 64 to beat his nemesis Nick Faldo by two. It was a moment of redemption for The Shark, who had suffered so many hard knocks in the majors, particularly at the Masters. It 1987 at Augusta, he found himself in a three-way play-off with Seve Ballesteros and Larry Mize. After Ballesteros was eliminated with a bogey, Norman was sitting in the catbird seat on the second play-off hole, safely on the eleventh green while Mize was forty yards off in the right rough, facing a seemingly impossible chip to a downhill green with water on the other side. Mize chipped in and brought the house down. In 1996, a green jacket seemed all but assured when Norman began the final round six shots ahead of playing partner Nick Faldo, after equaling the course record with an opening-round 63. In what would prove to be the nadir of Norman's career, his lead melted away, with his tee shots at the par-3 twelfth and sixteenth both finding water. He finished with a 78 to Faldo's winning 67. **OPPOSITE:** Greg Norman narrowly misses a chip on the fifteenth hole during his disastrous final round in the 1996 Masters. **BELOW:** At the 1994 Players Championship at the TPC Sawgrass, which he won in convincing fashion.

Nick Price was born in Durban, South Africa, to English parents, and grew up in Zimbabwe, which was then Rhodesia. Having won the Junior World Championship in 1974, he turned pro in 1977, initially playing South Africa's Sunshine Tour and then the European Tour. Price joined the PGA Tour in 1983 and promptly won the World Series of Golf, but suffered through a fallow period in which he was best known for a couple of close-but-no–Claret Jug finishes at the British Open in 1982 and 1988. Price revamped his swing working with South African swing shaman David Leadbetter and

transformed himself into a three-time major champion and world-beater. Price won fifteen of his eighteen PGA Tour victories during the 1990s. His wins at the British Open and the PGA in his storied 1994 season made him one of only three players to win two majors during the same year during the 1990s, together with Nick Faldo in 1990 and Mark O'Meara in 1998.
OPPOSITE: Travel poster for Turnberry, the site of Nick Price's 1994 British Open victory. **BELOW:** Price hugs the trophy after winning the 1994 PGA Championship at Southern Hills.

TURNBERRY On the Ayrshire Coast

EXPRESS SERVICES AND TOURIST, HOLIDAY AND WEEK-END TICKETS BY THE LMS

Paul Azinger, who grew up in Holyoke, Massachusetts, where his mother was a top-ranked amateur golfer, was one of the brightest American stars in the late 1980s and early 1990s, when players from overseas were dominating the game. A low-ball hitter with a strong grip, Zinger made up for what he lacked in technique with a deep competitive fire. After playing at Florida State, he turned pro in 1981. In 1987, he won three times on Tour and finished one shot behind Nick Faldo in the British Open, continuing to win at least one event for each of the next seven seasons. The year 1993 proved to be fateful for Azinger. He won the Memorial Tournament in memorable fashion, holing a bunker shot on the final hole to snatch victory from his good friend Payne Stewart, and it was Azinger who would deliver the eulogy at Stewart's memorial service following his tragic death in a plane crash. In August,

Azinger's career crescendo came at the PGA Championship at Inverness, when he birdied four of the last seven holes on Sunday to catch Greg Norman with a 68, and then won on the second hole of sudden death in a spine-tingling play-off with The Shark. Just a few weeks later, after halving his singles match against Faldo in the Ryder Cup, he was diagnosed with lymphoma in his right shoulder. He made a full recovery and returned to the Tour, continuing to enjoy success but never quite achieving the same competitive level. He won the Hawaiian Open for his twelfth Tour victory in 2000, and in 2002 made another Ryder Cup appearance. Azinger has been selected to captain the U.S. team in the 2008 Ryder Cup Match at Valhalla, in Louisville, Kentucky.

OPPOSITE: Paul Azinger chips in on the seventeenth hole in his singles match victory over Seve Ballesteros in the 1989 Ryder Cup at The Belfry.

The legend of "Long John" Daly was born at the 1991 PGA Championship at Crooked Stick, when as an unknown rookie he electrified the golfing world with his three-shot victory and overpowered Pete Dye's revamped layout with his parabolic drives. Indeed, Daly was the ninth and last alternate going into the event and only gained entry into the field when Nick Price dropped out at the last minute. Daly, who was raised in Dardenelles, Arkansas, and played golf for the Razorbacks, gained his good old boy image early in his career. His excesses, which prevented him from realizing the full potential of his enormous raw talent, have been well chronicled. They include battles with alcoholism and compulsive gambling, with Daly claiming to have lost between $50 million and $60 million at Las Vegas casinos over a fifteen-year period. When he won the British Open in 1995 for his second major, he had replaced drinking liquor with a massive consumption of Diet Cokes and candy bars. **OPPOSITE:** John Daly playing at Crooked Stick, outside Indianapolis, during his 1991 PGA victory.

Patty Sheehan was a feisty competitor on the LPGA Tour, who would perform cartwheels on the green after a big win. She joined the Tour in 1980, having been a top junior skier while growing up in Middlebury, Vermont. She won thirty-five events, including six majors, and placed in the top ten on the money list every year from 1982 to 1993. After letting the U.S. Open slip from her grasp in 1990, when she had a commanding nine-shot lead after thirty-six holes, she was the winner at Oakmont in 1992. She won a second U.S. Open at Indianwood Golf and Country Club in 1994. She also won consecutive LPGA Championships in 1983 and 1984, when she dusted the field by ten strokes, and another in 1993. In 2002, Sheehan was the jubilant captain of the winning U.S. Solheim Cup team at Interlachen in Minneapolis.

OPPOSITE: Patty Sheehan keeps her trophy dry after winning the Nabisco Dinah Shore at Mission Hills Country Club in 1996, the last of her six majors.

Fred Couples won the 1992 Masters in memorable fashion when his tee shot to the entrancing but dangerous par-3 twelfth came up short, but miraculously clung to the steep slope instead of rolling down into Rae's Creek. Couples calmly chipped up and made par, and then never looked back. Couples was also a top performer in international events, playing on five consecutive Ryder Cup teams between 1989 and 1997, and on the Presidents Cup team in 1994, 1996, 1998, and 2003. Paired with his friend Davis Love III, he won the World Cup four years running for the U.S., from 1992 to 1995. Couples has also enjoyed great success in the Skins Game, earning over $3.5 million, as well as in other made-for-TV events played in November and December, earning him the sobriquet "King of the Silly Season." **OPPOSITE:** Fred Couples is greeted by teammate Davis Love III after sinking a birdie putt to secure victory for the U.S. in the 1996 Presidents Cup match.

Lee Janzen is a deeply religious man with a sure and steady golf game, traits that are well suited to success in the U.S. Open. Janzen started focusing on golf after his family moved to Lakeland, Florida, when he was twelve. He had to overcome a severed artery in his right arm, suffered in a car accident when he was sixteen. After playing on a Florida Southern team that was the Division II national team champion in 1985 and 1986, Janzen was a relatively unknown young pro when he won the U.S. Open at Baltusrol in 1993 over Payne Stewart, tying the Open record of eight under par. Five years later, he won his second Open, at the Olympic Club, again beating Stewart. This time he shot a final-round 68 to make up a five-stroke deficit. Apart from his two

U.S. Open victories, Janzen has had a fairly low-key career, but he won eight tournaments between 1992 and 1998, including the Players Championship, the Kemper Open, and the Sprint International in 1995. Janzen's success in the Open is reminiscent of some other understated players with surefire swings who have shone in the event—such as two-time winner Andy North in 1978 and 1985, Larry Nelson, the 1983 champion, and Scott Simpson, who won at Olympic in 1987. **OPPOSITE:** Lee Janzen putting on the fourth hole during his victory at the 1993 U.S. Open at Baltusrol. **BELOW:** Being congratulated by Payne Stewart after winning the 1993 U.S. Open.

José Maria Olazábal was born and still lives in Fuenterrabía, just across the French border in Spain's Basque region, where both his grandfather and father worked at the venerable San Sebastian Golf Club. Olazábal turned pro in 1985, one year after winning the British Amateur over Colin Montgomerie at Formby, quickly becoming the heir apparent to Seve Ballesteros as Spain's leading golfer and a top international player. Olazábal has won more than twenty times on the European Tour, as well as six PGA events, beginning with the 1990 World Series of Golf at Firestone, when he destroyed the field to win by twelve shots. His greatest triumphs have come at Augusta, a course well suited to his game, where he has compensated for a few stray drives with a short game of sheer genius. Ollie won his first green jacket in 1994, following in the footsteps of Ballesteros to become the second Spaniard to win the Masters. In 1999, he finished ahead of Greg Norman to claim his second Masters title. **OPPOSITE:** José Maria Olazábal (in white shirt) on the way to victory in the final round of the 1994 Masters.

Dottie Pepper joined the LPGA Tour in 1988, after being named an all-American three times while attending Furman University. One of the premier players of the 1990s before injuries slowed her down, she won the Dinah Shore in 1992, beating Julie Inkster in a play-off, and again in 1999, with a record score of nineteen under par. She finished in the top ten in the money list ten times between 1991 and 2001. Pepper was a particularly fiery competitor and is best known for her outstanding record in the Solheim Cup. Playing on six U.S. Solheim Cup teams, she had an overall record of 13–5–2, and was 5–1 in her singles matches. Pepper is now a commentator for the Golf Channel. **OPPOSITE:** Dottie Pepper during the 2002 Solheim Cup Match at Interlachen in Minneapolis. **BELOW:** Interlachen Golf Club.

The possessor of a repeating piston of a swing and a warm, engaging personality, Nick Price was a particularly popular champion in the 1990s. Almost unbeatable when his putting was in synch, Price won his first major in 1992 at the PGA at Bellerive Country Club in St. Louis. The following year, he became the top-ranked player in the world, winning four times on the PGA Tour, including the Players Championship. The best was yet to come. In 1994, the floodgates opened with six victories, including the British Open at Turnberry, the PGA at Southern Hills, and the Canadian Open. Price's thrilling win at Turnberry was the crest of his career—when he sank a gigantic fifty-five-foot putt on the par-5 seventeenth for an eagle, pandemonium broke out. The front-runner, Jesper Parnevik, not realizing that he had a two-shot lead playing the eighteenth ahead of Price, fired at the flag on his second and came up short, making bogey to finish one back. Price was accompanied on all his victory marches by his trusty caddie Jeff "Squeaky" Medlin, a popular figure in his own right, who succumbed to leukemia in 1997. **OPPOSITE:** Nick Price stares down the eagle putt on the seventeenth hole in the final round of the 1994 British Open at Turnberry, lifting him to victory.

In the 1980s, Tom Weiskopf began focusing his energies on course design, forming a highly successful partnership with Jay Morrish, who had worked with Jack Nicklaus earlier in his career. Weiskopf also found time to win the 1995 U.S. Senior Open at Congressional. The tandem of Weiskopf and Morrish produced a number of outstanding courses in Arizona, where Weiskopf is based, including Forest Highlands, Troon North, and Estancia. They are also responsible for Double Eagle in Columbus and Shadow Glen in Kansas City. Weiskopf's personal favorite is Loch Lomond, completed in 1992, the site of the annual Scottish Open on the European Tour the week before the British Open. An enchanting course that skips along the shore of the bonnie Loch and over pleated streams and peat bogs, it features fairways that lie beneath Rossdhu House, the eighteenth-century Georgian mansion that serves as the clubhouse. Since striking out on his own, Weiskopf's design work has included the Desert Course at Cabo del Sol in Mexico; Lahontan Golf Club near Lake Tahoe; and the Falls Golf Club at the Lake Las Vegas resort. **OPPOSITE:** Lee Westwood putting on the sixth green during the 2006 Barclays Scottish Open at Loch Lomond Golf Club, designed by Tom Weiskopf and Jay Morrish.

Ben Crenshaw grew up in Austin, Texas, where he learned the game under the tutelage of Harvey Penick. In 1995, Crenshaw served as a pallbearer at Penick's funeral on the Wednesday before the Masters, then went on to win his second green jacket at age forty-three in one of the most heartwarming victories in the history of the game. Crenshaw played inspired golf throughout the tournament. After holing his final tap-in, he was overcome with emotion and collapsed in the arms of his veteran Augusta caddie, Carl Jackson. A keen and reflective student of golf's history, with a self-effacing manner, there has never been a more popular winner. **OPPOSITE:** Ben Crenshaw is overcome with emotion after winning the 1995 Masters. **BELOW:** At home in his golf library in 1990.

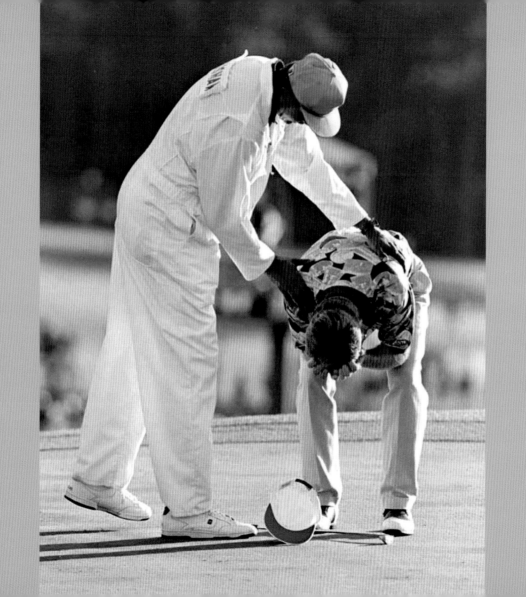

Corey Pavin was a throwback to an earlier style of play, a will-o'-the-wisp golfer who used finesse over brawn to win the U.S. Open and a bunch of events both on the PGA Tour and in Asia, New Zealand, and Europe. Born in Oxnard, California, Pavin starred on a UCLA golf team that included future Tour players Jay Delsing, Tom Pernice, Jr., Duffy Waldorf, and Steve Pate. Pavin always seemed to be in contention, winning fourteen times on Tour between 1984 and 1996, with a spellbinding short game in the tradition of Paul Runyan and Dave Stockton. Pavin found his path to glory at the 1995 U.S. Open at Shinnecock, when he started the final round trailing leader Greg Norman by three shots. His final-round 68 was emblazoned with one of the greatest closing shots in Open history, a boring, 238-yard four-wood that skipped on the green to six feet of the pin. The following year, Pavin won at Colonial. Then his game fell off a cliff. In 2006, ten years after his last Tour win, he came out of oblivion to win at Milwaukee, breaking the Tour record for nine holes with a scorching eight-under-par 26 on the front nine of the Brown Deer Park Golf Course. **OPPOSITE:** Corey Pavin putting for victory on the final hole of the 1995 U.S. Open at Shinnecock Hills.

The silky-swinging Steve Elkington grew up in Wagga Wagga, near the Australian outback. After learning the game at the Wagga Wagga Golf Club, he was recruited to play for the University of Houston, where he anchored the 1984 and 1985 NCAA championship teams. Elkington's notable wins on the PGA Tour include the Players Championship in 1991 and 1997, the season-opening Mercedes Championship in 1995, and the Doral Open in 1997 and 1999. He was also in the hunt in several majors. His lone major victory came in the 1995 PGA Championship at Riviera, when he sank a twenty-foot birdie putt in sudden death to dash Colin Montgomerie's chances. He also finished tied for second in the 2002 British Open at Muirfield, losing to Ernie Els in the four-man, four-hole play-off. "Elk" would undoubtedly have won more, but he was hampered by recurring health problems, including severe sinus trouble from an allergy to grass—or at least to grass in the United States. **OPPOSITE:** Riviera Country Club, sixteenth hole, the site of Steve Elkington's win in the 1995 PGA. **BELOW:** Elkington in action during the 1995 PGA.

Meg Mallon attended Ohio State University before joining the LPGA Tour in 1987. In 1991, she won the first of her two U.S. Women's Open titles, at Colonial in Fort Worth, and captured the LPGA Championship the same year. Her second victory in the Open came thirteen years later, the longest gap between Open victories in the history of the event. In the 2004 Open held at The Orchards in South Hadley, Massachusetts, a Donald Ross–designed gem, Mallon staved off Annika Sörenstam with a final-round six-under-par 65. She won the Canadian Women's Open a week later, becoming the first woman to win both the U.S. and Canadian titles in the same year. Mallon has also been a stalwart on the Solheim Cup team, making the U.S. team eight times through 2005. **OPPOSITE:** An ecstatic Meg Mallon after winning the U.S. Women's Open at The Orchards on July 4, 2004.

John Daly has lived and died by the motto "grip it and rip it," with a swing that goes so far past parallel that it is in a contortionist class of its own. Daly's unique swing generates enormous power—he has astounded galleries with his 300-yard-plus drives. His immense abilities, combining power with finesse, were on full display in his victory at the 1995 British Open at St. Andrews, earning him his second major. Playing in near gale-force winds in the final round, Daly's game was flawless. He had the victory seemingly sewn up when Italy's Costantino Rocca, needing birdie to tie, stubbed his chip shot from the Valley of Sin in front of the eighteenth green. In one of the most unlikely recoveries in golfing history, Rocca then holed his next shot,

a seventy-foot putt from the front of the green. But Daly proved to be rock-solid in the four-hole play-off, and when Rocca took a 7 at the Road Hole, the Claret Jug was his. With various troubles on and off the course, Daly has never been able to sustain the form he showed at St. Andrews, but he remains golf's popular Everyman and something of a folk hero. He has his own reality TV show on the Golf Channel and recorded an autobiographical country album titled *My Life*. **OPPOSITE:** The Road Hole at St. Andrews, No. 17. **BELOW:** Costantino Rocca congratulates John Daly at the end of their play-off in the 1995 Open at St. Andrews.

In the 1996 Masters, Nick Faldo was paired with Greg Norman in the final group, and while the haunting impression of that final round will always be Norman's irreversible free fall from a six-shot lead, it also featured a flawlessly played 67 by Faldo that gave him a five-stroke margin of victory. To Faldo's credit, he also displayed genuine sympathy for Norman, who finished with a 78. During the 1990s, Faldo anchored the Europeans in the Ryder Cup, accompanied by his no-nonsense caddie, Sweden's Fannie Sunesson. He played in a record eleven straight matches from 1977 to 1997, and holds the record for most wins and most points, with a record of 23–19–4. Faldo, who was notably withdrawn as a player, became the lead golf analyst for CBS television and the Golf Channel in 2007, displaying a dry sense of humor and engaging insight. **OPPOSITE:** Nick Faldo gives a handshake and encouragement to Greg Norman after winning the 1996 Masters.

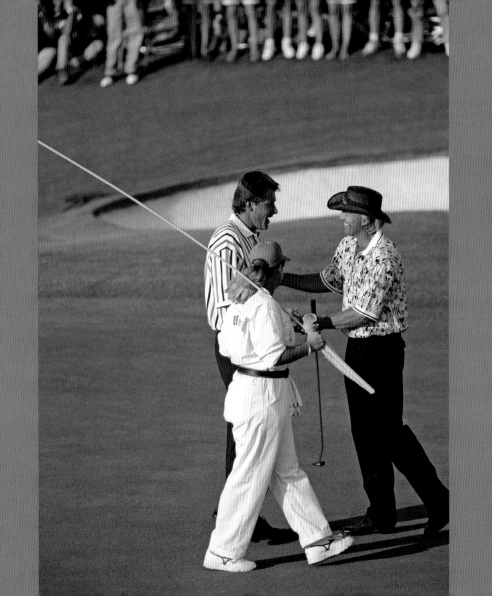

The brightest star on the LPGA Tour during the late 1970s and 1980s, Nancy Lopez won the LPGA Championship three times, but, like Sam Snead, victory in the U.S. Open always eluded her. She finished second four times, including once as an amateur in 1975. In 1997, near the end of her regular playing career, she came agonizingly close to achieving victory at Pumpkin Ridge in Portland, in one of the most memorable finishes in the history of the event.

Despite shooting four rounds in the 60s, a record in the Women's Open, she lost by one shot to the diminutive but doughty Alison Nicholas of England. In 2005, Lopez captained the winning American Solheim Cup team at Crooked Stick in Indiana. **OPPOSITE:** Nancy Lopez playing at Hershey Country Club in 1978. **BELOW:** Embracing a victorious Alison Nicholas after their duel at Pumpkin Ridge in the 1997 U.S. Women's Open.

Brad Faxon is a contemporary player who displays an appreciation for golf's traditions and an affinity for links golf. In that respect, as well as his other-worldly putting touch, he shares much in common with Ben Crenshaw. After starring at Furman University and turning pro in 1983, Faxon was a very steady performer for twenty years, before a knee injury in 2003 slowed him down. In 1995, he shot a scorching 28 on the front nine of Riviera in the PGA Championship, on his way to a final round of 63, which earned him a berth on the Ryder Cup team. With his friend, fellow PGA tour veteran and Rhode Island high school teammate Billy Andrade, Faxon started the Billy Andrade/Brad Faxon Charities for Children, Inc. Since 1999, Faxon and Andrade have hosted the CVS Charity Classic tournament played at Rhode Island Country Club each June, not far from Faxon's home in Barrington, with the proceeds going to benefit their charity. **OPPOSITE:** Brad Faxon playing out of trouble in the 1995 Ryder Cup at Rochester's Oak Hill.

Tom Lehman struggled to gain a foothold on the PGA Tour, but by the mid-1990s he had ascended to the top ranks, injecting a strong American presence back into the game along with other major winners such as Fred Couples, Corey Pavin, Davis Love, and Justin Leonard. A native Minnesotan and devout Christian, Lehman spent a number of years in the golfing wilderness. He played the Tour in anonymity from 1983 to 1985, and then spent six years playing overseas before regaining his PGA Tour card after dominating the Ben Hogan Tour in 1991. In 1996, he won the British Open at Royal Lytham & St. Annes to claim his sole major, the first American to win there since Bobby Jones had done so seventy years earlier. That same year, in a humdinger of a finish at the U.S. Open at Oakland Hills, Lehman and Steve Jones battled each other coming down the stretch, until Lehman's drive on the final hole trickled through the hourglass fairway into a bunker, and Jones hit a magnificent approach from the fairway to seal a one-stroke victory. Lehman capped off his year by winning the Tour Championship and climbing to the number one ranking in the world. An unflinching competitor, he won his singles matches in the Ryder Cup in 1995, 1997, and in the tumultuous U.S. victory in 1999. In 2006 at Ireland's K Club, Lehman was the popular captain of the U.S. team, which was KO'd by the Europeans. **OPPOSITE:** Tom Lehman acknowledges the gallery after winning the 1996 British Open at Royal Lytham and St. Annes.

Davis Love III, one of the most popular and thoughtful American pros, grew up immersed in the game as the son of the prominent instructor Davis Love, Jr., who lost his life in a 1988 plane crash. Indeed, Love was born shortly after his father almost won the 1964 Masters. Love starred as a three-time all-American at the University of North Carolina before turning pro in 1985. Known early in his career for his humongous drives, he throttled back his arcing swing to achieve greater consistency. In 1987, Love won the MCI Heritage Classic for his first Tour victory, an event he has reigned over with five wins. His nineteen career PGA victories also include the Players Championship in 1992 and 2003—a year in which he won four times. While Love contended in a bevy of majors during the 1990s, his shining moment came at the 1997 PGA Championship at Winged Foot, shooting three rounds of 66 in a commanding performance that saw him walk down the final fairway just as a rainbow broke through the firmament. He also teamed with his friend Fred Couples to win the World Cup four straight years from 1992 through 1995, with Love taking the individual title in 1995 at Mission Hills in China. Love also has a successful course design business with his younger brother and caddie, Mark. **OPPOSITE:** Davis Love III during his victory in the 1997 PGA Championship at Winged Foot. **BELOW:** Love and partner Fred Couples lift the trophy after winning the 1992 World Cup for the United States at Madrid's La Moraleja Golf Club.

Ernie Els, South Africa's golfing colossus, has continued the grand international golfing tradition of Gary Player, although a marked contrast to Player in both personality and physique. A gifted all-around athlete, Els was a junior tennis champion before deciding to devote himself to golf, winning the Junior World Golf Championship in San Diego in 1984, with Phil Mickelson finishing second. He turned pro in 1989 and put his stamp on the game early in his career, winning the first of his two U.S. Opens at parlous Oakmont in 1994. The strapping and modest Els awed the golf world with his combination of power and finesse, finishing tied with Loren Roberts and Colin Montgomerie, and then winning a roller-coaster twenty-hole play-off, beating Roberts on the second hole of sudden death. In 1997, he won his second U.S. Open, this time at a revamped Congressional, outside Washington, D.C., again withstanding the crucible of pressure in a tight finish when he parred in, hitting a five-iron onto the green on the seventeenth and finding the green on the par-3 eighteenth to finish one ahead of Montgomerie. Like Player, Els has also demonstrated his commitment to play around the world, with fifteen wins to date on the U.S. Tour and twenty-two on the European Tour, including victories in Dubai, Qatar, and at the Johnnie Walker Classic in Asia, as well as numerous wins in South Africa. **OPPOSITE:** Ernie Els chips in for birdie on the tenth hole on his way to winning the 1997 U.S. Open at Congressional Country Club.

Colin Montgomerie was Europe's top player throughout the 1990s, leading the Order of Merit or money list seven years running, from 1993 through 1999, and garnering some thirty European Tour victories to date. The son of the secretary of Royal Troon, his long, arching swing produces a highly reliable and accurate fade that seems invariably to split the fairway. Monty has repeatedly come close in the majors but has suffered a series of misfortunes, beginning with his runner-up finish in the memorable 1992 U.S. Open at Pebble Beach, when he was congratulated by Jack Nicklaus as the winner in the clubhouse, only to be undone by Tom Kite's remarkable closing round. In 1994, he lost to Ernie Els in the three-man play-off at Oakmont. The strapping South African was to prove his nemesis again in 1997, when Mongomerie three-putted the seventeenth hole at Congressional to finish a stroke back, while enduring a testy relationship with American spectators that earned him the nickname "Mrs. Doubtfire." Other close-but-no-cigar finishes in majors include a play-off loss to Steve Elkington in the 1995 PGA at Riviera. The bitterest disappointment of all came at the 2006 U.S. Open at Winged Foot, when he stood in the middle of the fairway on the final hole with a seven-iron in hand needing only a par for victory, but instead pushed his approach to the right and made double bogey. Montgomerie has been a tower of strength in his many Ryder Cup appearances, compiling an overall record in thirty-six matches of 20–9–7 from 1991 to 2006, and serving as the leader of the European team. **OPPOSITE:** Colin Montgomerie (center left) chats with teammate Darren Clarke on the practice range before the start of the 2006 Ryder Cup at Ireland's K Club. **BELOW:** Lining up a putt during the second round of the 1994 U.S. Open at Oakmont, which he would lose in a three-way play-off to Ernie Els.

Valderrama Golf Club, the top-ranked course in Continental Europe, is located at the more secluded western end of Spain's Costa del Sol, not far from Gilbraltar. Designed by Robert Trent Jones in 1975 and originally named Sotogrande New, the course was purchased in 1985 by Jaime Ortiz Patiño, heir to a Bolivian tin fortune. Patiño lavished attention on the course, bringing Jones back to redesign the layout from 1985 through 1990, and built a tiled Andalusian clubhouse. The course sways through cork oaks, with pampered fairways that make Valderrama the Augusta National of Spain.

In 1997, Valderrama became the first and so far only course on the Continent to host the Ryder Cup, with the European team captained by Seve Ballesteros bounding to victory. The course also hosts the Volvo Masters, which caps off the PGA European Tour's season. The clubhouse contains Patiño's private golf museum, an Aladdin's treasure of rare books, artwork, artifacts, and antique clubs and balls, including splendid examples of eighteenth- and nineteenth-century long-nosed drivers. **OPPOSITE:** Valderrama Golf Club, fifteenth hole, San Roque, Spain.

Seve Ballesteros's career is inextricably linked to the history of the Ryder Cup. His emergence as a top player coincided with the decision to allow Continental players to compete in 1979 on what had previously been the Great Britain and Ireland side. His participation gave the event a much-needed shot in the arm, the European side quickly becoming keenly competitive after many years of American dominance. Ballesteros brought a "take no prisoners" attitude to the competition, and was accused of poor gamesmanship by his American opponents over the years. Compiling an outstanding overall Ryder Cup record of 20–12–5, he was particularly invincible when paired with his compatriot José Maria Olazábal. In 1997, he put every fiber of his being into his role as captain, leading the European team to a historic 14 ½–13 ½ victory at Valderrama in the Ryder Cup Match. The Seve Trophy was introduced in 2000 as a Ryder Cup–style event played between teams from Continental Europe and Great Britain/Ireland. **OPPOSITE:** Teammates Seve Ballesteros (left) and José Maria Olazábal shake hands after their victory in the 1989 Ryder Cup at The Belfry.

José Maria Olazábal was riding high after winning the 1994 Masters when he began suffering excruciating foot pain the following year. Barely able to walk, he missed all of 1996 with what was misdiagnosed as arthritis but was eventually traced to a herniated disk in his lower back. After it had looked like he would never play again, Olazábal was the comeback winner at Augusta in 1999. He has been half of the Ryder Cup's most celebrated tandem, teaming with Seve Ballesteros in his Cup debut to lead Europe to its historic victory on American soil, at Muirfield Village in 1987. Playing together, the Spanish duo were nearly unbeatable, compiling a record of eleven wins, two losses, and two halves. Olazábal has continued to excel in the Ryder Cup, defeating Phil Mickelson in their singles match in 2006 at the K Club and teaming with compatriot Sergio García to take down Mickelson and Chris DiMarco. **OPPOSITE:** José Maria Olazábal receives the green jacket from Bernhard Langer after winning the 1994 Masters. **BELOW:** With teammate Sergio García before their fourball victory over Phil Mickelson and Chris DiMarco in the 2006 Ryder Cup.

Mark O'Meara was a steady winner on the PGA Tour but was never king of the hill until his double major year of 1998, when he won both the Masters and the British Open in razzle-dazzle fashion. The affable "Marko" also has served as a close friend, confidant, and mentor to the younger Tiger Woods, while some of Woods's intensity seems to have rubbed off on O'Meara. Overall, O'Meara has eighteen Tour victories and a well-known love affair with Pebble Beach, where he won the Crosby/AT&T National Pro-Am five times. In 1998, when he was forty-one, O'Meara won the Masters with a bang-bang finish, birdying both the seventeenth and eighteenth holes; he curled in a fifteen-foot putt to beat Fred Couples and David Duval by a stroke. In the Open at Royal Birkdale,

O'Meara's final-round 68 left him tied with little-known Brian Watts, whose success had come on the Japanese Tour, with O'Meara coming out ahead in the four-hole play-off. He also relishes international competition, and closed out his triumphant campaign in 1998 by defeating Woods in the final of the World Match Play at Wentworth. He teamed with Woods the following year to win the World Cup at the Mines Resort in Kuala Lumpur. **OPPOSITE:** Mark O'Meara tees off during the final round of the 2007 Senior British Open at Muirfield. **BELOW:** Arms upraised after holing the birdie putt on the eighteenth to win the 1998 Masters.

Julie Inkster has had a brilliant career on the LPGA Tour, winning thirty-one tournaments, including seven majors, since turning pro in 1983. As Julie Simpson, she matched the record of Glenna Collett Vare and Virginia Van Wie of winning the U.S. Women's Amateur three years in succession, pulling off the hat trick from 1980 to 1982. She won her first major in 1984, beating Pat Bradley on the first hole of a sudden-death play-off in the Nabisco Dinah Shore. Much of Inkster's success has come late in her career. She won five events in 1999, including the U.S. Women's Open at Old Waverly in Mississippi, setting a record for the Open of sixteen under par, as well as the LPGA Championship. In 2002, she won her second Open, firing a red-hot 66 in the final round at Prairie Dunes in Kansas to overcome Annika Sörenstam's two-stroke lead. With her Open victory in 1999, Inkster joined Pat Bradley as only the second woman to achieve the career grand slam of winning the Nabisco Dinah Shore, the du Maurier Classic, the U.S. Women's Open, and the LPGA Championship.

OPPOSITE: Julie Inkster celebrates a birdie putt on the sixteenth hole on the way to victory in the 2002 U.S. Women's Open at Prairie Dunes.

Justin Leonard, a native Texan who won the 1994 individual NCAA Championship for the Longhorns, joined the PGA Tour with high expectations that were quickly fulfilled. He won the 1997 British Open at Troon, displaying his superior short game and satin-smooth putting touch in overcoming a five-shot lead by Jesper Parnevik heading into the final round. Leonard looked like he would win a second Open in 1999, when he was the beneficiary of Jean van de Velde's cataclysmic eighteenth-hole collapse at Carnoustie, but he ended up losing to Paul Lawrie in the three-man play-off. Another near miss in the majors came at the 2004 PGA, when Vijay Singh won the three-man play-off at Whistling Straits that included Chris DiMarco. Leonard will be forever remembered for what ranks as the most scintillating single putt in Ryder Cup history, when his forty-five-foot birdie putt made a beeline for the seventeenth hole at The Country Club to give the United States its fabled comeback victory in 1999. A spontaneous victory celebration erupted on the green even though José Maria Olazábal still had a chance to halve the match, prompting charges of bad sportsmanship. When Olazábal missed his long putt, victory belonged to the Americans. **OPPOSITE:** Justin Leonard at the PGA Grand Slam of Golf at Poipu Bay, Hawaii in 1997. **BELOW:** Leonard erupts after sinking his long birdie putt to give the U.S. its thrilling victory in the 1999 Ryder Cup at Brookline.

Although the Swedish men golfers have had to take a backseat to their female counterparts, particularly Annika Sörenstam, Jesper Parnevik achieved the most success of a talented group that includes Anders Forsbrand, Joakim Haeggman, Pierre Fulke, and Per-Ulrik Johansson, with Henrik Stenson currently leading the Scandinavian brigade. The son of Bo Parnevik, the Bob Hope of Sweden, Parnevik is also well known for his eccentricities off the course, which include dining on volcanic sand. Earlier in his career he always wore the bill of his cap upturned, and his current wardrobe is decidedly avant-garde, featuring clothes by designer Johan Lindeberg that range from a tie-and-vest ensemble to bright purple trousers. A Ryder Cup member in 1997, 1999, and 2002, he played brilliantly in 1999 at Brookline to win 3 ½ out of 4

points in his matches. Parnevik has had success on both sides of the Atlantic, with five PGA victories between 1998 and 2001. In the majors, he has played his best golf at the British Open, losing by a shot to Nick Price at Turnberry in 1994 after bogeying the final hole, and finishing runner-up to Justin Leonard in 1997. Another claim to fame is that he introduced Tiger Woods to his future wife, Elin Nordegren, a Swedish model who worked as Parnevik's nanny. **OPPOSITE:** Jesper Parnevik on the sixth hole during the third round of the 2003 British Open at Royal St. George's. **BELOW:** Parnevik celebrates a chip-in on the twelfth hole with teammate Sergio García during their fourball victory over Jim Furyk and Phil Mickelson in the 1999 Ryder Cup.

Hal Sutton was brought up in Shreveport, Louisiana, the son of a wealthy oilman. His career has had two distinct phases, an early one when he, like Johnny Miller before him, was hailed as the heir apparent to Jack Nicklaus, and a late resurgence after he turned forty. An all-American at Louisiana's Centenary College, Sutton joined the Tour in 1982, and with his square-jawed and blond good looks, he resembled the Golden Bear both in build and golf game. In 1983, he was leading money winner and Player of the Year when he won the Players Championship and PGA Championship at Riviera, finishing one shot ahead of Nicklaus. Sutton lost his way from 1987 to 1997, and when he emerged from the golfing wilderness in 1998, he found himself in the Tiger Woods era. Sutton won six times between 1998 and 2001, including the 2000 Players Championship, when he went mano a mano with Woods, to give him a total of fourteen Tour wins. Sutton also spearheaded the American comeback in the 1999 Ryder Cup at Brookline, with a 3–1–1 record. A firebrand of a competitor, he was captain of the 2004 squad that went down to a decisive defeat at Oakland Hills. **OPPOSITE:** Hal Sutton (right) after winning the 1983 PGA by one stroke over Jack Nicklaus at Riviera Country Club.

Golf course architect Rees Jones, the younger son of legendary architect Robert Trent Jones, attended Yale and also studied landscape architecture at Harvard. He began his career working with his father in his hometown of Montclair, New Jersey, while his older brother, Robert Trent Jones, Jr., was based in the firm's California office. In 1974, Rees started his own firm, and in addition to designing a series of high-end private courses, he developed a reputation as "The Open Doctor," revitalizing and strengthening several classic U.S. Open venues—as his father had done at Oakland Hills and Baltusrol. Jones received acclaim for his sensitive restoration of The Country Club in preparation for the 1988 U.S. Open. That was followed by returning A. W. Tillinghast's Black Course at Bethpage State Park to its full glory before the 2002 U.S. Open, when it became the first public course to host the Open. Jones also remodeled Congressional, the site of the 1997 U.S. Open; Hazeltine, which had originally been designed by his father; and Torrey Pines's South Course in advance of the 2008 U.S. Open. His original creations include Atlantic Golf Club and The Bridge in the Hamptons; Huntsville Golf Club in Wilkes-Barre, Pennsylvania; Ocean Forest, hemmed by the Hampton River and the Atlantic in Sea Island, Georgia, and which hosted the 2001 Walker Cup; Redstone Golf Club (Tournament Course), site of the Shell Houston Open; and the Golf Club at Briar's Creek, routed along the Kiawah River on Johns Island, South Carolina. **OPPOSITE:** Ocean Forest Golf Club in Sea Island, Georgia, designed by Rees Jones, seventeenth hole.

In 1991, Payne Stewart won the first of his two U.S. Opens, coming from two strokes down with three holes to play at Hazeltine to catch Scott Simpson, the Open winner at Olympic in 1987. Stewart then won the eighteen-hole play-off by two shots the next day. Stewart came close to winning two more U.S. Opens, finishing one shot behind Lee Janzen at Baltusrol in 1993 and, in bit of déjà vu, one off Janzen's pace at Olympic in 1998. In 1999, Stewart achieved his greatest and gutsiest win, outdueling playing partner Phil Mickelson, a young Tiger Woods, and Vijay Singh in a scintillating finish at Pinehurst No. 2. Stewart poured in a fifteen-foot par putt on the eighteenth hole to win the championship, punching the air in one of the Open's defining moments. At the peak of his fame and popularity, Stewart died tragically in October of that year, leaving behind his wife and two young children, when the private plane on which he was traveling lost pressure over northern Florida, eventually crashing in South Dakota. **OPPOSITE:** An elated Payne Stewart after birdying the seventeenth hole at Troon during the 1989 British Open. **BELOW:** The indelible moment of winning the 1999 U.S. Open at Pinehurst No. 2.

Lee Westwood, who was born in Worksop in Nottinghamshire, was the big name in English golf in the late 1990s, combining power with a deft putting touch. While he has never conquered the majors, he has been one of Europe's top players, winning seventeen times on the European Tour, as well as winning the 1997 Australian Open and three successive Taiheyo Masters in Japan from 1996 to 1998. In 2000, he won five tournaments on the European Tour, including his second Deutsche Bank title and the Smurfit European Open, ending Colin Montgomerie's seven-year run atop the Order of Merit. Westwood's game has slipped in recent years, but he continues to be a major factor in Europe's Ryder Cup fortunes, having played on every European team since 1997, when he teamed with Nick Faldo. In 2006 at the K Club, Westwood was a captain's pick with Darren Clarke. He went undefeated in five matches, including teaming with Clarke to sink the top U.S. pairing of Tiger Woods and Jim Furyk in four-balls, bringing his career record to 14–8–3. Westwood is married to Laurae Coltart, sister of Scottish pro Andrew Coltart. **OPPOSITE:** Lee Westwood putting on the third green during the 2000 Dutch Open at Noordwijkse Golf Club. **BELOW:** In 2006 at the Dukes Course Skins Game in Scotland.

Vijay Singh has been one of Tiger Woods' principal rivals for golfing supremacy and one of the game's modern "Big Four" with Woods, Ernie Els, and Phil Mickelson. Singh had a harder and more circuitous route to the top than his rivals. Born in Lautoka, in Fiji, of Indian parentage, he was introduced to the game at age eleven by his father, Mohan, who was a good golfer. Singh developed a relentless will to succeed in golf and is renowned for practicing harder than any other player in the game, spending long hours pounding balls at the range. Tall and powerful, he modeled his swing after Tom Weiskopf's and studied old instruction books. Early in his career, after turning professional in 1982, Singh endured a period of exile when he was suspended from the Asian Tour in 1985 for allegedly lowering his score, which he denied. He then worked as the pro at the Keningau Club on Borneo and played the African or Safari Tour in the late 1980s, winning the Nigerian Open twice. Singh qualified for the European Tour in 1988, and then made it to the PGA Tour in 1993, where he quickly found success, winning five tournaments between 1993 and 1997. In 1998, he broke through to win the PGA Championship, the first of his three majors, threading his way through the ponderosa pines of Washington State's Sahalee Golf Club. **OPPOSITE:** Vijay Singh after winning the 2004 PGA Championship at Whistling Straits in Kohler, Wisconsin. **BELOW:** Sahalee Country Club, ninth hole, site of Singh's victory in the 1998 PGA Championship.

Phil Mickelson was a golfing prodigy, destined for greatness at an early age, and also a golfing rarity in playing left-handed. Reared in San Diego, he attended Arizona State, where he won the individual NCAA Championship three times, as well as the 1990 U.S. Amateur. In 1991, he became the last amateur to win a PGA tournament, taking the Tucson Open. Mickelson has had a vaunted career since turning pro in 1992, but for several years it looked as if he was jinxed in the majors and might never get the weight of expectations off his back. Mickelson's woes in the majors stemmed from two main factors. One was his golfing hubris—his aggressive, gambling style of play often cost him. The other was the downright difficulty of beating Tiger Woods. In the 2004 Masters, Mickelson broke through, winning in exhilarating and exultant fashion with a fifteen-foot birdie putt on the final hole. With his blond, boy-next-door good looks, sheepish grin, and analytical personality, Mickelson has been a very popular player. His first major win, setting up a continuing rivalry with Woods, was greeted with great fanfare. **OPPOSITE:** Phil Mickelson jumps for joy after holing his birdie putt on the final hole for victory in the 2004 Masters.

Annika Sörenstam, who dominated contemporary women's golf until a neck injury slowed her down in 2007, may well be the greatest woman golfer of all time. Born in Stockholm, she seemed headed for a career in pro tennis—her early sporting idol was Björn Borg—before deciding to focus on golf, playing at the Bro-Balsta Golf Club five minutes from her home. She came to the United States on a golf scholarship to the University of Arizona, leading the Wildcats to the 1991 NCAA Championship, and turned pro in 1992 after her sophomore year. Her first win on the LPGA Tour came at the 1995 U.S. Women's Open, when she came back to finish one ahead of Meg Mallon at the Broadmoor in Colorado Springs. She successfully defended the following year by firing a final-round 66 at Pine Needles, the Donald Ross diamond down the road from Pinehurst. Ten years later, in 2006, having established herself as a powerhouse in the women's game, she won her third U.S. Open, and the tenth major of her career, at historic Newport, defeating Pat Hurst in a play-off. Sörenstam began 2008 with sixty-nine wins on the LPGA Tour, third on the all-time list behind Kathy Whitworth and Mickey Wright, as well as sixteen other victories around the world. **OPPOSITE:** Annika Sörenstam putts in the first round of the 2006 U.S. Women's Open at Newport Country Club, which she went on to win.

TIGER WOODS BURNS BRIGHT—AND NEW STARS SHINE

324 | **THE WONDER CHILD OF GOLF**

Eldrick "Tiger" Woods has dominated and transformed modern golf, already leaving a greater stamp on the sport than any player in history since he turned professional in 1996. Born in Cypress, California, on December 30, 1975, Woods was an immense prodigy—he began to play at age two and appeared on television's *Mike Douglas Show* in a putting contest against Bob Hope before he turned three. Woods was coached in the psychological aspects of the game by his late father, Earl, a Green Beret in the U.S. Army who served in the Vietnam War, where he met and married Kultida Woods, who is Thai. Earl Woods instilled a fierce competitive spirit in his son, giving him his nickname after a Vietnamese soldier friend. Before turning pro, Woods had a now legendary amateur career, winning the U.S. Amateur in 1996 for a record third consecutive time in a spellbinding sudden-death final match against Steve Scott and taking the individual NCAA title while playing for Stanford, which he attended for two years. Through the 2007 season, Woods had won thirteen major tournaments, second all-time to Jack Nicklaus, and was on a pace to shatter Nicklaus's record of eighteen majors and Sam Snead's record of eighty-two PGA Tour victories. **OPPOSITE:** Tiger Woods teeing off on the eleventh hole during the third round of the 2007 BMW Championship played at Chicago's Cog Hill Golf and Country Club. **BELOW:** Woods putting at the seventh hole at Pebble Beach en route to his runaway win in the 2000 U.S. Open.

Vijay Singh has won thirty-one tournaments on the PGA Tour and a dozen more on the European Tour, of which nineteen have come since he turned forty in 2003. After winning the PGA in 1998, his second major victory came at the 2000 Masters, when he overcame the putting travails that had held him back in the past. In 2004, Singh chalked up one of the greatest single-season performances in history, winning nine times on Tour, starting with the AT&T Pebble Beach Pro-Am. He won the third major of his career that year, capturing the PGA at Wisconsin's Whistling Straits, Pete Dye's bodacious, bunker-strewn, man-made links overlooking Lake Michigan. After shooting rounds of 67, 68, and 69, Singh closed with a final-round 76 to fall into a tie with Justin Leonard and Chris DiMarco. After going all day without a birdie, he proceeded to pulverize his drive down the middle on the first play-off hole for a ho-hum birdie and won the three-hole play-off. His ninth win came in September at the Deutsche Bank Championship outside Boston, giving him more than $10 million in earnings for the year and a perch as the number one player in the world, bumping Tiger Woods from the top spot that he had occupied for 264 straight weeks. Singh has continued to add to his victory tally, winning the season-opening Mercedes Championship and the Arnold Palmer Invitational in 2007. **OPPOSITE:** Vijay Singh playing the fourth hole at Whistling Straits during the final round on his way to winning the 2004 PGA Championship.

David Duval's career has been one of the great enigmas of contemporary golf. The son of pro golfer Bob Duval, who played on the Champions Tour, Duval grew up in Jacksonville and was a four-time all-American at Georgia Tech before earning his PGA Tour card in 1995. After a number of runner-up finishes, Duval began to assert himself as the top player in the world. He won thirteen times on Tour between 1997 and 2001, including the 1997 Tour Championship and the 1999 Players Championship, while also teaming up with Tiger Woods to win the 2000 World Cup at Buenos Aires Golf Club. In 1999, he shot a fabulous final-round 59 on the Palmer Course at PGA West, which is no pushover, to win the Bob Hope Chrysler Classic, and in April of that year became the top-ranked player in the world. Duval finished second in the 1998 Masters behind Mark O'Meara and again in 2001 behind Woods. In 2001, he broke through to win the British Open at Royal Lytham, and it seemed a certainty that more majors would follow and that he would vie with Woods on the world stage for many years to come. But Duval was hampered by injuries and his game deserted him. While other major winners such as Ian Baker Finch and Sandy Lyle have suffered dramatic losses of form, no player in recent times has plummeted so swiftly and steeply from the pinnacle of the game as has Duval. In his heyday, Duval was known for his impassive demeanor; he has handled the decline in his fortunes with good grace and fortitude. **OPPOSITE:** David Duval blasts out of a bunker at Royal Lytham & St. Annes during his 2001 victory at the British Open.

In 1997, Tiger Woods won his first major, the Masters, in a display of power golf that not only obliterated the field but elevated the way golf is played to another level—much as Woods's role model Jack Nicklaus had done when he ran away with the 1965 Masters. After shooting 40 on the front nine of his opening round, Woods pummeled Augusta National and the competition, winning by a record twelve strokes and becoming the youngest Masters winner ever. Despite his breakout success, Woods embarked on a quest to remodel his swing, working with coach Butch Harmon, which led to a slump in 1999 before the results of Woods's improved mechanics were fully realized in his heroic 2000 season. During 2000, he won three consecutive majors, as Ben Hogan had done in 1953, but in even more dominating fashion. In the U.S. Open at Pebble Beach, his margin of victory was fifteen shots, eclipsing a record for the largest winning margin in a major that had endured since the days of Old Tom Morris and the dawn of the Open championship in 1862. Next came the Open at St. Andrews, when he reduced the sun-dried Old Course to little more than a pitch and putt, his winning score of nineteen under setting a record for low score to par in a major. With his Open victory, he also became at twenty-four the youngest player to achieve the career Grand Slam. He capped off his 2000 campaign by winning the PGA at Louisville's Valhalla Golf Club in one of the most thrilling head-to-head battles in the annals of the game, playing the final twelve holes in a birdie barrage of seven under par to tie Bob May in regulation, and then defeating May in the three-hole play-off.

OPPOSITE: Tiger Woods at the 2000 U.S. Open at Pebble Beach, which he won by fifteen shots. **BELOW:** Woods after winning the 1997 Masters in dominating fashion for his first major victory, ushering in a new era in golf.

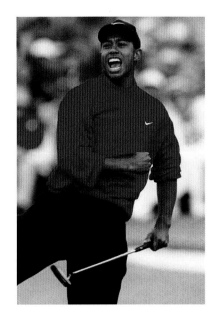

Retief Goosen, the quiet man from Pietersberg (now Polokane), South Africa, was something of a late bloomer, having to overcome both a lack of confidence and being struck by lightning on the golf course as a teenager. Goosen was enjoying success on the European Tour but was relatively unknown in the United States when he made a big splash, winning the U.S. Open in a particularly exciting championship in 2001 at Tulsa's Southern Hills. After Mark Brooks, the 1996 PGA champion, three-putted on the treacherous eighteenth green when two putts would have secured victory, Goosen also three-putted. With a positive outlook instilled by working with Belgian sports psychologist and ex–rock musician Jos Vanstiphout, the unflappable "Goose" prevailed in the eighteen-hole play-off the next day. That same year the thirty-two-year-old Goosen won the Scottish Open at Loch Lomond and the Madrid Open to take the European Order of Merit. He then teamed up with Ernie Els, South Africa's other golfing demigod, to win the World Cup at Gotemba in Japan in a play-off over New Zealand, Denmark, and the formidable U.S. duo of Tiger Woods and David Duval. **OPPOSITE:** Retief Goosen (left) with teammate Ernie Els on the way to winning the 2001 World Cup for South Africa at the Taiheiyo Club in Gotemba, Japan.

David Toms has been one of the top-tier golfers on the PGA Tour over the past decade, chalking up a dozen victories. Born in Monroe, Louisiana, he was an all-American at LSU and now lives in Shreveport. After turning pro in 1992, Toms won his first Tour event at the 1997 Quad City Classic, with his most recent victory coming at the 2006 Sony Open in Hawaii. Along the way, he won the inaugural Wachovia Open in 2003, despite stumbling with an 8 on the final hole. In 2001, a year in which he won three times, he collected the Wanamaker Trophy at the PGA Championship at Atlanta Athletic Club. Proving that discretion is the better part of valor, Toms elected to lay up short of the water guarding the par-5 eighteenth green, and then rolled in his twelve-foot birdie putt to give him a one-stroke victory over Phil Mickelson.

OPPOSITE: David Toms waits for his turn while Phil Mickelson putts at the 2001 PGA won by Toms at Atlanta Athletic Club.

Phil Mickelson has suffered more than his share of heartbreak in the U.S. Open, finishing runner-up four times. In 1999, he was stymied when Payne Stewart nailed his winning putt on the seventy-second hole at Pinehurst No. 2. In 2002, he was adopted as the favorite son of the boisterous New York fans at Bethpage Black, but ended up trailing Tiger Woods. In 2004, he again had the gallery rooting for him at Shinnecock, only to fall short to Retief Goosen after three-putting the seventeenth hole from short range. His bitterest disappointment surely came in 2007 at a perfidious Winged Foot, when needing par to win on the last hole, he drove into the trees on the left, was unable to extricate himself, and then found the greenside bunker with his third to finish with a double bogey and lose to Geoff Ogilvy. In his continuing quest to conquer the majors, Mickelson in 2007 replaced his long-time swing coach Rick Smith with Butch Harmon, Woods's former mentor, and works with short-game savant Dave Pelz. **OPPOSITE:** Phil Mickelson walks with Tiger Woods during the 2007 Deutsche Bank Championship played at the TPC Boston, where Mickelson defeated Woods in their final round show-down with a closing 66. **BELOW:** In action during the 2001 U.S. Open at Tulsa's Southern Hills.

In 2001, Tiger Woods opened the season by winning the Masters for his fourth consecutive major victory, giving him what has become known as the "Tiger Slam." The only player ever to achieve the single-season Grand Slam, Bobby Jones, did so in 1930, when the majors consisted of the U.S. and British Opens and the British and U.S. Amateurs. Tiger gave chase to the single-season Slam in 2002, when he won his second consecutive and third career Masters, followed by the U.S. Open at Long Island's Bethpage Black. His chance ended at the British Open at Muirfield, unraveled by a third-round 81 in abysmal weather. After a lull in 2003 and 2004, which saw the emergence of Phil Mickelson and Vijay Singh as his main rivals, by 2005 Woods had reinvented his swing for the second time, replacing coach Butch Harmon with Hank Haney. The 2005 Masters and Augusta National once again proved the stage where Woods served notice of his supremacy, this time in a nip-and-tuck showdown with Chris DiMarco. Woods holed a miraculous boomerang of a chip on the sixteenth hole to take the lead and then defeated DiMarco in the first hole of sudden death by birdying the eighteenth. After falling just short to Michael Campbell in the U.S. Open, Woods provided another sterling performance at St. Andrews, winning the Open for a second time over the Old Course. **OPPOSITE:** Tiger Woods shakes a finger at the twenty-five-foot birdie putt on the sixteenth hole that gave him a one-stroke lead over Bob May after the first hole of their play-off in the 2000 PGA at Valhalla in Louisville, Kentucky. It proved to be the margin of victory. **BELOW:** Tiger on the way to winning the 2006 PGA at Medinah, where he also won the PGA in 1999.

TODAY | THRU 15 | TOTAL

PGA CHAMPIONSHIP

TODAY	LEADERS	HOLE	TOTAL
E	WOODS	15	E
E	MAY	15	E
	PLAYOFF		

With his effortless power, lyrical tempo, and laid-back demeanor, Ernie Els has earned the nickname "The Big Easy." In 2002, Els won his third major and single British Open at Muirfield in a seesaw four-hole play-off with Aussies Steve Elkington and Stuart Appleby and unheralded Frenchman Thomas Levet, with Els finally finishing off Levet in the first hole of sudden death. Two years later he would be at the losing end of a play-off at Royal Troon to the lowball-hitting chip-shot artist Todd Hamilton, a regular winner on the Japanese Tour but a virtual unknown in his native United States. Els has had his share of disappointments at the Masters, a major that has continued to elude him. He has finished second twice, including in 2004, when he fell victim to Phil Mickelson's birdie putt on the final hole. **OPPOSITE:** Ernie Els and Todd Hamilton walk down the first fairway at Royal Troon in their play-off at the 2004 British Open. **BELOW:** Els playing to the eighteenth green in the third round of the 2004 Open.

Ben Crenshaw and his design partner, Bill Coore, are at the vanguard of contemporary course design, basing their approach on a return to the design principles of the golden era of golf course architecture in the 1920s. Their retro or "minimalist" style is one of steadfast adherence to natural features and the lay of the land, with an attention to detail that makes their courses look handcrafted. Their designs range from the Plantation Course at the Kapalua Golf Club in Maui, home of the Mercedes Championship Tour event, to Bandon Trails, opened in 2005 as the most recent addition to the Bandon Dunes Resort on the Oregon Coast, to the private Friar's Head Golf Club on the bluffs overlooking Long Island Sound in Riverhead, New York. In June 1995, Crenshaw and Coore completed Sand Hills Golf Club after spending two years developing an ideal routing through the vast landlocked dunes of central Nebraska, creating a supreme inland links on an immense scale. Sand Hills has been consistently ranked by *Golfweek* as the best American course opened since 1960. **OPPOSITE:** View of the par-3 second hole out to the par-5 third hole at the Bandon Trails Course at the Bandon Dunes Resort in Oregon, designed by Bill Coore and Ben Crenshaw.

Australia's Karrie Webb dominated women's golf with a wellspring of victories, including six majors, between her rookie season on the LPGA Tour in 1996 and 2002. Webb then suffered a victory drought while her rival Annika Sörenstam continued to reap wins in record numbers. She returned to form in 2006 when she won five tournaments, including the Kraft Nabisco Championship for her seventh career major, while losing in a play-off to Se Ri Pak in the LPGA Championship. Although shy and unassuming, Webb is a tough competitor with thirty-five career wins on the LPGA Tour. In her stellar seasons of 2000 and 2001, she won back-to-back U.S. Women's Opens, in 2000 at the Merit Club in Libertyville, Illinois, where she was five shots ahead of Meg Mallon and Cristie Kerr, and in 2001 at Pine Needles in North Carolina. She also won the Women's British Open three times—in 1995 and 1997, before it was recognized as a major by the LPGA, and again in 2002. Webb is only the sixth woman to achieve the LPGA career Grand Slam, and by virtue of winning all five majors recognized during her career, she can also claim the career Super Slam. **OPPOSITE:** Karrie Webb playing in the inaugural Ginn Clubs & Resorts Open in Orlando, Florida, in 2006.

Jim Furyk, who grew up near Pittsburgh, was coached by his father, Mike Furyk, the head pro at Uniontown Country Club. Mike wisely chose not to tinker with his son's highly unconventional but repetitive swing, which has a pronounced curlicue at the top that brings it back on line during the downswing. He has also putted cross-handed since he was seven. A long, accurate driver and excellent putter despite these unorthodox techniques, Furyk has enjoyed steady success on the PGA Tour since turning pro in 1992, winning at least one event each year between 1998 and 2003. After contending in a number of majors, he broke through to win the 2003 U.S. Open at Olympia Fields, tying the all-time Open scoring record of 272. Furyk is currently at the peak of his game, winning both the Wachovia Championship and the Canadian Open in 2006, on his way to becoming the number two ranked player in the world in September 2006 and partnering with Tiger Woods that month in the Ryder Cup at the K Club. Furyk, like Woods, finished second in the 2007 U.S. Open at Oakmont, one shot behind Argentina's Angel Cabrera.

OPPOSITE: Jim Furyk at the Golf Challenge in Sun City, South Africa, in 2006.

BELOW: Furyk birdies the eighteenth hole in the third round during his victory at the 2003 U.S. Open at Chicago's Olympia Fields.

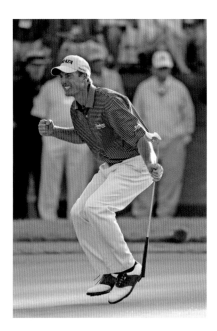

Annika Sörenstam began smashing records on the LPGA Tour in the late 1990s, and the Swedish star's success snowballed entering the new millennium. In 1998, she became the first LPGA player to record a sub-70 season scoring average, finishing at 69.99, a mark she subsequently lowered. In 2001, she won eight LPGA events and became the first and only woman ever to shoot a 59 in competition—at the Standard Register PING tournament. In 2002, she won eleven LPGA tournaments, tying Mickey Wright's single-season record, and won twice overseas, giving her a phenomenal thirteen victories in twenty-five starts. That same year, she won her second consecutive Kraft Nabisco Championship. In 2003, Sörenstam won two more majors, the LPGA Championship and the Women's British Open, making her the sixth player to complete the LPGA career Grand Slam. Her 2005 season was the pièce de résistance, when she won ten out of the twenty tournaments she entered, including two more majors. That year Sörenstam became the only LPGA player ever to win the same major three years in a row, when she captured the McDonald's LPGA Championship, and also won the third Kraft Nabisco of her career. **OPPOSITE:** Annika Sörenstam celebrates on the way to defeating Angela Stansford in their singles match at the 2003 Solheim Cup, won by the European team at Barsebäck Golf Club in Sweden.

For the past decade, Ernie Els has been one of Tiger Woods's main rivals, and one of modern golf's Big Four with Woods, Phil Mickelson, and Vijay Singh. In 2003, he started off the season by shattering the all-time PGA Tour scoring record with a score of thirty-one under par for four rounds to win the Mercedes Championship at Kapalua, an event he had lost to Woods in sudden death in 2000 after both eagled the final hole in regulation. That same year he won five events on the European Tour, including the Heineken Classic at Royal Melbourne and the Johnnie Walker Classic played at Australia's Lake Karrinyup. In 2004, he won a record sixth World Match Play Championship at Wentworth. Els has also regularly represented South Africa in the Alfred Dunhill and World Cup competitions, teaming with Wayne Westner to win the World Cup at Erinvale in Cape Town and with Retief Goosen to win at Gotemba in Japan in 2001. In 2005, he required knee surgery after a freak sailing accident while on a family holiday in the Mediterranean but came back at the end of the season, winning the Dunhill Championship at South Africa's Leopard Creek Golf Club. **OPPOSITE:** Ernie Els tees off on the fifteenth hole of the Leopard Creek Country Club in Malelane, South Africa, in the 2004 Dunhill Golf Championship. **BELOW:** Winning the 2004 Heineken Classic at Royal Melbourne.

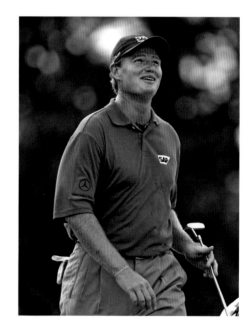

Scott Verplank grew up in Dallas, learning the game at Brookhaven Country Club, before starring for the Oklahoma State University Cowboys as a four-time all-American and taking individual NCAA champion honors in 1984. In 1984, he also won the U.S. Amateur at Oklahoma's Oak Tree Golf Club. The following year, while still an amateur, he won the Western Open in a sudden-death play-off over Jim Thorpe, making Verplank the first amateur to win on the PGA Tour since Doug Sanders captured the Canadian Open in 1956. Verplank would himself win the Canadian Open in 2001. He has had to contend with diabetes since he was nine, as well as battling elbow and shoulder injuries, but has been a consistently solid player, winning five times on Tour. His most recent victory came at the 2007 Byron Nelson Championship—the first played since Nelson's death on September 26, 2006—when he fired a final-round 66 for a one-stroke victory. For Verplank, who lost in a four-way play-off in 2001, winning the tournament was charged with emotion, a dream come true that was tinged with sadness. He had played several rounds with Nelson as a teenager growing up in Dallas, and had received encouragement from Nelson throughout his career. Nelson's widow, Peggy, clutched one of his fedoras in her hand as she hugged Verplank on the eighteenth hole. Verplank was also a captain's pick for both the 2002 and 2006 Ryder Cup teams, becoming the first American to make a hole in one in the competition when he aced the fourteenth hole at the K Club in his match against Padraig Harrington. **OPPOSITE:** Scott Verplank shows off his Orange County Choppers custom motorcycle and the trophy after winning the 2007 EDS Byron Nelson Championship at the TPC Four Seasons Resort Las Colinas, outside Dallas.

Darren Clarke, who hails from Dungannon in Northern Ireland and plays out of Royal Portrush, has been a larger-than-life figure in European golf in recent years. He has won a total of ten times on the European and U.S. tours since turning pro in 1990, after playing college golf at Wake Forest. His best-publicized victory came in the 2000 World Golf Championship Match Play event at La Costa Country Club, when he beat David Duval, at the time ranked number two in the world, in the semifinals, and then vanquished Tiger Woods in the final. Clarke is known for his gusto on and off the course, enjoying fine cigars and champagne after his victories. In August 2006 Heather, his wife and the mother of their two young sons, lost a brave battle against breast cancer. Not long afterward, Clarke announced that he would be available to play in the 2006 Ryder Cup and was selected by team captain Ian Woosnam. Clarke, who has been a stalwart of the European side since 1997, received an outpouring of sympathy from players and fans alike. He won all three of his matches at the K Club outside Dublin, giving the Europeans a huge emotional lift as they went on to trounce the Americans. **OPPOSITE:** Darren Clarke reacts after holing a 110-foot putt on the twelfth hole of his singles match against Zach Johnson in the 2006 Ryder Cup at the K Club.

Se Ri Pak has been one of the premier players in the women's game since the late 1990s, with five major victories. She is also the most successful of the large and expanding coterie of Korean players who have prospered on the LPGA Tour, including Mi Hyun Kim, Grace Park, Jeong Jang, and Meena Lee. Driven hard to succeed by her father, Pak burst onto the U.S. scene in her rookie season of 1998, winning both the LPGA Championship and the U.S. Women's Open at Kohler. At twenty, she was the youngest golfer ever to win the Women's Open, squeaking past Jenny Chuasiriporn on the second hole of sudden death after the two remained deadlocked following an eighteen-hole play-off. After slumping in 2004 and 2005, she returned to the spotlight in 2006, pulling off a dramatic sudden-death victory over a resurgent Karrie Webb in the 2006 LPGA Championship when she knocked her two-hundred-yard second shot on the first play-off hole right next to the pin. Pak also made the cut in a men's tournament on the Korean PGA Tour and was in contention to win before finishing tenth. **OPPOSITE:** Se Ri Pak on her way to winning the 1998 U.S. Women's Open on Blackwolf Run at the Kohler Resort in Wisconsin. **BELOW:** Teeing off at the 2006 Evian Masters in Evian-les-Bains, France.

Greg Norman, who was the top-ranked golfer in the world for a good part of the late 1980s and early 1990s, won twenty times on the PGA Tour, including two British Opens and the 1994 Players Championship, fourteen events on the European Tour, and a slew of tournaments in Australia and Asia. Nowadays, Norman focuses his energies on golf course architecture, having emerged as a perceptive and hands-on designer, and on his international business ventures. Norman has designed courses in every corner of the earth. His work in Australia, influenced by the Sand Belt masterpieces of Alister MacKenzie, includes the Moonah Course at the National Golf Club on the Mornington Peninsula; the Grand Golf Club in Queensland; and the ultra-exclusive Ellerston, designed for the late Australian media magnate Kerry Packer. In Europe, his notable designs include Doonbeg in Ireland's County Clare and Barcelona's new El Prat. In the Americas, the TPC at Sugarloaf in Duluth, Georgia, is the highly acclaimed home of the AT&T National; the Four Seasons Resort Great Exuma at Emerald Bay is a pristine links cut through the mangrove thickets of Exuma in the Bahamas; while Temenos Golf Club, wrapped around the Merrywing Salt Pond, is the first course built on Anguilla. **OPPOSITE:** Ellerston Golf Club in Australia's Hunter Valley, designed by Greg Norman, ninth hole.

Mike Weir, born in Brights Grove, Ontario, is Canada's charmingly boyish golfing hero, and became the first Canadian ever to win a professional major when he captured the 2003 Masters. Weir, who played his college golf at Brigham Young and turned pro in 1992, initially played on the Canadian Tour and began playing the PGA Tour full-time in 1998. In 1999, he fittingly won the Air Canada Championship in Vancouver for his first PGA victory. After winning the 2000 WGC–American Express Championship at Valderrama and the 2001 Tour Championship, 2003 proved to be Weir's breakout year. He won the Bob Hope Desert Classic and the Los Angeles Open before arriving at Augusta. Weir's final round, a bogey-free 67, showed him to be a short-game virtuoso, but he still finished tied with the hard-luck Len Mattiace, whose 65 was only blemished by a bogey on the last hole. Weir then won the play-off on the first hole of sudden death. Weir's victory also made him only the second left-handed player to win a major after New Zealand's Bob Charles, although Phil "Lefty" Mickelson has now followed suit with three majors of his own. Neck and back injuries greatly hampered Weir's performance in 2005, but he appears to be on the comeback trail. In the 2007 Presidents Cup at Royal Montreal, with the crowd cheering his every shot, Weir pulled off a stunning upset of Tiger Woods in their singles match on the final day, defeating Woods on the eighteenth hole. He then went on to win the Fry Electronics Open in Arizona in October 2007. **OPPOSITE:** Mike Weir with Tiger Woods during their match in the final round of the 2007 Presidents Cup, in which Weir was the upset victor.

The Presidents Cup kicked off in 1994 as the biennial match between the United States and an International Team, a competition along the lines of the Ryder Cup that excludes European players to allow players from the rest of the world to compete. While the format is similar to the Ryder Cup, with twelve players per side, the Presidents Cup includes an additional six matches. The inaugural match, won by the United States, was held at the Robert Trent Jones Golf Club in Virginia, appropriately close to Washington, D.C. President Gerald Ford, known for his love of the game and occasional wayward tee shots, served as honorary chairman. The 2003 event, held at the Links Course at the Fancourt Resort in South Africa, designed by International Team captain Gary Player, was highly memorable. When the match ended all square, Player and U.S. team captain Jack Nicklaus selected Ernie Els and Tiger Woods under the tie-breaker format as their picks to play a sudden-death match for all the marbles. After three holes of intense drama, with darkness descending and Woods and Els deadlocked, Nicklaus and Player agreed to call it a tie and share the Cup. In 2007, the Presidents Cup was held at Royal Montreal, with the U.S. team including resurgent veterans Steve Stricker and Woody Austin and up-and-coming stars Hunter Mahan, Lucas Glover, and Charles Howell III. The Americans were victorious for the first time on foreign soil, bringing their overall record to 5–1–1 in the competition. **OPPOSITE:** The eighteenth hole at the Fancourt Hotel and Country Club in George, South Africa, at the foot of the Outeniqua Mountains, site of the 2003 Presidents Cup.

In 2003, Annika Sörenstam received a sponsor's invitation to play in the Colonial Invitational on the men's Tour, held at Fort Worth's Colonial Country Club. She became the first woman to play in a PGA event since Babe Zaharias, who qualified for the 1945 Los Angeles Open. One of the longest and straightest drivers in women's golf, Sörenstam shot a solid opening-round 71 despite the distraction of a huge gallery rooting for her and the media frenzy. Trying to make the cut, she fell short with a second-round 74. That same year, she also competed in the Skins Game with Fred Couples, Phil Mickelson, and Mark O'Meara, finishing second. Not surprisingly, Sörenstam has been the linchpin of the European Solheim Cup team since 1994. She went 4–1 in leading the Europeans to a particularly gratifying victory in 2003, when the match was held in Sweden at Barsebäck, a fine old links course near Malmö, with views over the sea to Copenhagen. In 2007, she missed much of the year with a neck injury, losing her top spot in the official rankings to Lorena Ochoa, but returned to tee it up in the debut of her own event on the LPGA Tour—the Ginn Tribute hosted by Annika Sörenstam—at RiverTowne Country Club near Charleston, South Carolina. **OPPOSITE:** Annika Sörenstam eyes her putt on the tenth green during the Colonial Invitational at Fort Worth's Colonial Country Club.

After winning his first major at Augusta in 2004, Phil Mickelson went on to win two more, establishing himself as Tiger Woods's main American rival and one of the modern Big Four with Woods, Vijay Singh, and Ernie Els. Mickelson is one of the longest drivers in the game, but the most exciting part of his repertoire is his daredevil short game with its famous full-swing flop shot. He has now won more than thirty tournaments on the PGA Tour, with four-win seasons in 1996, 2000, and 2005. His second major came at the 2005 PGA Championship at Baltusrol, when he birdied the final hole thanks to one of his flop shots from off the green, finishing one ahead of Steve Elkington and Thomas Bjørn. Then he opened 2006 by winning his second green jacket in three years, with South Africa's Tim Clark two shots back. **OPPOSITE:** Phil Mickelson (right) tips his cap after winning the 2005 PGA Championship at Baltusrol. **BELOW:** Smiling on the way to the twelfth tee during the final round of the 2005 PGA.

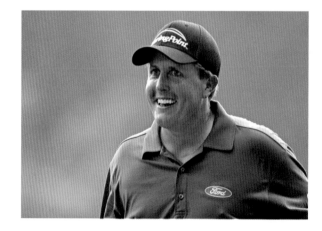

Tom Doak has been at the forefront of the movement back to the principles of classic golf course architecture, emphasizing naturalism, a minimalist approach to earthmoving, and attention to the ground game features that are an intrinsic part of British links golf. Doak dedicated himself early on to a career as a golf course architect, studying landscape architecture at Cornell and receiving a scholarship for post-graduate study that sent him to the British Isles, where he caddied at St. Andrews over the summer and spent seven months observing every course of note. Doak apprenticed with Pete Dye and also wrote about course architecture with refreshing and unusual candor, reviewing in his *Confidential Guide* many of the more than a thousand courses he had seen in his travels. Considered a controversial figure because of his strongly held views, Doak has received a number of plum assignments in recent years. He has made the most of these, designing courses that are a sheer joy to play while showcasing his design philosophy. His chef d'oeuvre is the Pacific Dunes Course at the Bandon Dunes Resort, where he was able to fulfill his dream of designing a monumental links course in the spirit of Royal County Down—with broad fairways running through a tableau of blown-out sand dunes, blankets of huckleberry, and garlands of yellow gorse—on cliffs high above the Pacific coastline. Doak also created a pair of eye-dazzling antipodean links, at the Cape Kidnappers Resort in New Zealand, which was formerly the Summerlea sheep station high above Hawkes Bay, and Barnbougle Dunes, on the northern coast of Tasmania, with views of Bridport Bay. **OPPOSITE:** Barnbougle Dunes in Tasmania, designed by Tom Doak, seventh hole.

Michael Campbell, New Zealand's premier golfer, was born in the small town of Hawera near Mount Taranaki on the North Island before his family moved to Wellington. Although Campbell is predominantly of Maori descent, his great-great-great-grandfather John Logan Campbell emigrated from Scotland in the 1840s, eventually becoming the mayor of Auckland. After turning pro in 1993, Cambo came to the fore in 1995 when he led the British Open at St. Andrews after three rounds, finishing one shot out of the play-off between winner John Daly and Costantino Rocca. Campbell enjoyed success on the European and Australasian tours before his monumental victory in the 2005 U.S. Open, joining Sir Bob Charles as the only Kiwis ever to win a major. Campbell went through sectional qualifying in Europe to earn a place in the field at Pinehurst, shooting 69 in the final round to hold off a charging Tiger Woods, who was tripped up by bogeys on the sixteenth and seventeenth holes. That same year, he carried away the HSBC World Match Play Championship at Wentworth, knocking off Retief Goosen in the semifinals and beating Ireland's Paul McGinley in the final. **OPPOSITE:** Michael Campbell shares a laugh with Tiger Woods after his two-stroke victory over Woods in the 2005 U.S. Open at Pinehurst No. 2.

Spain's Sergio García, who started playing when he was three, became a junior prodigy and is now one of Europe's leading stars as he closes in on thirty. After winning the British Amateur in 1998, García burst onto the golfing scene as an exuberant nineteen-year-old at the 1999 PGA at Medinah, finishing second to Tiger Woods after closing his eyes to hit a six-iron shot onto the green after his ball lodged against a tree trunk on the sixteenth hole. Since 2001, "El Niño" has won half a dozen events on the PGA Tour, including the Colonial and the Byron Nelson, and another six tourneys on the European Tour, including the 2005 European Masters—but a victory in the majors has so far eluded him. He has contended a number of times, having worked hard to correct an exaggerated lag in his downswing, but a balky putter has held him back in recent years. He charged out to the lead after three rounds in the 2007 British Open at Carnoustie, wielding a belly putter that proved the antidote for his putting troubles, and was on the cusp of winning his first major coming to the ferocious final hole on Sunday. His hopes were cruelly dashed when his par putt for victory singed the cup, and he lost in the ensuing play-off to Padraig Harrington. García has been at his best in the competitive cauldron of the Ryder Cup, compiling a cracking 14–3–3 record since 1999. He teamed with Luke Donald to take down the top U.S. pairing of Tiger Woods and Jim Furyk in their foursomes match at the K Club in 2006.

OPPOSITE: Sergio García escapes from up against a tree at the sixteenth hole in the final round of the 1999 PGA at Medinah. **BELOW:** Teeing off at the first play-off hole in the 2007 Open at Carnoustie.

After winning the 2001 U.S. Open, Retief Goosen emerged as one of the game's top five players with Tiger Woods, Phil Mickelson, Vijay Singh, and fellow South African Ernie Els. The possessor of a graceful, powerful swing, "The Goose" is also a streaky long putter. After joining Gary Player and Els as the third South African to win the U.S. Open, Goosen repeated in 2004 at Shinnecock Hills. He was the only player in the field in the final round who was able to handle the scalped and virtually unputtable greens, holing putts left and right. That same year he won the Smurfit European Open and the season-ending Tour Championship, shooting a final-round 64 to beat Woods. The year 2005 saw the globetrotting Goosen win the International on the PGA Tour, the Linde German Masters, the South African Open, and the Volvo Masters–China on the Asian Tour, while in 2007 he claimed the Qatar Masters. **OPPOSITE:** Retief Goosen playing from the bunker at the fourteenth hole en route to his 2004 U.S. Open win at Shinnecock.

The past few years have seen a flowering of English golf, with Luke Donald leading a crop of players consisting of Justin Rose, Paul Casey, David Howell, Nick Dougherty, and Ian Poulter—who is best known for a wardrobe that would make a peacock proud. Donald was born in Hemel Hempstead in Hertfordshire, a place name fit for Henry Higgins, and played collegiate golf at Northwestern. Donald turned pro in 2001, and by January 2002 had climbed to number seven in the official world rankings. In 2004, he won the European Masters and the Scandinavian Masters, and in 2006 the Honda Classic for his second victory on the PGA Tour. In the 2006 Ryder Cup, the European squad that shellacked the Americans included Donald, Casey, Howell, and English veteran Lee Westwood. Donald won his singles match over Chad Campbell and teamed with Sergio García to win another two points. Donald also partnered with Casey, who played college golf at Arizona State, to give England the WGC–World Cup in 2004 at Real Club de Golf de Sevilla. Fellow Englishman Justin Rose came on strong in 2007, winning the European Tour Order of Merit by capturing the Volvo Masters at Valderrama to finish up the year and vault into the top ten in the world rankings. **OPPOSITE:** Justin Rose playing in the Dunlop Phoenix Tournament at the Phoenix Golf Club in Miyazaki, Japan, in 2002. **BELOW:** Paul Casey (left) and Luke Donald raise the trophy after winning the 2004 World Cup for England in Seville, Spain.

Geoff Ogilvy established himself as an Australian golfing giant in 2006, when he came through the crash-and-burn U.S. Open at Winged Foot unscathed. Born in Adelaide, Ogilvy played the European Tour in 1999 and 2000 before joining the U.S. Tour and moving to Scottsdale, where he has also been involved in a business venture selling Australian meat pies. Ogilvy's stock was rising after he won the Tucson Open in 2005 and the 2006 WGC-Accenture Match Play Championship, where he beat Davis Love in the final, but his fame skyrocketed with his Open victory. Ogilvy finished in dramatic fashion, holing a chip shot from off the fringe on the seventeenth and getting up and down for par on the eighteenth, while Phil Mickelson's drive landed in jail on the final hole and Colin Montgomerie blocked his approach and both blew their chances with double bogeys. Ogilvy's win was the first by an Australian in a major since Steve Elkington's 1995 PGA Championship and made him, with David Graham, one of the only two Australians ever to win the U.S. Open. **OPPOSITE:** Geoff Ogilvy teeing off during his final round victory over Davis Love III to capture the 2006 Accenture World Match Play Championship at the La Costa Resort in Carslbad, California. **BELOW:** Driving at the 2006 PGA at Medinah.

Tiger Woods's career so far has had three distinct phases. First came his brilliant debut in 1997 and early 1998, when he astounded the golfing world with his whirlwind of a swing that launched projectiles of unprecedented distance. Then came a stretch in 2000 through 2002 when he seemed virtually unbeatable, winning six majors, four of them in succession. He has now entered a more mature phase of his career and appears more dominant than ever, even if the competition is less awestruck. In 2006, after missing the cut at the U.S. Open following his return to competition after the death of his father, he won the British Open at Royal Liverpool (Hoylake), defending his title. In doing so he displayed superb course management and self-discipline, hitting his driver only once all week and missing just four fairways. In August, he cruised to victory at the PGA at Medinah, where he had won the PGA in 1999 by one shot over an exuberant newcomer, Sergio García. Woods finished the year with six consecutive victories on the PGA Tour, a streak that he extended to seven at the start of 2007. **OPPOSITE:** Tiger Woods putting on the final hole during his victory at the 2006 British Open at Royal Liverpool in Hoylake, England. **BELOW:** An emotional Woods is congratulated by his caddie, Stevie Williams, after his victory in the 2006 British Open.

Padraig Harrington, who in 2007 became the first Irishman to win the British Open since Fred Daly sixty years earlier, was born in Ballyroan in County Dublin and learned to play at the Stackstown Golf Club, a course his father had a hand in building. After an outstanding amateur career that included playing on the victorious Walker Cup team at Porthcawl in 1995, Harrington joined the European Tour in 1996. Over the next decade, he established himself as one of Europe's premier players and a genial competitor, winning eleven times on the Tour. After finishing second at the Players Championship in both 2003 and 2004, he joined the winner's circle on the PGA Tour in 2005, winning the Honda Classic in a play-off with Vijay Singh and the Barclays Classic. Earlier in 2007, in what would prove to be a harbinger of his Open victory, Harrington became the first Irish player to win the Irish Open in twenty-five years when he bested Bradley Dredge in a sudden-death play-off at Adare Manor. In a wild finish at Carnoustie, Harrington plunked two balls in the Barry Burn on the final hole, and then scrambled for a double-bogey 6 that got him in a play-off with Sergio García. He birdied the first play-off hole, giving him the cushion he needed to win the four-hole play-off by a stroke. Harrington has played in the Ryder Cup Match since 1999 and regularly represents Ireland in international events. He teamed with Paul McGinley to win the World Cup for Ireland in 1997 at the Ocean Course on Kiawah Island, thirty-nine years after Harry Bradshaw and Christy O'Connor triumphed at Mexico City. **OPPOSITE:** Padraig Harrington chipping across the burn on the seventy-second hole of the 2007 Open at Carnoustie, on his way to a double bogey 6. **BELOW:** Waving the Irish flag after his victory over Sergio García in the play-off.

In recent years, Cristie Kerr has emerged as one of the premier American players on an LPGA Tour that has become increasingly international. After a stellar amateur career in Miami, where she was coached by Jim McLean at Doral, she turned pro in 1996. She began winning in 2002, after a slow start, with ten victories through 2007. By 2003, she had also shed fifty pounds, transforming her image into that of a svelte, blond star. In 2007, after going 0 for 41 in the majors, she won the U.S. Women's Open at Pine Needles in decisive fashion, playing the final thirty-six holes in six under par to finish five under. Kerr's putter, which she purchased in a Korean golf shop while playing in the Korean Open, never failed her, and she finished two ahead of Mexico's Lorena Ochoa, the top-ranked player in the world, and eighteen-year-old Tour rookie Angela Park. Off the course, Kerr has been heavily involved in raising money for breast cancer research. **OPPOSITE:** Cristie Kerr launching an iron during the first round of the 2007 U.S. Women's Open at Pine Needles. **BELOW:** Kerr savors her victory.

Aaron Baddeley, who was born in Lebanon, New Hampshire, is one of a quartet of young Aussie stars with Adam Scott, Nick O'Hern, and Geoff Ogilvy, the 2006 U.S. Open champion. With veteran cohorts Robert Allenby, Peter Lonard, and Stuart Appleby, they are making big waves for Australian golf on the PGA Tour. "Badds" won the Australian Open in 1999, when he was still an amateur, and repeated the following year, by which time he had turned pro. In 2006, he won the Verizon Heritage at Hilton Head for his maiden victory on the U.S. Tour, following up with a win at the FBR (Phoenix) Open in 2007. Baddeley had a two-shot lead over Tiger Woods going into the final round of the 2007 U.S. Open at Oakmont, but struggled to a final-round 80 and finished tied for thirteenth. **OPPOSITE:** Aaron Baddeley plays a bunker shot at the MasterCard Masters held at Melbourne's Huntingdale Golf Club in December 2003.

Mexico's Lorena Ochoa was crowned *La Reina* of the LPGA Tour in 2006, winning the Player of the Year Award and being named AP Female Athlete of the Year. In 2007, she officially became the number one ranked woman player, succeeding Annika Sörenstam, who missed part of the season with an injury. Ochoa, who learned the game at the Guadalajara Country Club, dominated women's collegiate golf while playing for the University of Arizona in 2001 and 2002. She won a record eight consecutive collegiate events in her sophomore year before turning pro. In 2006, after losing to Karrie Webb in a play-off at the Kraft Nabisco Championship, she won six tournaments, including the Samsung World Championship with a closing-round 65. Her Tour victories that year also included an emotional win in her native country, where she is immensely popular—the Corona Morelia Championship held at the Tres Marías Golf Club in Morelia, Michoacán. Her 2007 season was even more sensational, as she pulled off her first major in convincing fashion, finishing four clear of the field in the British Women's Open, which was held for the first time on the Old Course at St. Andrews. She ended the year on a tear, taking the ADT Championship in November for her eighth win in 2007, when she nailed a six-iron to thirty inches from the pin for a closing birdie and a two-shot margin over Natalie Gulbis. **OPPOSITE:** On the way to winning the Women's British Open at St. Andrews in 2007. **BELOW:** Playing in the Corona Morelia Championship at the Tres Marías Golf Club in her native Mexico in 2007.

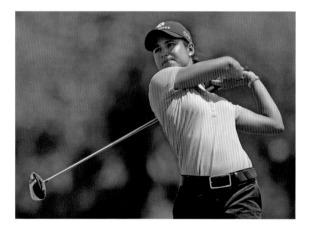

Golf has been booming in Mexico, driven by tourism but also sparked by the star power of Guadalajara's Lorena Ochoa, who has risen to the top spot in women's professional golf. The LPGA, PGA, and Champions Tours each now feature regular events in Mexico. The LPGA's Corona Morelia Championship is held at the Jack Nicklaus–designed Tres Marías Golf Club in Michoacán. The PGA Tour's Mayakoba Golf Classic, inaugurated in February 2007, is held at the El Camaleón Course that Greg Norman carved through mangrove jungles and limestone canals on the Riviera Maya. The Champions Tour journeys south of the border for the Puerto Vallarta Blue Agave Golf Classic. At the center of the golf boom is Los Cabos, at the southern tip of the Baja Peninsula, where the Sea of Cortez meets the Pacific at Land's End. The corridor between the sedate San José del Cabo and the boisterous nightlife of Cabo San Lucas is a desert garden of golfing delights, with courses designed by Jack Nicklaus, Robert Trent Jones, Jr., Tom Weiskopf, Roy Dye, and Tom Fazio. The fairways are flanked by *palo verde,* wild plum, and ironwood trees and bordered by organ pipe and paddled cactus, overlooking the midnight-blue Pacific where the right whales make their winter migration from Alaska.

OPPOSITE: Lorena Ochoa putts on the eighteenth hole during her 2007 victory at the Corona Morelia Championship, held at Mexico's Tres Marías Golf Club.

Natalie Gulbis is the LPGA Tour's reigning sex symbol, but she also has plenty of game. One of a crop of talented young American players that includes Morgan Pressel, Cristie Kerr, and Paula Creamer, Gulbis turned pro in 2001 when she was eighteen, after playing one year at the University of Arizona. She placed in the top ten in four consecutive major championships, beginning with the 2005 LPGA Championship, and then broke through in 2007 to capture her first LPGA victory along the shores of Lake Evian at the Evian Masters in France. She played on the winning Solheim Cup teams in 2005 and 2007. Gulbis has her own reality TV show on the Golf Channel, writes a monthly golf advice column for *FHM Magazine,* and models in her own calendar each year. **OPPOSITE:** Natalie Gulbis tees off during the 2006 ADT Championship at Trump International Golf Club in West Palm Beach, Florida.

Australian Adam Scott, who hails from Adelaide, is one of modern golf's young superstars, climbing to third in the world rankings in early 2007. Scott turned pro in 2000, concentrating on the European Tour early on, but is now also a regular on the U.S. Tour. With his leading-man good looks and soft-spoken but articulate charm, Scott is a popular player who is just entering his prime. He won for the first time on the PGA Tour in 2003, and followed up by capturing the Players Championship and Booz Allen Classic in 2004. The 2005 campaign saw success in Asia, where Scott won the Johnnie Walker Classic, a European Tour event, at the Jack Nicklaus–designed Pine Valley Golf Resort in Beijing, and the Singapore Open at the Sentosa Golf Club's Serapong Course. In 2006, he capped off his season by winning the Tour Championship, and got off to a hot start in 2007 by winning the Shell Houston Open at the Rees Jones–designed Redstone Golf Club. Scott has shared the limelight with fellow up-and-coming Aussie stars Geoff Ogilvy, the 2006 U.S. Open winner, and Aaron Baddeley, who led going into the final round of the 2007 Open at Oakmont. **OPPOSITE:** Adam Scott blasting out while playing in the 2005 Australian Open at the Moonah Links Open Course. **BELOW:** Holding the trophy after winning the 2005 Johnny Walker Classic at Pine Valley Golf Resort in Beijing.

Paula Creamer is one of the rising stars on the LPGA Tour, together with Morgan Pressel and Natalie Gulbis. As an eighteen-year-old in her rookie season of 2005, she finished second on the money list to Annika Sörenstam. That same year, she won the Sybase Classic in New Rochelle, New York, making her the second-youngest first-time winner in LPGA history after Marlene Bauer Hagge. She went on to win the Evian Masters in France in 2005 as well, and earned a spot on the winning Solheim Cup team. She chalked up two more wins in 2007 and another Solheim Cup appearance, defeating Maria Hjorth in their singles match. Creamer, known as "The Pink Panther," is partial to pink outfits on the course, sports a pink golf bag, and uses a pink golf ball during the last round of every tournament. **OPPOSITE:** Paula Creamer playing in the Sky 72 Skins Game at the Sky 72 Golf Club in Incheon, South Korea, in 2007.

Zach Johnson, a modest and likeable young pro from Cedar Rapids, won the 2007 Masters, making him the second mild-mannered Iowan to win a major, the first having been 1955 U.S. Open winner Jack Fleck, the dark horse from Davenport. While others folded on the firm, fast, and recently elongated Augusta National, Johnson displayed nerveless putting down the stretch with birdies on thirteen, fourteen, and sixteen to hold off Tiger Woods, who finished two shots back with a pair of South Africans, the up-and-coming Rory Sabbatini and Retief Goosen. Johnson's one-over-par total was the highest winning score since 1956, when Jack Burke, Jr., won in

difficult conditions. A product of Drake University who joined the Tour in 2004, Johnson was little known to golf fans before his big breakthrough, despite having played on the 2006 Ryder Cup team. He followed up his Masters victory by beating Ryuji Imada in a play-off to win the AT&T National (formerly Bell South Classic) tournament at the TPC Sugarloaf, a tournament he had also won in 2004, giving him all three of his Tour victories in the Peachtree State. **OPPOSITE:** Zach Johnson playing in the final round on the way to winning the 2007 AT&T National. **BELOW:** Sharing a laugh with Phil Mickelson after winning the 2007 Masters.

Morgan Pressel had an outstanding amateur career and is one of the new wave of talented young golfers on the LPGA Tour who seem destined for stardom. In 2005, when she was seventeen, she won the U.S. Women's Amateur as well as the North and South Women's Amateur at Pinehurst. She qualified for the 2001 U.S. Women's Open as a twelve-year-old, the youngest qualifier ever. Pressel came close to becoming the first amateur since Catherine LaCoste to win the Open, in 2005 at Cherry Hills. She was tied for the lead coming down to the final hole, finishing two shots back when Birdie Kim holed her bunker shot for victory in one of the most memorable moments in the history of the U.S. Women's Open. In 2007, Pressel won the Kraft Nabisco for her first major and became the youngest woman ever to win a major. She capped off the year by defeating Annika Sörenstam in their singles match in the Solheim Cup to lead the U.S. to victory at Halmstad Golf Club in Sweden. Pressel is the niece of former tennis star Aaron Krickstein. **OPPOSITE:** Morgan Pressel playing in the final round of the 2007 U.S. Women's Open at Pine Needles in North Carolina.

A new and glorious chapter in the history of Argentine golf was written in 2007 when Angel Cabrera won the U.S. Open at Oakmont, becoming the first Argentine player to win the U.S. Open. Cabrera, who together with José Coceres has been the most successful of the Argentine pros on the international circuit, was born in Villa Allende in Córdoba, four hundred miles northwest of Buenos Aires. He began as a caddie at the Córdoba Golf Club, leaving school when he was ten. Córdoba is also the home course of Eduardo *"El Gato"* ("The Cat") Romero, another of Argentina's top pros, who sponsored Cabrera when he was starting out. Cabrera, known as *"El Pato"* ("The Duck") for his distinctive gait, kept his cool to fend off both Tiger Woods and Jim Furyk by a shot. It was almost a double Open year for Argentina when Andrés Romero, an unsung twenty-six-year-old from Tucumán, nearly won the British Open at Carnoustie, playing a surreal final round in which he made ten birdies and briefly held the lead before a double bogey, bogey finish left him one shy of the Padraig Harrington–Sergio García play-off that went to the Dubliner. Argentina has a venerable golfing tradition, particularly in the British Open, beginning with José Jurado, who finished second to Tommy Armour in the 1931 Open at Carnoustie. Roberto De Vicenzo, the behemoth of Argentine golfers, won the Open at Hoylake in 1967, while his contemporary, Antonio Cerda, was runner-up to Max Faulkner in 1951 and to Ben Hogan at Carnoustie in 1953. **OPPOSITE:** Argentina's Angel Cabrera waves to the crowd on the eighteenth hole at Oakmont after winning the 2007 U.S. Open. **BELOW:** Cabrera hugs the trophy.

Michelle Wie, who grew up in Honolulu, is one of the best-known golfers on the planet, despite not having won in a professional tournament to date. A golfing prodigy, she started playing the game at age four and was coached by her father, B. J. Wie. By the time she turned sixteen in October 2005, Wie was six feet one inch tall and able to drive the ball as far as the top men pros, cranking out tee shots that averaged 280 yards. In 2003, she became the youngest player ever to make the cut in an LPGA event, at the Kraft Nabisco, where she played in the final group on Sunday with Annika Sörenstam and winner Patricia Meunier-Lebouc of France. Wie turned pro a week before she turned sixteen, although she was not eligible to become a member of the LPGA Tour until her eighteenth birthday. She is best known at this early stage in her career for her attempts to compete on the men's PGA Tour and against men in other professional events. In 2004, she played in the Sony Open in Hawaii, becoming the fourth woman and the youngest ever to play in a PGA event. She shot rounds of 72 and 68 to miss the cut by a single stroke. Wie also was in contention to qualify for the 2006 U.S. Open at Winged Foot, finishing first in the local qualifying tournament but missing out on one of the sixteen spots in the sectional qualifying event at Canoe Brook in New Jersey. While she has yet to win an LPGA event, she had considerable success on the Women's Tour before injuring her wrist in 2007 and playing poorly after her return. She enrolled at Stanford, the alma mater of her golfing idol, Tiger Woods, in the fall of that year. **OPPOSITE:** Michelle Wie tees off in the 2006 Omega European Masters played at Crans-sur-Sierre, Switzerland, where Bradley Dredge of Wales was the winner.

In the long and rich history of the royal and ancient game, no player has displayed the wondrous alchemy of explosive power, short-game legerdemain, and indomitable willpower achieved by Tiger Woods. As a front-runner in major tournaments, Woods has been invincible, holding a 13–0 record going into the final round with a lead or a share of the lead. During 2007, Woods was upset in the Masters by Zach Johnson, finishing tied for second, and was one shot shy of Angel Cabrera in the U.S. Open. But he finished the season in rousing and record-setting fashion. He captured the PGA Championship at a steamy Southern Hills, winning back-to-back PGAs for the second time in his career, with a third-round 63 propelling him to victory. He continued on a tear, winning the inaugural FedEx Cup play-offs with victories in the BMW Championship and a cakewalk in the Tour Championship played at East Lake. He also hosted a new event on the PGA Tour, the AT&T National, played at Congressional outside Washington, D.C., which benefited the Tiger Woods Foundation. Tiger looks certain to bestride the world of golf, both on and off the course, for many years to come. **OPPOSITE:** Tiger Woods teeing off on the sixth hole during the first round of the 2005 British Open at St. Andrews, the second time Tiger would win the Open on the Old Course. **BELOW:** Tiger with the Golden Bear before their match at the Battle of the Bighorn against Sergio García and Lee Trevino in Palm Desert, California.

TIGER WOODS BURNS BRIGHT—AND NEW STARS SHINE

INDEX

Editor: Margaret L. Kaplan
Designer: Robert McKee
Production Manager: Jules Thomson

Cataloging-in-Publication Data has been applied for and may be obtained from the Library of Congress. ISBN: 978-0-8109-7281-0

Text copyright © 2008 Robert Sidorsky

Published in 2008 by Abrams, an imprint of Harry N. Abrams, Inc. All rights reserved. No portion of this book may be reproduced, stored in a retrieval system, or transmitted in any form or by any means, mechanical, electronic, photocopying, recording, or otherwise, without written permission from the publisher.

Printed and bound in China
10 9 8 7 6 5 4 3 2 1

Abrams books are available at special discounts when purchased in quantity for premiums and promotions as well as fundraising or educational use. Special editions can also be created to specification. For details, contact special markets@hnabooks.com or the address below.

HNA ■■■■■
harry n. abrams, inc.
a subsidiary of La Martinière Groupe
115 West 18th Street
New York, NY 10011
www.hnabooks.com